T0214257

Lecture Notes in Computer Science 12216

More information about this series at http://www.springer.com/series/7409

Gavriel Salvendy · June Wei (Eds.)

Design, Operation
and Evaluation of
Mobile Communications

First International Conference, MOBILE 2020
Held as Part of the 22nd HCI International Conference, HCII 2020
Copenhagen, Denmark, July 19–24, 2020
Proceedings

 Springer

Editors
Gavriel Salvendy
University of Central Florida
Florida, FL, USA

June Wei
University of West Florida
Pensacola, FL, USA

ISSN 0302-9743 ISSN 1611-3349 (electronic)
Lecture Notes in Computer Science
ISBN 978-3-030-50349-9 ISBN 978-3-030-50350-5 (eBook)
https://doi.org/10.1007/978-3-030-50350-5

LNCS Sublibrary: SL3 – Information Systems and Applications, incl. Internet/Web, and HCI

This Springer imprint is published by the registered company Springer Nature Switzerland AG
The registered company address is: Gewerbestrasse 11, 6330 Cham, Switzerland

Foreword

The 22nd International Conference on Human-Computer Interaction, HCI International 2020 (HCII 2020), was planned to be held at the AC Bella Sky Hotel and Bella Center, Copenhagen, Denmark, during July 19–24, 2020. Due to the COVID-19 coronavirus pandemic and the resolution of the Danish government not to allow events larger than 500 people to be hosted until September 1, 2020, HCII 2020 had to be held virtually. It incorporated the 21 thematic areas and affiliated conferences listed on the following page.

A total of 6,326 individuals from academia, research institutes, industry, and governmental agencies from 97 countries submitted contributions, and 1,439 papers and 238 posters were included in the conference proceedings. These contributions address the latest research and development efforts and highlight the human aspects of design and use of computing systems. The contributions thoroughly cover the entire field of human-computer interaction, addressing major advances in knowledge and effective use of computers in a variety of application areas. The volumes constituting the full set of the conference proceedings are listed in the following pages.

The HCI International (HCII) conference also offers the option of "late-breaking work" which applies both for papers and posters and the corresponding volume(s) of the proceedings will be published just after the conference. Full papers will be included in the "HCII 2020 - Late Breaking Papers" volume of the proceedings to be published in the Springer LNCS series, while poster extended abstracts will be included as short papers in the "HCII 2020 - Late Breaking Posters" volume to be published in the Springer CCIS series.

I would like to thank the program board chairs and the members of the program boards of all thematic areas and affiliated conferences for their contribution to the highest scientific quality and the overall success of the HCI International 2020 conference.

This conference would not have been possible without the continuous and unwavering support and advice of the founder, Conference General Chair Emeritus and Conference Scientific Advisor Prof. Gavriel Salvendy. For his outstanding efforts, I would like to express my appreciation to the communications chair and editor of HCI International News, Dr. Abbas Moallem.

July 2020   Constantine Stephanidis

HCI International 2020 Thematic Areas
and Affiliated Conferences

Thematic areas:

- HCI 2020: Human-Computer Interaction
- HIMI 2020: Human Interface and the Management of Information

Affiliated conferences:

- EPCE: 17th International Conference on Engineering Psychology and Cognitive Ergonomics
- UAHCI: 14th International Conference on Universal Access in Human-Computer Interaction
- VAMR: 12th International Conference on Virtual, Augmented and Mixed Reality
- CCD: 12th International Conference on Cross-Cultural Design
- SCSM: 12th International Conference on Social Computing and Social Media
- AC: 14th International Conference on Augmented Cognition
- DHM: 11th International Conference on Digital Human Modeling and Applications in Health, Safety, Ergonomics and Risk Management
- DUXU: 9th International Conference on Design, User Experience and Usability
- DAPI: 8th International Conference on Distributed, Ambient and Pervasive Interactions
- HCIBGO: 7th International Conference on HCI in Business, Government and Organizations
- LCT: 7th International Conference on Learning and Collaboration Technologies
- ITAP: 6th International Conference on Human Aspects of IT for the Aged Population
- HCI-CPT: Second International Conference on HCI for Cybersecurity, Privacy and Trust
- HCI-Games: Second International Conference on HCI in Games
- MobiTAS: Second International Conference on HCI in Mobility, Transport and Automotive Systems
- AIS: Second International Conference on Adaptive Instructional Systems
- C&C: 8th International Conference on Culture and Computing
- MOBILE: First International Conference on Design, Operation and Evaluation of Mobile Communications
- AI-HCI: First International Conference on Artificial Intelligence in HCI

Conference Proceedings Volumes Full List

38. CCIS 1224, HCI International 2020 Posters - Part I, edited by Constantine Stephanidis and Margherita Antona
39. CCIS 1225, HCI International 2020 Posters - Part II, edited by Constantine Stephanidis and Margherita Antona
40. CCIS 1226, HCI International 2020 Posters - Part III, edited by Constantine Stephanidis and Margherita Antona

http://2020.hci.international/proceedings

First International Conference on Design, Operation and Evaluation of Mobile Communications (MOBILE 2020)

Program Board Chairs: **Gavriel Salvendy, University of Central Florida, USA, and June Wei, University of West Florida, USA**

- Ibrahim Arpaci, Turkey
- Younghoon Chang, China
- Shuchih Chang, Taiwan
- Shin-Horng Chen, Taiwan
- Alain Chong, China
- David Douglas, USA
- Sumeet Gupta, India;
- Bruce Chien-Ta Ho, Taiwan
- Chang-Tseh Hsieh, Taiwan
- Cheng-Kui Huang, Taiwan
- Jui-Chen Huang, Taiwan
- Noor Ismawati Jaafar, Malaysia
- Kai Koong, USA
- Ting-Peng Liang, Taiwan
- Binshan Lin, USA
- Shu-Ping Lin, Taiwan
- Manlu Liu, USA
- Yuan Liu, China
- June Lu, USA
- Abdul Samad Shibghatullah, Malaysia
- Tsang Wah, Hong Kong
- Bob Xu, UAE
- Jiaqin Yang, USA
- Shuiqing Yang, China
- Peiyan Zhou, China

The full list with the Program Board Chairs and the members of the Program Boards of all thematic areas and affiliated conferences is available online at:

http://www.hci.international/board-members-2020.php

HCI International 2021

The 23rd International Conference on Human-Computer Interaction, HCI International 2021 (HCII 2021), will be held jointly with the affiliated conferences in Washington DC, USA, at the Washington Hilton Hotel, July 24–29, 2021. It will cover a broad spectrum of themes related to Human-Computer Interaction (HCI), including theoretical issues, methods, tools, processes, and case studies in HCI design, as well as novel interaction techniques, interfaces, and applications. The proceedings will be published by Springer. More information will be available on the conference website: http://2021.hci.international/:

General Chair
Prof. Constantine Stephanidis
University of Crete and ICS-FORTH
Heraklion, Crete, Greece
Email: general_chair@hcii2021.org

http://2021.hci.international/

Contents

Human-Computer Driving Collaborative Control System for Curve Driving

Zhenhai Gao[1], Yiteng Sun[1]([⊠]), Hongyu Hu[1], Xingtai Mei[2], Lei He[1], Fei Gao[1], and Tianyao Zhang[1]

[1] State Key Laboratory of Automobile Simulation and Control, Jilin University, Changchun 130022, China
swatsyt@126.com

[2] Automotive Engineering Research Institute of Guangzhou Automobile, Guangzhou, China

Abstract. Curve driving has high requirements on the driver's hand, foot and eye coordination ability. Therefore, the bend is a frequent accident section. In this article, the performance of novice drivers and experienced drivers driving in curves were compared. Then, we found the coordination relationship between the longitudinal acceleration and the lateral motion of the vehicle according to the steering behavior of experienced drivers and vehicle movement state. Based on this coordination relationship, a human-computer driving control system is proposed. The control system aims at reducing the difficulty of driving in curves, and assisting the driver to control the longitudinal acceleration according to the driver's steering operation. Finally, the system was verified by means of real car experiments. By comparing acceleration changes and steering angles with or without a cooperative control system, the feasibility and effectiveness of the control system for reducing the difficulty of driving in curves is confirmed.

Keywords: Longitudinal and lateral coordination · Human-computer driving · Driver behavior · Driving assistant system

1 Introduction

Lateral motion of a vehicle is assumed to be the main task in the real driving situation. Nowadays, most cars are designed to have moderate understeer characteristics. This is due to the fact that when a car with oversteer characteristics turns, the turning radius will decrease with the increase of vehicle speed, and there is a risk of side slipping or even overturning. The turning process also requires certain coordination of the driver's hands, feet, and eyes. Especially, when the driver enters a corner at a high speed, it is difficult to control the vehicle's lateral and longitudinal movements cooperatively to make the vehicle move smoothly.

In previous research, the Electric Power Steering (EPS) [1] can effectively reduce the steering torque exerted by the driver, make the steering lighter, which can avoid oversteering after turning. It also provides support for subsequent active steering technologies.

© Springer Nature Switzerland AG 2020
G. Salvendy and J. Wei (Eds.): HCII 2020, LNCS 12216, pp. 1–15, 2020.
https://doi.org/10.1007/978-3-030-50350-5_1

In the study of critical instability, Bosch proposed the Vehicle Dynamics Control System (VDC) [2], which regulates the engine torque and the wheel brake pressures using traction control components to minimize the difference between the actual and the desired motion. It was later developed into an Electronic Stability Program (ESP) [3] and applied to real cars to improve the safety of the car during turning and reduce rollover accidents.

In the study of normal curve driving, Japanese Y. Shibahata and other scholars found that the Direct Yaw moment Control (DYC) [4] by proper distribution of traction and braking forces on the right and left tires could provide a very effective means of stabilizing vehicle characteristics, specifically for acceleration and deceleration, and enlarging the limit of vehicle maneuverability. M. Yamakado and other scholars introduced the G-Vectoring Control (GVC) [5], a coordinated control method for trading off longitudinal motion against lateral motion, which can reduce the steering wheel correction during turning and improve the handling experience.

In recent years, the researches on curves of automatic driving focus more on Lane Keeping System (LKS) based on EPS active steering [6, 7]. When the driver steers the steering wheel, the EPS provides assistance. When the driver is not operating, the EPS is controlled to steer actively to achieve lane keeping.

Aiming at the problems that the driver has difficulty in controlling the vehicle's longitudinal and lateral movements at the same time, and the control mode between the driver and the system, this paper proposes a hybrid intelligent control of human and vehicle from the perspective of co-driving. The optimized curves driving control method allows the assist system to work in coordination with the driver's behaviors, giving full play to the advantages of human-vehicle hybrid intelligent control.

By comparing and analyzing the differences in the driving behaviors of experienced drivers and novice drivers in curve, and according to the coordinated control law of experienced drivers, a human-computer driving control system is proposed. The curve coordinated control method, that is, the system applies a longitudinal acceleration control to the vehicle according to the current steering behavior of the driver. By shifting the vertical load generated by the change of the vehicle's longitudinal acceleration, the car's steering characteristics are adapted to the current state in the curve, which reduces the driver's workload. And reduces the difficulty of controlling the longitudinal and lateral movement of the vehicle, make it easier to handle the car in the curve. In addition, the change of acceleration during the curve is gentler, and the peak value of the lateral and longitudinal resultant acceleration is reduced.

2 Mechanism Analysis of Curved Driving

In order to explore the control mechanism of different types of drivers during curve driving, we selected 4 experienced drivers with driving mileage of more than 50,000 km and 4 novice drivers with driving mileage of less than 10,000 km. The experimental curve is shown in Fig. 1. The outer diameter of the curve is 50 m and the width of the curve is 7.5 m. The driver enters the curve at a speed of 50 km/h. After entering the curve, the driver can freely control the car. In addition, we collected vehicle speed, steering wheel angle, brake cylinder pressure, throttle position, longitudinal acceleration, lateral acceleration and other values during the experiment. By comparing the acceleration trajectories of the novice drivers and the experienced drivers in the curve, the control law of the drivers is summarized. From the perspective of the impact of the car's steady response, the improvement of the control strategy and the optimization of the curve driving are analyzed.

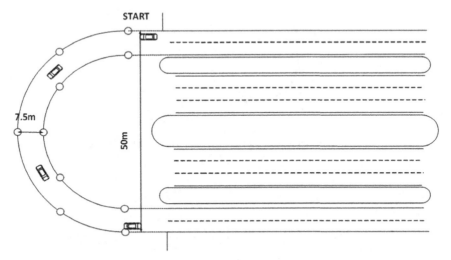

Fig. 1. Schematic diagram of test site

2.1   Comparison of Control Strategies for Turn-in

The acceleration trajectory diagram is drawn from the longitudinal acceleration Ax as the abscissa and the lateral acceleration Ay as the ordinate during the curve driving, which can reflect the driver's control rule in the curve.

The experienced driver started a left turn at time t0 in the acceleration trajectory diagram Fig. 2a and decelerated at the same time. At this time, the absolute values of the lateral acceleration Ay and the longitudinal acceleration Ax started to increase (at time t1). Then the driver adjusted the braking intensity. The absolute value of longitudinal acceleration decreased slightly, and the absolute value of lateral acceleration continued to increase (time t2). In the end, the lateral acceleration reached the maximum, the longitudinal acceleration decreased to approximately zero (time t3), and the bending process was completed. Due to the driver's continuous coordination of longitudinal and lateral movements, the trajectory of lateral and longitudinal acceleration is approximately an arc, and the absolute values of the longitudinal and lateral resultant accelerations at t1, t2, and t3 do not change significantly.

The novice driver made a left turn at time t0 in Fig. 2b. Firstly, he decelerated with a lower braking strength (time t1), and then with a higher braking intensity (time t2). After that he kept the braking intensity to continue turning (time t3). Finally, the brake pedal was released and the cornering process was ended (time t4). The comparison shows that the novice driver's ability to control longitudinal and lateral movements is weak. The acceleration trajectory is not smooth, and the absolute values of the resultant accelerations at t1, t2, t3, and t4 are significantly different. This is because the lateral movement of the car produced by the steering wheel cannot be coordinated with the longitudinal movement produced by the pedal.

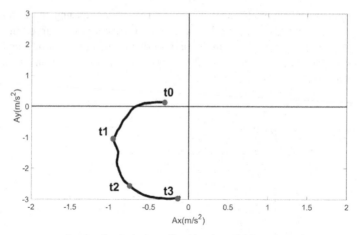

a. Acceleration trajectory of an experienced driver at turn-in stage

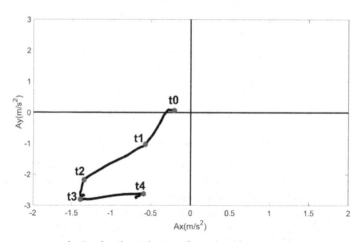

b. Acceleration trajectory of a novice driver at turn-in stage

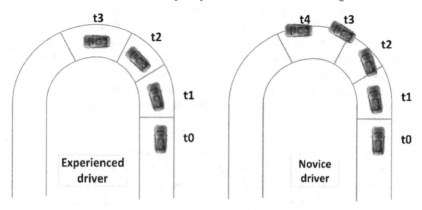

c. Comparison of experienced and novice drivers at turn-in stage

Fig. 2. (a) Acceleration trajectory of an experienced driver at turn-in stage. (b) Acceleration trajectory of a novice driver at turn-in stage. (c) Comparison of experienced and novice drivers at turn-in stage

2.2 Comparison of Control Strategies for Exit

During the exit stage, the acceleration trajectory of the experienced driver is still similar to an arc (Fig. 3a). The driver prepared to exit from time t0. With the decrease of the lateral acceleration, the driver accelerated (time t1). Subsequently, the accelerator pedal

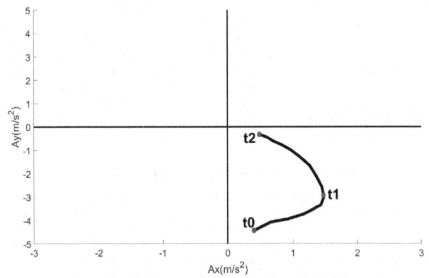

a. Acceleration trajectory of an experienced driver at exit stage

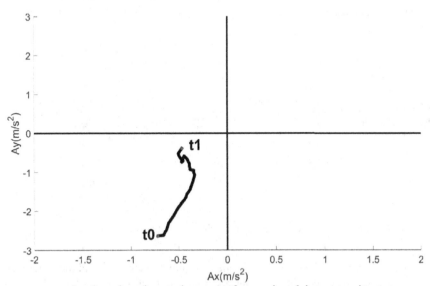

b. Acceleration trajectory of a novice driver at exit stage

Fig. 3. (a) Acceleration trajectory of an experienced driver at exit stage. (b) Acceleration trajectory of a novice driver at exit stage

was released, and the lateral and longitudinal accelerations were reduced at the same time. Then, the car resumed straight driving at a constant speed. However, the novice driver's acceleration trajectory is approximately a straight line (Fig. 3b). From t0 to t1, the lateral acceleration continued to decrease, but the longitudinal acceleration did not change significantly.

As can be seen from the acceleration trajectory diagram, experienced drivers and novice drivers have significantly different operating strategies, that is, experienced drivers cooperate with deceleration behavior during the turn-in stage, and have an acceleration behavior when exiting a curve. In all stages, the acceleration trajectory of the experienced driver is approximately a smooth arc. And the absolute value of the resultant acceleration does not change abruptly. However, the novice driver's hands, feet and eyes coordination ability is weak, and the vehicle's longitudinal and lateral movement cannot be coordinated at the same time during the curve, so the acceleration trajectory is a combination of multiple straight lines.

2.3 Effect of Longitudinal Acceleration on Steady-State Response

The control strategy of experienced drivers mainly affects the steady state response of the car by changing the vertical load of the front and rear axles. When there is braking behavior during cornering, the front axle load increases significantly and the rear axle load decreases accordingly. Within a certain load range, the change in tire cornering stiffness is the same as the load increase and decrease trend, so the front axle cornering stiffness increases and the rear axle cornering stiffness decreases. Therefore, when braking in a corner, the difference between the absolute values of the front and rear wheel side slip angles ($\alpha1 - \alpha2$) will be reduced, which will reduce the tendency of the car to understeer. Then, the vehicle attitude is easier to fit the curve (phase 2 in Fig. 4).

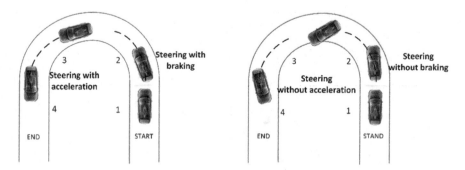

Fig. 4. Effect of longitudinal acceleration changes on understeer trend in curves

When accelerating at the stage of exit, the load moves backward, and the difference between the absolute values of the front and rear wheel side slip angles ($\alpha1 - \alpha2$) increases. The tendency of understeer of the car increases, and the attitude of the car is easier to approach the straight line (phase 4 in Fig. 4), which avoids more correction behaviors.

3   Human-Computer Driving Collaborative Control System

3.1   Three-Parameter Cooperative Control Algorithm

According to the study of the above mentioned mechanism, and following the curve control of experienced drivers, a human-computer driving control system is proposed. The human-vehicle hybrid intelligence method is used to solve the driver's hand-foot-eye coordination problem. In curves, the driver controls the lateral movement of the vehicle. At the same time, the system controls longitudinal movement according to the driver's steering wheel angle and the current vehicle speed. Coordinate with the lateral movement of the car, reduce the difficulty of the driver's operation, and make the car easier to drive.

The control strategy refers to the acceleration trajectory diagram of experienced drivers, so that the acceleration trajectory of the vehicle is approximately elliptical, as shown in Fig. 5. The ideal right-turn acceleration trajectory (shown in the blue line in Fig. 5) and the left-turn acceleration trajectory (shown in the black line in Fig. 5) are circular arcs, which helps to prevent lateral and longitudinal acceleration from exceeding the limit of road adhesion.

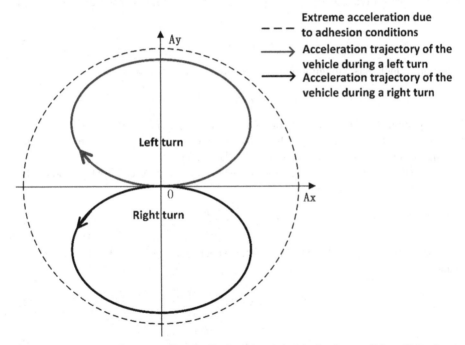

Fig. 5. Coordination of lateral and longitudinal acceleration and adhesion conditions (Color figure online)

The left-turn ellipse equation is

$$\frac{Ax^2}{a^2} + \frac{(Ay - b)^2}{b^2} = 1 \tag{1}$$

The parametric equation is

$$Ax = a\cos\theta \tag{2}$$

$$Ay = b\sin\theta + b \tag{3}$$

In the equation: Ay is the lateral acceleration of the vehicle, Ax is the longitudinal acceleration. a is the length of the major axis of the ellipse, b is the length of the minor axis of the ellipse and θ is the parameter of the eccentric angle.

The derivative of Eq. (3) is

$$\dot{Ay} = b\cos\theta\,\dot{\theta} \tag{4}$$

Substitute Eq. (4) into Eq. (2)

$$Ax = \frac{a\,\dot{Ay}}{b\,\dot{\theta}} \tag{5}$$

When the car is driving at a constant speed, the moment at the rear wheel ground point is

$$F_{Z1}L = mgl_2 \tag{6}$$

When the vehicle has a longitudinal acceleration, the moment becomes

$$F_{Z1}L = mgl_2 - mAxh \tag{7}$$

In the equation: F_{Z1} is the ground normal reaction force acting on the front wheels; L is the wheelbase of the vehicle; l_2 is the distance from the center of mass to the rear axle; h is the height of the center of mass and m is the mass of the car.

Due to the influence of the axial load transfer, the normal force of the ground on the front axle changes as follows:

$$F_{Z1} = -\frac{mAxh}{L} \tag{8}$$

The normal forces of the left and right front wheels and the left and right rear wheels change to

$$\Delta w_{Z1} = \Delta w_{Z2} = -\frac{mAxh}{2L} \tag{9}$$

$$\Delta w_{Z3} = \Delta w_{Z4} = \frac{mAxh}{2L} \tag{10}$$

Similarly, when the vehicle has a lateral acceleration Ay at the same time (as shown in Fig. 6), the normal forces of the left and right front wheels and the left and right rear wheels change as follows:

$$\Delta w_{Z1} = -\frac{mAxh}{2L} - \frac{mAyh}{2d} \tag{11}$$

$$\Delta w_{Z2} = -\frac{mAxh}{2L} + \frac{mAyh}{2d} \tag{12}$$

$$\Delta w_{Z3} = \frac{mAxh}{2L} - \frac{mAyh}{2d} \tag{13}$$

$$\Delta w_{Z4} = \frac{mAxh}{2L} + \frac{mAyh}{2d} \tag{14}$$

In the equation: d is the wheel track. w_{Z1}, w_{Z2}, w_{Z3} and w_{Z4} are ground normal reaction forces acting on the front left wheel, front right wheel, rear left wheel, and rear right wheel, respectively.

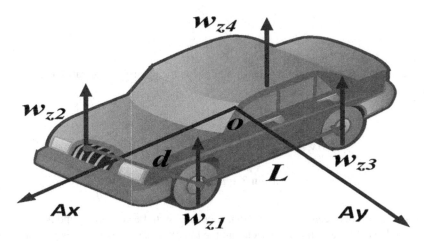

Fig. 6. Force diagram of tires with lateral and longitudinal acceleration

The previous experimental results show that the derivative of the vertical load transfer of the front outer wheels in the curve is approximately constant [8], that is,

$$\frac{dw_{Z2}}{dt} = -\frac{mh}{2}\left(\frac{\dot{Ax}}{L} - \frac{\dot{Ay}}{d}\right) = C \tag{15}$$

Take Eq. (4) and the derivative of Eq. (2) into Eq. (15) to get

$$\frac{dw_{Z2}}{dt} = -\frac{mh}{2}\left(-\frac{a\sin\theta\,\dot{\theta}}{L} - \frac{b\cos\theta\,\dot{\theta}}{d}\right) = C \tag{16}$$

$$\dot{\theta} = \frac{2dCL}{mh(ad\sin\theta + bL\cos\theta)} \tag{17}$$

Take Eq. (17) into Eq. (5) to get

$$Ax = \frac{amh(ad\sin\theta + bL\cos\theta)}{2bdCL}\dot{Ay} \tag{18}$$

From Eq. (18), it can be known that in the human-vehicle coordinated control system, the longitudinal movement of the car controlled by the system, that is, the longitudinal acceleration Ax and the derivative of the lateral acceleration $\dot{A}y$ have a certain relationship. The derivative of the vehicle's lateral acceleration depends on the driver's control of the steering wheel. Therefore, when the driver turns the steering wheel to control the lateral movement of the car, the system can choose a suitable longitudinal acceleration to coordinate.

In the ideal case, when the driver turns the steering wheel, the corresponding car curvature is 1/R, and the lateral acceleration is Ay. The relationship between them is as follows [9].

$$\frac{1}{R} = \frac{\delta}{iL} \tag{19}$$

$$Ay = \frac{V^2}{R} = \frac{\delta}{iL}V^2 \tag{20}$$

In the equation: δ is the steering wheel angle, i is the steering gear ratio and V is the vehicle speed.

Take Eq. (20) into Eq. (18)

$$Ax = \frac{amh(da\sin\theta + Lb\cos\theta)}{2dCL}\left(\frac{\dot{\delta}}{iL}V^2\right) \tag{21}$$

$$Ax = \frac{amh(da\sin\theta + Lb\cos\theta)}{2idCL^2}\left(V^2\dot{\delta} + 2\delta V\dot{V}\right) \tag{22}$$

The relationship between the longitudinal acceleration to be controlled and the steering wheel angle is obtained. It can be seen that the longitudinal acceleration is proportional to the steering wheel angle and vehicle speed. Therefore, the longitudinal acceleration correction value can be determined by parameters such as the steering wheel angle and vehicle speed.

3.2 Judgment of Status and Conditions Precedent

The turning process is divided into five stages, as shown in Fig. 7, which are the turn-in stage I and II, the apex stage III, and the exit stages IV and V.

Firstly, the system should determine whether the vehicle is in a turn-in state or exit state. The steering wheel angle is defined as a positive value on the right side of the initial position and a negative value on the left side. Therefore, during the entire left turn, the steering wheel angle is negative. In addition, during the stage I and II, the driver continues to turn the steering wheel to the left, so the derivative of the steering wheel angle is also negative. However, during the stage IV and V, the driver continues to turn the steering wheel to the right, the derivative of the steering wheel angle is positive. Since the steering wheel position is always to the left of the initial position, the steering angle is negative.

$$n = -\frac{\delta\dot{\delta}}{|\delta\dot{\delta}|} = \pm 1 \tag{23}$$

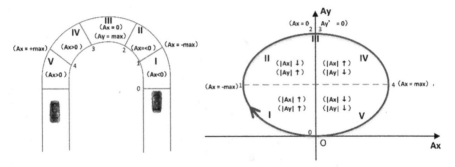

Fig. 7. Comparison diagram of five-stage vehicle state and acceleration trajectory in the curve

Therefore, Eq. (23) can be used to determine whether the vehicle is in the turn-in or exit phase (see Table 1).

Table 1. Turn-in and exit state partitioned table

States	δ	$\dot{\delta}$	$\dot{\delta}\dot{\delta}$	n
Turn-in of left turn	−	−	+	−1
Exit of left turn	−	+	−	1
Turn-in of right turn	+	+	+	−1
Exit of right turn	+	−	−	1

Based on the driver's lateral control, the strategy for the system to automatically adjust the longitudinal acceleration can be written as

$$Ax = -\frac{\dot{\delta}}{\left|\dot{\delta}\dot{\delta}\right|}k\left(V^2\dot{\delta}+2\delta V\dot{V}\right) \tag{24}$$

In the equation, k is the auxiliary intensity coefficient, which constitutes three parameters with the steering angle δ and vehicle speed V.

At the same time, in order to avoid the sudden intervention of the system in non-turning conditions such as lane changing and other daily driving conditions, the opening conditions of the system should be limited. System intervention is mainly determined by vehicle speed, steering wheel angle, and lateral acceleration (see Fig. 8).

The system will only work if three conditions are met: the vehicle speed is greater than 20 km/h, the steering wheel angle is greater than 10° and the absolute value of lateral acceleration is greater than 2 m/s². For the acceleration function at the exit stage, two additional conditions must be met. That is, the vehicle speed is less than 50 km/h and the absolute value of lateral acceleration is less than 4 m/s². This is to avoid excessive speed and frequent acceleration/deceleration switching in curves.

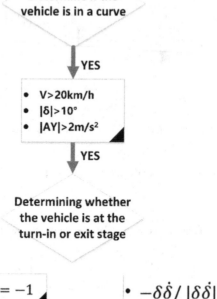

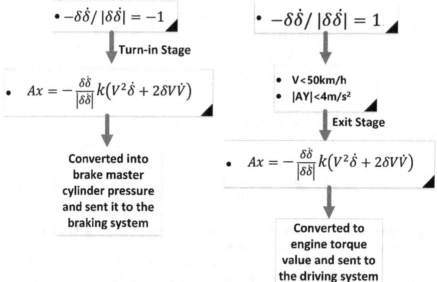

Fig. 8. Data flow diagram of collaborative control system

4 Real Vehicle Test Verification

4.1 Comparison of the Effects With/Without Control Systems

The control algorithm is carried on a real car for experiments. The experimental scenario is shown in Fig. 1. After accelerating through straight sections, the car reaches the starting point at a speed of 40 km/h and the drivers could drive freely in curves. Record the driver's performance with or without the collaborative control system.

Figure 9 shows the acceleration trajectory of the vehicle in a curve with or without a collaborative control system. It can be clearly seen from the figure that with the help of the control system, the acceleration trajectory (orange line) is smoother than that without the system (black line). And the change in resultant acceleration is also gentler. When the system is not turned on, the peak lateral acceleration is 4.92 m/s^2. However, with the system, the peak lateral acceleration is reduced to -4.1 m/s^2. And the system can effectively reduce the peak resultant acceleration from 4.99 m/s^2 to 4.21 m/s^2 to avoid reaching the road adhesion limit. In addition, due to the system's auxiliary control of longitudinal movement in curves, the driver can pay more attention to the lateral movement of the car. This makes the steering wheel angle fluctuations smaller and the changes slighter (see Fig. 10), which can effectively reduce driving difficulty.

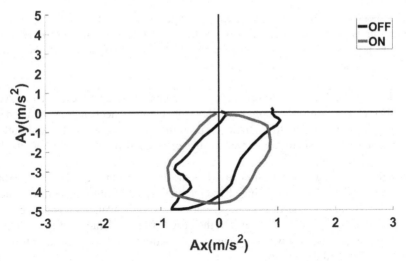

Fig. 9. Acceleration trajectory of the vehicle with or without the control system (Color figure online)

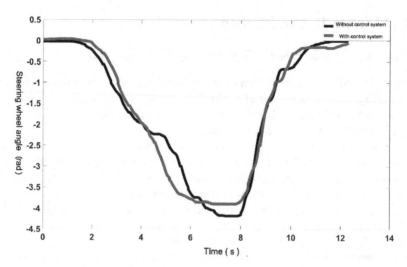

Fig. 10. Steering wheel angle with or without the control system

5   Conclusion

From the perspective of human-computer driving, a collaborative control system for curve driving is proposed. According to the steering wheel manipulation by the driver, the system performs longitudinal acceleration control in accordance with the current lateral motion state.

- Simulating the coordinated control regularities of experienced drivers in the curve, a three-parameter coordinated control method for steering wheel angle, vehicle speed, and system auxiliary strength coefficient is proposed. It can coordinate the longitudinal acceleration of the car in the curve, so that ordinary drivers can drive as well as experienced drivers.
- Through the vertical load transfer caused by the change of the vehicle's longitudinal acceleration, the vehicle's steering characteristics are adapted to the current state in the curve. Braking at the turn-in stage can reduce the tendency of understeer and make it easier for the vehicle to fit into the curve. The acceleration of the exit stage can increase the tendency of understeer, and the attitude of the car is easier to fit the straight line after the cornering.
- The cooperative control system reduces the workload of the driver's longitudinal manipulation in the curve and the difficulty of hand-foot-eye coordination. The system makes the car easier to handle, and the acceleration change of the car in the curve is slighter.

Acknowledgments. We acknowledge Zhang Yichi, Zhu Naixuan and Sheng Yuhuan for technical assistance, Liu Jiaqi for assistance with translation. Funding: Supported by National Science Foundation of China (grants 51775236 51675224 U1564214) and National Key Research and

Development Program (grant 2017YFB0102600). Competing interests: Authors declare no competing interests. Data and materials availability: All data is available in the main text or the supplementary materials.

References

1. Kim, J.H., Song, J.B.: Control logic for an electric power steering system using assist motor. Mechatronics **12**(3), 447–459 (2002)
2. Woerdt, A., Erhardt, R.P., Pfaff, G.: VDC, the vehicle dynamics control system of Bosch. In: Proceedings of the International Congress Exposition (1995)
3. Liebemann, E.K., et al.: Safety and performance enhancement: the Bosch Electronic Stability Control (ESP). No. 2004-21-0060. SAE Technical Paper (2004)
4. Shibahata, Y., Shimada, K., Tomari, T.: Improvement of vehicle maneuverability by direct yaw moment control. Veh. Syst. Dyn. **22**(5-6), 465–481 (1993)
5. Yamakado, M., et al.: Study of mechanism improving target course traceability in G-Vectoring Control. Veh. Syst. Dyn. **56**(5), 832–851 (2018)
6. Marino, R., Scalzi, S., Netto, M.: Nested PID steering control for lane keeping in autonomous vehicles. Control Eng. Pract. **19**(12), 1459–1467 (2011)
7. Zhang, H., Luo, Y., Jiang, Q., Li, K.: Lane keeping system based on electric power steering system. In: SAE-China, FISITA (eds.) Proceedings of the FISITA 2012 World Automotive Congress. LNEE, vol. 194, pp. 83–97. Springer, Heidelberg (2013). https://doi.org/10.1007/978-3-642-33829-8_9
8. Yamakado, M., Abe, M.: An experimentally confirmed driver longitudinal acceleration control model combined with vehicle lateral motion. Veh. Syst. Dyn. **46**(S1), 129–149 (2008)
9. Guo, K.: Principles of vehicle handling dynamics (2011)

Wearable Services Adoption Study from a Perspective of Usability

Zhongwei Gu[1] and June Wei[2(✉)]

[1] Shanghai Dianji University, Pudong, Shanghai, China
zwgu@qq.com
[2] University of West Florida, Pensacola, FL, USA
jwei@uwf.edu

Abstract. This paper explores the adoption of wearable services from the perspective of usability. Firstly, three factors influencing the usability of wearable services are proposed, namely device characteristics, APP characteristics, network characteristics. Secondly, we put forward an adoption framework based on usability of wearable service. The empirical analysis results from the structural equation model analysis show that device characteristics, APP characteristics and network characteristics have significant impacts on the usability of wearable services, and usability significantly affected use intention. It indicates that the characteristics of wearable devices are very important and consumer satisfaction needs to be improved urgently. The conclusions of the study can provide references for the usability and adoption of wearable services, and point out the direction of product development for wearable device manufacturers.

Keywords: Wearable service · Usability · Device characteristics

1 Introduction

Wearable service refers to a new service model that comprehensively utilizes various wearable devices, wearable apps and related technologies (sensors, cloud computing, big data and wireless network etc.), and has the capability of scenario computing and natural human-computer interaction, so as to be applied in healthcare, entertainment, social commerce and other fields. At present, the world is entering the era of 5G plus Internet of Things (IoT), which indicates that wearable services will definitely enter a period of rapid development. Wearable devices market is expected to reach 500 million dollars in 2021 [1]. However, due to the limitations of wearable devices, the backward of APP software and the imperfect of communication network, the adoption of wearable services will bring certain negative effects. These factors include wearables' comfortability, beauty, durability, size, input/output efficiency, store capacity, connection and transmission speeds etc. These disadvantages are determined by the characteristics of wearable devices, APP, communication network etc. which will affect the usability and thus the adoption of wearable services.

© Springer Nature Switzerland AG 2020
G. Salvendy and J. Wei (Eds.): HCII 2020, LNCS 12216, pp. 16–22, 2020.
https://doi.org/10.1007/978-3-030-50350-5_2

Traditional adoption studies are mostly based on classic technology adoption theories such as TAM, but the main factors of TAM model are subjective rather than objective description of technology itself. Therefore, the TAM model has a limited role in guiding the research on wearable service adoption. Compared with perceived usefulness (PU) and perceived ease of use (PEOU) factors in TAM model, usability is a more objective concept. The research of many scholars has shown that usability is an important factor in the success and wide adoption of mobile services [2, 3]. Wearable services are similar to mobile services, so this paper hopes to study the adoption of wearable services from the perspective of usability, propose a wearable service adoption model based on usability and carry out empirical analysis. It is hoped that it can provide reference for the research on factors influencing the usability of wearable services and the adoption of wearable services, and provide guidance and suggestions for the product R&D and design of wearable device manufacturers.

2   Conceptual Model and Hypotheses

2.1   Conceptual Model

Combined with the above literature and research on wearable manufacturers, this article finally builds a wearable service adoption model based on usability (Fig. 1 below). Among them, five variables will be evaluated, including device characteristics, network characteristics, APP characteristics, usability and use intention.

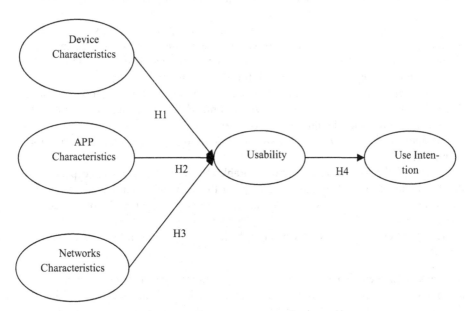

Fig. 1. Conceptual model of wearable adoption

2.2 Hypotheses

Device Characteristics. As a new kind of device, wearable device is quite different from traditional desktop device and handheld device. Many scholars point out that the important factors restricting the development of wearable devices include battery life, input and output mode, storage capacity and so on [4]. Wearable devices are closer to our bodies than handheld or desktop devices. These devices stay with us longer even at night (for example, bracelet used for monitoring sleep). So, the device must have comfortable wearing with higher durability and endurance. For outdoor activities, these devices also need to be beautiful, not too large or too heavy, and in some cases need better waterproof ability. Of course, the capabilities that other mobile devices have, such as processing speed, storage capacity etc., also need to be considered. Now consumers have high expectations for wearable devices and diversified demands, which bring new challenges to hardware manufacturers. To sum up, these factors will directly or indirectly affect the usability of wearable services. Therefore, the following hypothesis can be made:

H1: wearable device characteristics significantly affect the usability of wearable services.

APP Characteristics. Due to the limitation of screen size, the User Interface (UI) design and interaction design of wearable APP have higher requirements. The layout of the content presented in the software's user interface needs to help reduce search time, improve user efficiency in completing tasks, and increase user satisfaction. Hsiao et al. believe that the personalized design of wearable devices will affect consumers' choices [5]. More and more personalized demands require UI design that is not only convenient for users but also customized by users.

In order to improve user experience, the interaction process of the software can be minimized by using voice interaction or visual recognition, such as using the intelligent voice assistant to control the software operation of the wearable device, authentication payment through fingerprint or face scan for identification.

At the same time, due to the limitation of computing power and storage capacity, the APP function of wearable devices will be limited. The software should not be too large and the functions should not be too many. Therefore, the development tools and development process of APP are also different from the development of traditional mobile APP.

In a word, the APP development of wearable devices must be able to keep pace with the development of hardware and make up for the shortage of hardware. The characteristics of APP software for wearable devices are very important factors influencing consumer adoption. Therefore, the following hypothesis is proposed:

H2: APP characteristics of wearable devices significantly affect the usability of wearable services.

Networks Characteristics. Before, due to the immaturity of network communication technology, sometimes users were disappointed with it. The main reasons were the slow speed of data transmission, the instability of network access and the low coverage rate, which greatly affected the efficiency of users to achieve the predetermined target. With the commercialization of 5G, network connection speed and transmission rate will be gradually solved. But the issue of coverage could still constrain the growth of wearables.

Especially in sparsely populated countries, network coverage is a challenge, given the wild or time-critical use scenarios.

At the same time, with the development of the IoT, there are more and more types of wearable devices and more and more complex usage scenarios. In the era of internet of everything, the interconnection and compatibility between various heterogeneous networks are becoming more and more important. If we want to break down the barriers between each device and platform, we need to make the network compatible with each other, so that users can switch easily and freely. Xia et al. believes it is important to make wearable devices compatible [6]. Therefore, the following hypothesis is proposed:

H3: network characteristics of wearable devices significantly affect the usability of wearable services.

Usability. Usability is an important variable that affects users' willingness to adopt it. Coursaris et al. summarized 45 empirical research literatures on mobile usability. Efficiency will have an impact on usability, and then the usability of the whole system [7]. In the same way, the effectiveness and high satisfaction to users will make users feel that the system has good usefulness, thus increasing users' intention and adoption of the system. These three essential attributes of usability also apply to wearable services.

This article adds wearablity to the usability concept defined by ISO 9241-11. That is, usability includes efficiency, effectiveness, satisfaction, and wearablity. The biggest difference between wearables and mobile devices is wearablity. The term "wearablity" refers to the capability to provide services through dress or wear without the need for handheld or manual operation.

Of course, wearablity, as one of the core characteristics of wearable devices, is a key attribute that constitutes the usability of wearable services. Wearablity will determine whether people can comfortably use wearable devices, which will largely affect people's PEOU of wearable services, thus influencing users' adoption of wearable services. Therefore, through the above analysis, the author believes that usability will have a critical impact on the adoption of wearable services by users. So, the following hypothesis is proposed:

H5: usability significantly affects use intension to adopt wearable services.

3   Research Method

This paper developed some new measurement items for questionnaires, and adopted 7-point Likert method. We conducted a small sample pre-survey. Preliminary investigation had chosen 50 persons with a wearable device or mobile device using experience. Finally the concrete measurement item and the literature sources are shown in Table 1.

The questionnaire respondent were selected from undergraduate students, graduate students and IT professionals in China. A total of 330 questionnaires were collected, of which 269 were valid. Men accounted for 52% and women make up 48 percent of the population. The majority of respondents were between the ages of 18 and 35 (84.8%). The total proportion of students is 37.9%. Among the students, 82.9% have a bachelor's degree or above, 34.9% have a monthly income below 3,000 yuan, and 37.1% have a monthly income between 3,000 and 6,000 yuan. All of them are Chinese citizens, so the questionnaire respondent were selected in line with the current research requirements of wearable devices in mainland China.

Table 1. Improved measurement scale

Variable		Indicators	Index content	Source
1	Device Characteristics (D)	D1	Wearable devices must be durable, waterproof and dustproof	Literature [8]
		D2	Wearables should be comfortable to wear	New item
		D3	Wearable battery life is important	Literature [4]
		D4	The information input of wearable devices should be more convenient	Literature [9]
		D5	Wearables have more computing power and are faster	Literature [9]
		D6	Wearable devices should have the right storage capacity	Literature [9]
2	APP Characteristics (A)	A1	UI layout design of wearable device APP is very important	New item
		A2	Interactive process design of wearable device APP is very important	New item
		A3	I hope my wearable device can customize the UI interface and functions	New item
3	Network Characteristics (N)	N1	I think compatibility between networks is important	New item
		N2	I want my wearable device to connect to other devices quickly	New item
		N3	I want the wireless Internet to download as fast as possible	Literature [12]
		N4	I hope the signal on the wireless network is stable	Literature [12]
		N5	I hope wireless coverage can be higher	Literature [12]
Usability (U)		U1	Wearables should be comfortable to wear.	New item
		U2	Wearable services can improve my productivity.	Literature [11]
		U3	Wearable services can improve my work.	Literature [11]
		U4	I'm happy with the wearable service	Literature [11]
Use Intension (UI)		UI1	I'm willing to buy wearables and try out some apps	Literature [10]
		UI2	I am willing to provide necessary personal information to wearables providers	Literature [10]
		UI3	I will try to use wearable devices in the future	Literature [10]

4   Data Analysis and Results

4.1   Reliability and Validity Analysis

First, the Bartlett sphericity test was performed using SPSS24.0. The results showed that the KMO value of the sample data was 0.894. Four factors were extracted from principal component analysis, the variance interpretation rate was 74.696%, and the load values of each index's corresponding factors were all greater than 0.5, while the factor load values of the cross variables were all less than 0.5, indicating that the samples had good convergent validity and discriminant validity.

Through confirmatory factor analysis the mean variance extraction (AVE) of all variables is greater than 0.6, indicating that the scale has good convergent validity, and the composite reliability (CR) is higher than 0.8, indicating that the scale has good reliability.

4.2 Structural Model: Hypothesis Testing

This article uses LISREL to test the model's hypotheses, as shown in Table 2. Data analysis results showed that all the hypotheses were significant at the $p < 0.05$ level, with H1, H3 and H5 being significant at the $p < 0.001$ level.

Table 2. Hypotheses testing results and path coefficient

Hypothesis	Testing results	Path coefficient
H1	Supported	0.44***
H2	Supported	0.15**
H3	Supported	0.34***
H4	Supported	0.95***

5 Discussion and Conclusion

Discussion. Data analysis results show that wearable device characteristics, APP, network characteristic and usability all have positive significant effect. The device characteristic's influence on usability is the largest, the path coefficient of device characteristics is 0.44. This shows that consumers still pay great attention to the special value brought by wearable hardware products. Consumers have high expectations for wearable device characteristics, such as durability, endurance, size and comfortability. This also indicates that the gap between device characteristics and consumer ideal is the most obvious in the process of wearable services at present. Secondly, the path coefficient of network characteristics is 0.34, indicating that good network communication is a necessary condition for the use of wearable services, and consumers are well aware of this. Thirdly, the path coefficient of APP characteristic, 0.15, also significantly affects the usability of wearable services, indicating the importance of APP, which can be adapted to hardware, bring personalized customization functions to consumers, and improve the efficiency, effectiveness and satisfaction of wearable services.

The hypothesis that the usability of wearable services has a significant impact on consumers' use intentions has also been verified, with a path coefficient of 0.95, indicating that improving the usability of wearable services is the best way to fundamentally improve consumers' use intentions.

Conclusion. This paper proposes a new attribute of wearable service usability, namely: wearablity. This new attribute is put forward for the first time on the basis of integrating all kinds of literature in academia and business circles. Although the adoption of wearable services has been mentioned in the previous research literature, the number of literatures is small, and the perspectives are different. Studying the adoption of wearable services from a usability perspective is a useful attempt.

References

1. Gartner: The forecast of global wearable device shipments in 2015–2021. Forward - Industry Research Institute, Gartner (2017)
2. Han, J., Pei, J., Yin, Y.: Mining frequent patterns without candidate generation. ACM Sigmod Rec. **29**(2), 1–12 (2000)
3. Pasquier, N., Bastide, Y., Taouil, R., et al.: Efficient mining of association rules using closed itemset lattices. Inf. Syst. **24**(1), 25–46 (1999)
4. Liu, D., Cai, S.: Research on influencing factors of wearables user adoption behavior based on the comparative analysis of iWatch and xiaomi. Prod. Res. (11), 68–73, 6 p. (2016)
5. Yang, J., Wang, Q.-P., Hu, H.-N., et al.: New progress in wearable device endurance research. Micro Nano Electron. Technol. **53**(7), 425–430 (2016)
6. Hsiao, K.-L.: Android smartphone adoption and intention to pay for mobile Internet. Libr. Hi Tech **31**(2), 216–235 (2013)
7. Integration technology of smart home and wearable devices. Hunan Normal University (2015)
8. Coursaris, C., Kim, D.: A qualitative review of empirical mobile usability studies. In: AMCIS 2006 Proceedings, p. 352 (2006)
9. Gu, Z., Xu, F., Wei, J., et al.: The empirical study on the influencing factors of consumers' initial trust in wearable commerce. J. Manag. Rev. **27**(7), 168–176 (2015)
10. Buchanan, G., Farrant, S., Jones, M., et al.: Improving mobile internet usability. In: Proceedings of the 10th International Conference on the World Wide Web, pp. 673–680 (2001)
11. Nielsen, J.: Usability Engineering. Morgan Kaufmann, Burlington (1994)
12. Hung, S.Y., Ku, C.Y., Chang, C.M.: Critical factors of WAP services adoption: an empirical study. Electron. Commer. Res. Appl. **2**(1), 42–60 (2003)

How Does Mobile Devices Usage Contribute to Individual's Creativity in Cross-Cultural Settings?

Shangui Hu[1]([✉]), Hefu Liu[2], and Guoyin Wang[1]

[1] School of Business, Anhui University of Technology, Ma'anshan, Anhui, China
stanleyhff@hotmail.com, wgycch@hotmail.com
[2] School of Management, University of Science and Technology of China, Hefei, China
liuhf@ustc.edu.cn

Abstract. The prevalence of mobile device usage is changing the main domains of the current world. In light of increasing international expatriation to meet the demands of overseas success, more empirical research should be conducted to investigate the under-studied usage of mobile device in cross-cultural contexts. The current research was designed to explore relationships among mobile device usage, intention to share knowledge, individual creativity and cultural distance. We identified that the impacts of informational and socializing usage of mobile device contribute to individual's intention to share knowledge, thereby positively influencing individual's creativity. However, cultural distance was identified as a boundary condition impairing the positive effects of mobile device usage on individual's intention to share knowledge in cross-cultural environment. The implications and limitations of this research are also discussed.

Keywords: Mobile device usage · Intention to share knowledge · Creativity · Cultural distance · Cross-cultural settings

1 Introduction

Mobile device usage has become ubiquitous and influences people's lives in various domains by changing the way people communicate and interact with each another (Yan et al. 2019; Brown and Palvia 2015). Although there has been growing scholarly interests in researching the impacts of mobile device usage, inconsistent findings have been reached with both positive and negative effects stirred by mobile device usage on individual performance (Hu et al. 2017; Karr-Wisniewski and Lu 2010). On one hand, evidence has shown that mobile devices such as smartphones enhance interpersonal relationships and role performance (Lee et al. 2017). On the other hand, mobile device usage may bring disturbance, addiction and break down work-life balance as a noisy channel (Brown and Palvia 2015; Kauffman et al. 2017).

Although literature has indicated the significant effects of mobile device usage on individual development, there is scarcity of evidence testing empirically its functionalities in cross-cultural environment. This becomes an urgent issue since globalization

© Springer Nature Switzerland AG 2020
G. Salvendy and J. Wei (Eds.): HCII 2020, LNCS 12216, pp. 23–32, 2020.
https://doi.org/10.1007/978-3-030-50350-5_3

increases the mobility of expatriates who show more reliance on mobile devices when they travel to foreign countries wherein they suffer a lot from cultural shock and conflicts (Hu et al. 2018, 2020). Although few studies have identified that application of information technology influences individual development in cross-cultural environment (Hu et al. 2017, 2018), there is a great necessity to further identity the relationships between mobile device usage and personal development, such as, creativity, the key competence in the 21st century for individual and business success (Miron-Spektor and Beenen 2015). Moreover, how cultural boundaries impact mobile device usage in cross-cultural settings deserve scholarly attention as well.

The current research aims to answer the important yet unclear question. More specifically, we endeavor to clarify how two dimensions of mobile device usage impact two dimensions of intention to share knowledge respectively, thereby enhancing individual creativity. Further, we explore how cultural distance as a boundary condition in cross-cultural environment acts as a noisy channel to disturb the positive effects exerted by mobile device usage.

The remainder of the paper is organized as follows. A literature review is conducted in Sect. 2. Thereafter, research model and hypotheses are developed, which is followed by research methodology and results. Following that, a discussion section interprets research results and suggests implications and limitations.

2   Research Model and Theoretical Development

Based on the extant literature review about mobile device usage, intention to share knowledge, individual creativity and cultural distance, we propose the research model outlining the relationships between those variables. And the research model is depicted in Fig. 1.

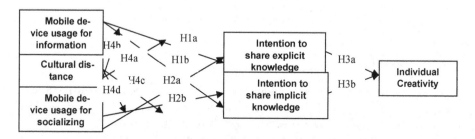

Fig. 1. Research model

2.1   Mobile Devices Usage and Intention to Share Knowledge

Mobile device usage helps expatriates to integrate into the new community with better understandings and change cultural identification to conform to the majority group (Safdar and Berno 2016). Thereafter getting acquainted with the new environment, expatriates are more likely to share explicit knowledge including their work reports, manuals, methodologies, and research theories with their colleagues and leaders (Bock et al.

2005). Further, mobile device usage for information purpose also encourages expatriates to interact and establish good interpersonal relationships with others from different cultural backgrounds. And this finally enhances individual's intention to share implicit knowledge. Based on the above statement, we hypothesize that:

Mobile device usage for information purpose is positively related to intention to share explicit knowledge: H1a, and intention to share implicit knowledge: H1b.

Likewise, expatriates tend to rely on mobile device usage for direct socializing purpose. Interaction and communication through mobile device usage offers conveniences for expatriates to establish interpersonal relationship and integrate into the mainstream culture (Hu et al. 2020; Chung et al. 2014). In this way, they are more likely to share explicit and implicit knowledge. Thus we hypothesize that:

H2a: Mobile device usage for socializing purpose is positively related to intention to share explicit knowledge, and positively related to intention to share implicit knowledge: H2b.

2.2 Intention to Share Knowledge and Individual Creativity

During the process of knowledge sharing, positive psychological changes happen to expatriates including trust, self-efficacy, self-confidence (Hu et al. 2017, 2018; Ogunmokun et al. 2020). And those factors have been identified as antecedents for individual creativity (Perry-Smith and Mannucci 2017; Al-Kurdi et al. 2020). Relevant evidences have identified the positive association between expatriate's knowledge sharing and individual creativity (Gong et al. 2013; Ali et al. 2019; Sigala and Chalkiti 2015; Liao and Chen 2018). Based on the above statement, we hypothesize that:

Expatriate's intention to share explicit knowledge (H3a) and intention to share implicit knowledge (H3b) are positively related to individual creativity.

2.3 The Moderating Roles of Cultural Distance

As a dominant stressor disturbing expatriate's psychological comfort, cultural distance comprehensively represents culturally-rooted patterns how individuals from different cultural backgrounds think, feel and act (Hofstede 1997). The more distant one culture is from another one, the more negative effects and less psychological comfort would happen to expatriates (Redmond 2000). In other words, perceived cultural distance may hamper expatriate's mobile device usage to enhance their intention to share knowledge because of unpredicted uncertainties existing in culturally-distant host culture. Based on the above statement, we hypothesize:

Cultural distance negatively moderates the relationship between informational mobile device usage and intention to share explicit knowledge (H4a), and intention to share implicit knowledge (H4b);

Cultural distance negatively moderates the relationship between socializing mobile device usage and intention to share explicit knowledge (H4c), and intention to share implicit knowledge (H4d).

3 Research Methodology

A survey methodology was employed. The survey was conducted at two Chinese public universities with samples of international students who show reliance on mobile device usage during their learning process. 400 questionnaires were delivered to the international students. 381 questionnaires were finally collected back with a returning rate of 95.3%. After deleting the incomplete ones, a total of 340 questionnaires were used for the current research analysis.

A six-item scale was adapted from Hughes et al. (2012) to measure mobile device usage. Intention to share knowledge was measured with a 5-item scale developed by Bock et al. (2005). Among the five items, two were used to measure the intention to share explicit knowledge and 3 were used to measure the intention to share implicit knowledge. Individual creativity was measured with a 4-item scale, which was adapted from Farmer et al. (2003). A 6-item scale was adapted from Chen et al. (2010) to measure the cultural distance.

4 Results

4.1 Assessment of Variables

Table 1 indicated good discriminant validity of all constructs.

Table 1. Measurement of constructs

Constructs	Dimensions	Items	Cronbach's α	Loadings	CR	AVE
Mobile device usage	Informational socializing	3 3	0.829 0.619	0.844–0.885 0.704–0.835	0.900 0.806	0.750 0.581
Intention to share knowledge	Explicit knowledge Implicit knowledge	2 3	0.831 0.833	0.925–0.925 0.862–0.871	0.922 0.900	0.856 0.750
Creativity		4	0.842	0.778–0.871	0.895	0.682
Cultural distance		6	0.880	0.644–0.859	0.911	0.633

4.2 Hypothesis Testing

Regression analysis was conducted to examine the hypotheses. Figure 2 Structural model results indicated that all hypotheses were supported with data statistics.

Further, results indicated that cultural distance negatively moderates the relationships between two dimensions of mobile device usage and two dimensions of intention to share knowledge respectively (Fig. 3, 4, 5 and 6).

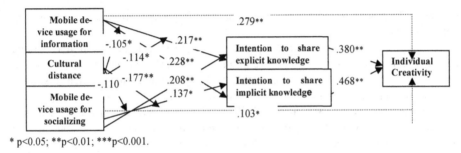

* p<0.05; **p<0.01; ***p<0.001.

Fig. 2. Structural model results

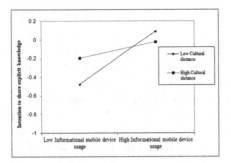

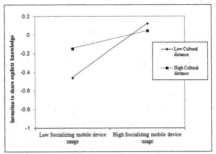

Fig. 3. Moderating effect of cultural distance on the relationship between informational mobile device usage and intention to share explicit knowledge

Fig. 4. Moderating effect of cultural distance on the relationship between socializing mobile device usage and intention to share explicit knowledge

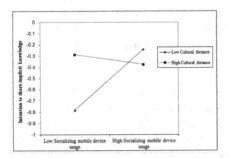

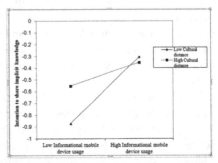

Fig. 5. Moderating effect of cultural distance on the relationship between socializing mobile device usage and intention to share implicit knowledge

Fig. 6. Moderating effect of cultural distance on the relationship between informational mobile device usage and intention to share implicit knowledge

5 Discussion

The purpose of the current research is to empirically investigate the relationships between mobile device usage, intention to share knowledge, individual creativity and cultural distance. The research findings are interesting and important, and make the following contributions.

First, the current research makes significant contributions to the literature of mobile device research by uncovering its usage on individual development (creativity). Moreover, the empirical research was conducted in cross-cultural settings, which fills in the previous research gaps. With the rapid growth of mobile technology significantly diffusing over the whole world (Shiyadeh et al. 2013; Al-Adwan et al. 2018), more research is expected to further explore how mobile device influences individual development. The research findings suggest that mobile device usage, either for information purpose or socializing purpose, is positively associated with individual creativity in cross-cultural environment. Previous research ever indicated that mobile device usage is associated with cultural intelligence and self-efficacy (Hu et al. 2018) and moderates the relationship between multicultural experiences and individual creativity (Hu et al. 2017). However, to the best of our knowledge, there is no previous research examining the direct relationship between mobile device usage and individual creativity. And this research has addressed the gap by unveiling the underlying mechanism through which mobile device usage exerts effects on individual creativity.

Second, the current research also contributes to the creativity research. As the key competence in the 21st century (Miron-Spektor and Beenen 2015), creativity has attracted a lot of scholarly attention. Scholars endeavor to explore the antecedents impacting creativity development from various perspectives (Dong et al. 2017; Perry-Smith and Mannucci 2017). Meanwhile, there is still paucity of literature researching the correlations between personal attributes, contextual conditions and creativity in cross-cultural settings (Hu et al. 2017). The current research takes the perspective of combining the information technology and creativity, which is seldom addressed by prior research. The research findings suggest that mobile device usage, either for information or socializing purpose, acts as a positive role impacting individual creativity through the conduit of intention to share knowledge in cross-cultural settings. Moreover, results indicate that intention to share explicit knowledge and implicit knowledge is a reliable resource to enhance individual creativity. And this seems to be particularly significant for international expatriates for survival and success in cross-cultural environment (Vezzali et al. 2016).

Finally, the current research also contributes to cross-cultural studies by identifying that cultural distance still makes a noisy channel to mitigate the positive effects of two dimensions of mobile device usage on individual intention to share explicit and implicit knowledge, thereby enhancing creativity. In this regard, the combination of information technology and psychology research contributes significantly to cross-cultural studies. And the research findings about the boundary effects of cultural distance keep consistent with previous research (Sougand and Yamin 2010; Chen et al. 2010).

The current research also makes significant implications for expatriates and business management. First of all, management and expatriates should acknowledge the enabling roles of mobile device, particularly in cross-cultural settings. To be more specific, management and expatriates should be fully aware of the positive functionalities of mobile device usage. This research indicates that informational mobile device usage and socializing mobile device usage are reliable resources for enhancing individual's intention to share explicit and implicit knowledge. Further, mobile device usage is positively associated with individual creativity through the conduit of intention to share knowledge. In this vein, subordinates' or expatriates' mobile device usage in cross-cultural settings should be encouraged at working places. On one hand, mobile device usage facilitates expatriates to spread information and attain useful information from local peers and experts, which contributes to their creativity by stipulating their intention to share knowledge. Furthermore, studies have also confirmed that exchanging information purpose of using mobile device contributes to expatriate's cultural capability and self-efficacy (Hu et al. 2018, 2020). In this vein, management should encourage their subordinates assigned for international expatriation to exchange information a lot with overseas company's peers and leaders. This social behavior not only brings much smoother flow of information resources for the company's business operation, but also contributes more to expatriate's acquaintance of local business culture and successful adaptation to a foreign environment. On the other hand, mobile device usage offers more opportunities for expatriates to socialize with locals and make friends. Studies have identified that associations with locals contribute to expatriate's cultural intelligence and cross-cultural adjustment (Hu et al. 2020). Similarly, the current research indicates that socializing purpose of mobile device usage is positively related to creativity by enhancing expatriate's intention to share knowledge. In this vein, expatriate's mobile device usage to interact and communicate with local peers and experts should be encouraged. When expatriates use mobile device for socializing purposes, they are exchanging ideas with locals and integrating into the mainstream culture, which is conducive to their cross-cultural adjustment. During the process of interaction and communication, they are also learning new cultural and professional knowledge to restructure their thinking styles and mindset for new ideas, which finally benefits their creativity. Thus ubiquitous socializing networking systems including Apps in the host country could be installed in expatriate's mobile devices. For example, if expatriates have been sent to China, the widely-used socializing software called Wechat should be installed in expatriate's mobile phones or PCs because more than 1 billion active users use Wechat every month and text 45 billion messages every day for living and working purposes according to the statistics released by the company.

Second, management should fully acknowledge the significance of employee's creativity in international business operations. Increasing global competition requires management to take measures to develop their subordinates' creativity. In the current research, two factors were confirmed to contribute to enhancing creativity. Just as mentioned, mobile device usage for information and socializing purposes is conducive to individual's creativity. Relevant measures including allowing expatriate's to install and use Apps in the working places should be advocated for exchanging work-related or cultural-related information. Further, the research also confirms that intention to share explicit and implicit knowledge is an antecedent for developing creativity. In this regard, any measures encouraging expatriate's intention to share their knowledge with other people from different cultural backgrounds should be taken. From the perspective of two categories of knowledge, this could be realized in two ways. One way is to organize activities to encourage behaviors sharing reports, official documents, manuals, methodologies and models. Those activities are organized to increase employee's intention to share explicit knowledge. The other way is to take measures to increase employee's sense of belonging and harmonious leader-member and teammates relationships. Feel-at-home company climate stipulates employee's intention to exchange implicit knowledge including their experiences, know-how, know-where, know-whom, and expertise. And this is also the conduit to transfer the positive effects of mobile device usage on individual creativity.

Last but not the least, management should be highly cautious about the potential negative effects of cultural distance. The current research has identified that cultural distance is detrimental to exert negative effects on expatriate's psychological comfort and final performance. Previous research also confirmed that cultural distance seriously impacts interpersonal relationships and intercultural communication (Redmond 2000; Galchenko and van de Vijver 2007). In this vein, management should be fully aware of the cultural differences of another country's cultural knowledge, including cultural traditions, customs, and taboos. For example, in Japan, business culture does not allow their staff to express their ideas freely and publicly, which is widely advocated in western countries on the contrary. In China, Chinese culture is highly distant from western countries in many aspects, wherein Chinese culture is rooted in collectivism, whilst western countries advocate individualism. Thus western expatriates may find it hard to comprehend the prevalence of Guanxi in China business operations (Chen and Peng 2008). Failure to deal with cultural distance may lead to fatigue of communication and exchange of ideas during the process of socializing with the locals through mobile device usage. And this may finally separate expatriates from the mainstream culture and result in final psychological problems and business failure (Sit et al. 2017). Training programs designed for expatriates to familiarize the main cultural differences between home and host countries become a critical part before expatriate's international expatriation. During their expatriation, activities facilitating better interaction and mitigating the negative effects stirred by cultural distance should be considered as partial work of human resources management. For example, company's yearly get-together party may be a good choice for subordinates from different cultural backgrounds to exchange their ideas and demonstrate the charm of their cultural differences.

6 Limitations and Future Research Directions

The current research is subject to some limitations. First, the research adopted a self-reported questionnaire to measure related variables in the model. The research method contains possible common forms of bias although it has been found not to be a big issue here. Second, the research findings are also limited by cross-sectional approach. Third, the sampling may be another limitation because more than 97% participants are from Asian and African countries. The research findings should be cautiously extended to other parts of the world.

Acknowledgement. The research was financially supported by Anhui Provincial Natural Science Foundation under Grant 1908085MG238 and 2019' National Education Sciences Planning Project of China under Grant BBA190019.

References

Al-Adwan, A.S., Al-Adwan, A., Berger, H.: Solving the mystery of mobile learning adoption in higher education. Int. J. Mob. Commun. **16**(1), 24–49 (2018)

Ali, I., Ali, M., Leal-Rodriguez, A.L., Albort-Morant, G.: The role of knowledge spillovers and cultural intelligence in enhancing expatriate employees' individual and team creativity. J. Bus. Res. **101**, 561–573 (2019)

Al-Kurdi, O., El-Haddadeh, F.R., Tillal, E.: The role of organisational climate in managing knowledge sharing among academics in higher education. Int. J. Inf. Manag. **50**, 217–227 (2020)

Bock, G.W., Zmud, R.W., Kim, Y.G., Lee, J.N.: Behavioral intention formation in knowledge sharing: examining the roles of extrinsic motivators, social-psychological forces and organizational climate. MIS Q. **29**(1), 87–111 (2005)

Brown, W., Palvia, P.: Are mobile devices threatening your work-life balance? Int. J. Mob. Commun. **13**(3), 317–337 (2015)

Chen, G., Kirkman, B.L., Kim, K., Farh, C.I.C., Tangirala, S.: When does cross-cultural motivation enhance expatriate effectiveness? A multilevel investigation of the moderating roles of subsidiary support and cultural distance. Acad. Manag. J. **53**(5), 1110–1130 (2010)

Chen, X.P., Peng, S.: Guanxi dynamics: shifts in the closeness of ties between Chinese coworkers. Manag. Organ. Rev. **4**(1), 63–80 (2008)

Chung, S., Lee, K.Y., Choi, J.: Exploring digital creativity in the workspace: the role of enterprise mobile applications on perceived job performance. Comput. Hum. Behav. **42**, 93–109 (2014)

Dong, Y., Bartol, K.M., Zhang, Z.-X., Li, C.: Enhancing employee creativity via individual skill development and team knowledge sharing: influences of dual-focused transformational leadership. J. Organ. Behav. **38**(3), 439–458 (2017)

Farmer, S.M., Tierney, P., Kung-Mcintyre, K.: Employee creativity in Taiwan: an application of role identity theory. Acad. Manag. J. **46**(5), 618–630 (2003)

Galchenko, I., van de Vijver, F.J.R.: The role of perceived cultural distance in the acculturation of exchange students in Russia. Int. J. Intercult. Relat. **31**(2), 181–197 (2007)

Gong, Y., Kim, T.-Y., Lee, D.R., Zhu, J.: A multilevel model of team goal orientation, information exchange, and creativity. Acad. Manag. J. **56**(3), 827–851 (2013)

Hofstede, G.: Cultures and Organizations: Software of the Mind. McGraw-Hill, New York (1997)

Hu, S., Liu, H., Gu, J.: What role does self-efficacy play in developing cultural intelligence from social media usage? Electron. Commer. Res. Appl. **28**, 172–180 (2018)

Hu, S., Gu, J., Liu, H., Huang, Q.: The moderating role of social media usage in the relationship among multicultural experiences, cultural intelligence, and individual creativity. Inf. Technol. People **30**(2), 265–281 (2017)

Hu, S., Liu, H., Zhang, S., Wang, G.: Proactive personality and cross-cultural adjustment: roles of social media usage and cultural intelligence. Int. J. Intercult. Relat. **74**, 42–57 (2020)

Hughes, D.J., Rowe, M., Batey, M., Lee, A.: A tale of two sites: Twitter vs Facebook and the personality predictors of social media usage. Comput. Hum. Behav. **28**(2), 561–569 (2012)

Karr-Wisniewski, P., Lu, Y.: When more is too much: operationalizing technology overload and exploring its impact on knowledge worker productivity. Comput. Hum. Behav. **26**, 1061–1072 (2010)

Kauffman, R.J., Kim, K., Lee, S.Y., Hoang, A.P., Ren, J.: Combining machine based and econometrics methods for policy analytics insights. Electron. Commer. Res. Appl. **25**, 115–140 (2017)

Lee, K.Y., Lee, M., Kim, K.: Are Smartphones helpful? An empirical investigation of the role of Smartphones in users' role performance. Int. J. Mob. Commun. **15**(2), 119–143 (2017)

Liao, S., Chen, C.: Leader-member exchange and employee creativity: knowledge sharing: the moderated mediating role of psychological contract. Leadersh. Organ. Dev. J. **39**(3), 419–435 (2018)

Miron-Spektor, E., Beenen, G.: Motivating creativity: the effects of sequential and simultaneous learning and performance achievement goals on product novelty and usefulness. Organ. Behav. Hum. Decis. Process. **127**, 53–65 (2015)

Ogunmokun, O.A., Eluwole, K.K., Avci, T., Lasisi, T.T., Ikhid, J.E.: Propensity to trust and knowledge sharing behavior: an evaluation of importance-performance analysis among Nigerian restaurant employees. Tour. Manag. Perspect. **33**, 100590 (2020)

Perry-Smith, J., Mannucci, P.V.: From creativity to innovation: the social network drivers of the four phases of the idea journey. Acad. Manag. Rev. **42**(1), 53–79 (2017)

Redmond, M.V.: Cultural distance as a mediating factor between stress and intercultural communication competence. Int. J. Intercult. Relat. **24**, 151–159 (2000)

Safdar, S., Berno, T.: Sojourners: the experience of expatriates, students, and tourists (Chapter 10). In: Sam, D.L., Berry, J.W. (eds.) The Cambridge Handbook of Acculturation Psychology, 2nd edn, pp. 173–196. Cambridge University Press, Cambridge (2016)

Shiyadeh, S., Rad, M., Jooybari, M.: The effect of mobile learning on the future of learning in Iran. Res. J. Appl. Sci. Eng. Technol. **6**(14), 2668–2675 (2013)

Sigala, M., Chalkiti, K.: Knowledge management, social media and employee creativity. Int. J. Hosp. Manag. **45**, 44–58 (2015)

Sit, A., Mak, A.S., Neill, J.T.: 'Does cross-cultural training in tertiary education enhance cross-cultural adjustment? A systematic review. Int. J. Intercult. Relat. **57**, 1–18 (2017)

Sougand, G., Yamin, M.: Cultural distance and the pattern of equity ownership structure in international joint ventures. Int. Bus. Rev. **19**, 457–467 (2010)

Vezzali, L., Gocłowska, M.A., Crisp, R.J., Stathi, S.: On the relationship between cultural diversity and creativity in education: the moderating role of communal versus divisional mindset. Think. Skills Creat. **21**, 152–157 (2016)

Yan, K., Tan, J., Fu, X.: Improving energy efficiency of mobile devices by characterizing and exploring user behaviors. J. Syst. Architect. **98**, 126–134 (2019)

A Direct Transaction Model for Energy Blockchain Mobile Information System Based on Hybrid Quotation Strategy

Wei Hu[(⊠)] and Li Huanhao

School of Economics and Management, Shanghai University of Electric Power, Yangpu District, Shanghai 200090, China
2625904776@qq.com

Abstract. This paper designs a direct transaction model for energy blockchain mobile information system based on hybrid quotation strategy, aiming to improve the smartness, real-time property and information security of the direct transaction between distributed power generation companies (DPGCs) and users. Specifically, the continuous auction mechanism was adopted to improve the matching efficiency between the transaction parties, injecting fresh impetus to the power market. In the blockchain system, the serial number of the transaction script was marked with a special label to prove the power quantity being transacted, such that the two parties can exchange the digital proof of transaction power and the transaction fee. Next, the hybrid quotation strategy was introduced to minimize the impacts of frequent fluctuations in the electricity transaction price of the continuous auction market. In this way, the two parties can flexibly adjust their quotations according to the changes of market information. The case study shows that our model outperformed the traditional centralized transaction model in efficiency and mobile power information security. The research findings provides a reference for further research on the application of block chain technology in distributed energy mobile power information transaction.

Keywords: Mobile power information security · Hybrid information quotation strategy · Blockchain · Continuous auction mechanism · Digital proof of power quantity

1 Introduction

With the deepening of power market reform, China has lifted the ban on distributed power generation companies (DPGCs) participating in the power market as sellers [1]. The State Council issued the Opinions on Further Deepening the Reform of the Power System (hereinafter referred to as the Opinions), which requires to reestablish electricity as a commodity and replace traditional planned power supply with market transaction. The Opinions clearly defines the status of the DPGCs in the power market, and permits the DPGCs to directly sell electricity to users. The direct transaction has only one precondition: the DPGCs need to pay the grid company a wheeling fee, depending on

G. Salvendy and J. Wei (Eds.): HCII 2020, LNCS 12216, pp. 33–51, 2020.
https://doi.org/10.1007/978-3-030-50350-5_4

the level of the access voltage. The power transaction between the DPGCs and users is decentralized, many-to-many, and small in scale. Nevertheless, it is still not possible for the DPGCs to sell electricity directly to users, due to the absence of an effective communication channel for information, energy and value between the two parties. In fact, most DPGCs can only obtain a certain price subsidy by putting their electricity onto the grid. To realize the direct transaction between the DPGCs and the users, the key is to establish a secure, decentralized, and transparent transaction model. With the development of communication industry and energy Internet, the application of intelligent terminal is more and more extensive. Mobile intelligent terminals store data, property information and personal privacy. The communication between mobile terminals in traditional trading mode is centralized. The mobile transaction information transmitted in the terminal is forwarded through the intermediate device of the server [2]. The traditional centralized transaction model does not support the direct transaction, owing to its high operating cost of the transaction center, the lack of trust between the two parties, and the risk of tampering with the transaction data. It cannot effectively guarantee the communication security between DP and power users and secure storage of terminal privacy transaction data [3].

Based on distributed databases and peer-to-peer decentralized network, the blockchain is by nature a suitable technique for the power market, whether in operating mode, topology and security. This technique boasts high security, strong transparency and tamper resistance, thanks to smart contact, distributed decision-making, collaborative autonomy, marking a new trend for the power market [4, 5]. The research and application of blockchain technology in the power market are still in infancy, yet preliminary results have been achieved at home and abroad. For example, Yang H et al. [6] creates a blockchain-based power transaction framework for direct purchases of big users, and explains the framework from four aspects, namely, market access, transaction, settlement and physical constraint. Xu C et al. [7] constructs an optimized operation framework for microgrid based on the blockchain, and minimizes the total operating cost of the system by suppressing the fluctuation in DP output. Sawa, Toshiyuki [8] enumerates the key issues of the demand-side energy transaction plan and automatic response system, which are based on the blockchain. Zhang N et al. [9] clarifies the way to apply blockchain technology in the power transaction of decentralized distribution network, and in the transaction of virtual power resources based on virtual power plants. Wu Geng et al. [10] designs the blockchain technology that supports point-to-point transactions in networked microgrids, and offers a plan to verify the adaptability of the integration between blockchain and grid techniques. Shi Quansheng et al. [11] develops a cross-province generation right transaction model based on blockchain technology. Peck et al. [12] Moore explores the research framework of blockchain technology in energy Internet, and deliberates the possible applications of the framework. Mengelkamp E et al. [13, 14] points out that the bid and offer prices are quoted at specified times in the call market, instead of being adjusted timely as per the market changes. Considering the development needs of the existing power system, the above studies have probed into the application of smart contract, collaborative autonomy and other blockchain techniques in various fields, including the direct purchases by big users, the cross-province transaction of generation rights and the automatic response to seller-side demand. The research findings provide valuable references to further research into the structure and flow of the blockchain-based model for the power market. However, none of the existing studies manages to further analyze the following issues under the scenarios of the power market: the structure of the power market, the efficiency of real-time transaction and collaborative scheduling of power market mobile information commodities under partial decentralization, as well as the mobile information transaction mechanism, terminal privacy data security and default compensation between the DPGCs and the users.

From the perspective of technical integration, this paper, considering the similar network topologies of the blockchain and power market, examines the structure and flow of blockchain-based model for power mobile information transaction, and realizes the direct, autonomous, point-to-point transaction between the DPGCs and the users without relying on trust. Next, a continuous double auction mechanism was proposed in light of the formation of power market transactions and the quotation constraints. Under this mechanism, the buyer and the seller quote their prices to the continuous double auction market according to hybrid quotation strategy, and adjust their prices flexibly as per the change in market equilibrium price. In this way, the power market mobile information system transactions become much more efficient [15].

The article is organized as follows: First, we use the continuous auction mechanism to enhance the active degree of the electricity trading market. Then, we add specific marks to the serial numbers in the transaction script to prove the transaction power data, and realize the exchange of the proof and cost of the transaction power numbers in the block chain system. Next, we propose a mixed quotation strategy to reduce the influence of frequent fluctuation of electricity market price information, so that both parties can adjust the quotation according to the change of information flexibly. Finally, we propose a trading model of energy block chain mobile information system based on mixed quotation strategy, which proves that the trading model can effectively guarantee the secure storage of terminal trading data.

2 Fitness Between Blockchain Technology and the DP Mobile Information System

2.1 Blockchain Technology

A blockchain consists of a series blocks generated chronologically using cryptography [16]. As shown in Fig. 1, each block contains a body and a header. The body records the information of all transactions in the previous period, while the header realizes most functions of the blockchain. The hash value of the previous block can be found in the header of the current block, which is calculated by the hash function according to the header of the previous block. The blocks are linked in turns by the hash values into a block chain. The body and header are connected by the Merkle root, in which each node has a corresponding hash value. It only takes one signature on the root node to verify the completeness of all the nodes on the Merkle tree. The Merkle root changes with any variation in the transaction information within the block. As an important data structure of the blockchain, the Merkle root can rapidly sort out and check the presence and integrity of block data.

Blockchain technology as a special method to record, store and represent distributed data. It applies to any decentralized trust network. Without relying on trust, blockchain technology boasts excellent performance in decentralization and traceability, making it a promising architectural paradigm of future databases.

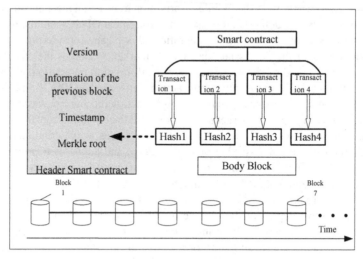

Fig. 1. Basic structure of the blockchain

2.2 Applicability Analysis

The energy blockchain is an organic integration between blockchain and energy Internet. In the energy blockchain, the blockchain provides technical support to the energy Internet and facilitates the construction of the DP utilization system; in return, the energy Internet offers the market and application fields to realize the technical value of blockchain [17, 18].

The blockchain can greatly bolster the DP utilization in China, because it prevents data from being tampered with and ensures high transparency and traceability. In the *Opinions*, the State Council highlighted the importance and urgency of the market-oriented reform of the power system. To promote the reform, it is of great significance to design a direct transaction model for the energy blockchain mobile information system based on hybrid quotation strategy.

The DP development is dominated by the removal of centralized management and the rise of direct, point-to-point transaction based on mobile information system. The fitness between the DP and the blockchain technology is mainly reflected in the following three aspects:

(1) Decentralization: The blockchain supports the direct, point-to-point transaction between a massive number of users through the decentralization technology, which naturally fits with the scattered distribution of energy and load in the DP. In addition,

the blockchain keeps the transaction information secure with distributed accounting, dissemination and storage.

(2) Security and sharing of data: The block chain technology and distributed storage provide a new path for mobile information system to realize data traceability. Each block header in the blockchain encapsulates the hash value of the leading block. Therefore, data blocks are constructed as end-to-end data chains to ensure the traceability of data in the whole blockchain. The distributed storage ensures that the data can be Shared. In the trading of energy blockchain information system, blockchain technology realizes data traceability and information sharing.

(3) Smartness and contracting: The smart contract is a decentralized, trustworthy and sharable program deployed on the blockchain. The blockchain-based smart contract can regulate transaction behaviors, ensure transaction information security and guarantee fair profit distribution, as the DP transactions are increasingly smart.

The energy blockchain verifies and stores the transaction data from all energy nodes, ranging from power plants, DPGCs to transport networks, with chained encryption blocks. Based on the consensus mechanism, the energy blockchain makes decisions by the hybrid quotation strategy through continuous double auction, and automatically completes the transaction processing with the smart contract, forming a brand-new decentralized energy Internet. In this way, the energy, information and value can flow effectively in DP transactions.

3   Continuous Double Auction Mechanism

The continuous double auction market mainly involves the transaction entities, transaction duration, market information, and price mechanism. In this paper, the DP consumers, independent sellers and ordinary users are allowed to engage in the continuous double auction mechanism for DP market transactions. The transaction model of continuous double auction is defined as follows: in a many-to-many market, the buyers and sellers quote bid and offer prices in multiple rounds in a transaction cycle, and conclude a transaction once the bid and offer prices are matched. Considering the prediction accuracy of DP output and load, the transaction duration was set to 1 h. The bid and offer prices must be quoted according to the quotation rules of the continuous double auction market. The buyer with the highest bid price is called the optimal buyer, while the seller with the lowest offer price is called the optimal seller.

During the transaction, the buyers are prioritized in descending order of their bid prices, and the sellers are prioritized in ascending order of their offer prices. The entities quoting the same prices are prioritized in chorological order. The sellers and buyers are matched by the order of price and time. The transaction occurs when the bid price of the optimal buyer is greater than the offer price of the optimal seller. In this case, the price of the party making the earlier quotation should be taken as the transaction price. This process will be repeated until the bid price is lower than the offer price, marking the end of a round of transaction. Then, the transaction information will be publicized to the market entities. The transaction process of the continuous double auction market is illustrated in Fig. 2.

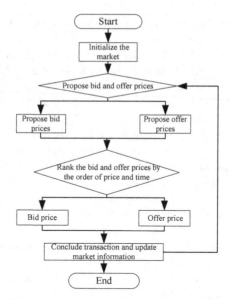

Fig. 2. Transaction flow in continuous double auction market

As shown in Fig. 2, the transaction in the continuous double auction market can be detailed as follows:

Step 1: The market is initialized, and the buyers and sellers quote their prices.
Step 2: Judge if the bid and offer prices meet the rules in the continuous double auction market. If yes, accept the bid and offer prices, and rank them by the order of price and time; otherwise, return the prices to the quoters, and ask them to quote their prices again.
Step 3: Match the bid and offer prices according to the transaction rules and conclude the transaction.
Step 4: Publicize the status information in the market according to the information publicity rules, including the price and power quantity of the transaction concluded between the buyer and the seller, as well as the quoted prices and number of the buyers and sellers in the market.
Step 5: All market entities can view the prices quoted by the optimal buyer and the optimal seller and the mean transaction price in the market, and adjust its price continuously for the next transaction according to the market information and the quotation strategy.
Step 6: The current round of transaction ends when all power being sold have been bought or the transaction duration expires.

4 Direct Transaction Model for Energy Blockchain Mobile Information System Based on Hybrid Quotation Strategy

4.1 Principle of Transaction Settlement Based on Digital Proof of Power Quantity

After being matched, the DPGC and the user will exchange the purchase price and the digital proof of the power quantity through the blockchain. In this paper, the transaction is settled by the bitcoin protocol: the user transacts with the DPGC with bitcoins, while the DPGC transfers the power asset by the token system.

In essence, the token is a digital proof of the power asset in the blockchain. The bitcoins of the transaction are marked by the serial number in the input script of the transaction, turning into colored coins. Thus, the colored coins are, in nature, bitcoins. It only takes a few bitcoins to create a digital record of the power asset in the blockchain. The serial number ($Sequence\_N$) is a 32-bit character in the input script, in which the last 6 digits form the label of the transaction type Zag_Zp. Here, Zag_Zp = 110011 (hexadecimal value: 0x33) means colored coins are transferred in the transaction, and Zag_Zp = 100101 (hexadecimal value: 0x25) means colored coins are created in the transaction. In other cases, the ordinary bitcoin is used in the transaction. The label of the transaction type can be extracted by the following formula:

$$Zag\_Zp = Sequence\_N \,\&\, 0x3F \qquad (1)$$

where & is bitwise AND operation. If Zag_Zp = 110011, colored coins are created in the transaction; if Zag_Zp = 0x33, colored coins are transferred in the transaction; otherwise, the ordinary bitcoin is used in the transaction.

The bitcoin transaction has a lower bound for the transaction quantity. The colored coins only serve as a proof of the power quantity, and has a very small bitcoin amount. Thus, a padding variable was introduced to meet the lower bound. Similar to the label of the transaction type, the padding variable was calculated from the 7th to the 12th digits in the serial number. The calculation process is detailed below:

Step 1: Express the padding variable:

$$Value = Padding + Ve \qquad (2)$$

Step 2: Extract the 7th to the 12th digits from the serial number:

$$Padding\_N = Sequence\_N \,\&\, 0x0FC0 \qquad (3)$$

Step 3: Calculate the value of the padding variable

$$Padding = 2^{Padding\_N} \qquad (4)$$

where $Value$ is the bit value in the output script; $Padding$ is the padding variable; Ve is the actual value of colored coins. By formulas (2)–(4), the user can calculate the number of colored coins he/she receives according to the bitcoin value he/she receives and the serial number of the input script. The calculated result can serve as the digital proof of the power quantity.

To sum up, the DPGCs embed colored coins in the blockchain network for point-to-point transactions. During the transaction, the DPGC transfers a number of colored coins proportional to the power quantity to the user, while the user pays the DPGC the corresponding number of bitcoins. However, the DPGC, upon receiving the bitcoins, may refuse to transfer the token to the user or fail to supply power to the user due to system failure and other reasons, causing losses to the user. To avoid this problem, the arbitration chain was introduced to save the message digests generated from all transaction blocks in the transaction chain. The arbitrary chain will arbitrate the possible disputes according to the transaction information, and effectively maintain the order of market transactions.

4.2 Hybrid Information Quotation Strategy

Under the hybrid information quotation strategy, the quotations are automatically adjusted based on the mobile power trading information through autonomous learning, and automatically submitted to the market through a multi-agent system. This strategy mainly covers the profit-based equilibrium price estimation, confidence function-based profit analysis, quotation strategy, and balance mechanism.

(1)   Profit-based equilibrium price estimation

In the power market, the generation cost or valuation is relatively fixed. Thus, the quoted price for the power depends on the profit margin. When the market is first opened, each transaction entity sets a profit margin according to the equilibrium price of the latest n transactions in the market, which will be slightly increased by a random value after each successful transaction, and slightly reduced by a random value after each failed transaction. Of course, the profit margin of any entities should not be negative, that is, the bid price should not be lower than the buyer's valuation of the commodity, and the offer price should not be lower than the seller's cost. Since the DP market involves multiple sellers and users, the two parties do not have the power to fundamentally influence the market, pushing the transaction price towards the profit-based equilibrium price, in the pursuit of the maximal profits. While it is impossible to acquire the equilibrium price of the market in advance, the equilibrium price can be estimated based on the moving average of the profit margin weighted by the prices of the latest n transactions:

$$p = \sum_{i=m-n}^{n} (1 + \alpha_i) \cdot p_i \tag{5}$$

where p_i and α_i are the price and profit weight of the i-th transaction, respectively.

(2)   Confidence function-based profit analysis

The confidence functions refer to the subjective probabilities P(x) calculated by the two parties of the transaction according to the bid and offer prices in the latest L transactions (HL). The probabilities depict the likelihood that the price x quoted by a party can be accepted by the other party. Thus, the seller's confidence function can be expressed as:

$$p(\alpha) = \frac{TAG\,(\alpha) + WS\,(\alpha)}{TAG\,(\alpha) + WS\,(\alpha) + IG\,(\alpha)} \tag{6}$$

where TAG(α) is the number offer prices in the HL greater than α and accepted by the buyer; (α) is the number of offer prices in the HL greater than α; IG(α) is the number of offer prices in the HL smaller or equal to α. Thus, $p(\alpha)$ describes the subjective probability that the offer price of α will be accepted by the buyer. If $\alpha = 0.00$, then $P(0.00) = 1$; meanwhile, there must exists a positive number M such that $P(M) = 0$.

Similarly, the buyer's confidence function can be expressed as:

$$q(\beta) = \frac{TBL(\beta) + AL(\beta)}{TBL(\beta) + AL(\beta) + RNG(\beta)} \tag{7}$$

where TBL(β) is the number bid prices in the HL smaller than β and accepted by the seller; AL(β) is the number of bid prices in the HL smaller than β; RNG(β) is the number of bid prices in the HL greater than β. Thus, $q(\beta)$ describes the subjective probability that the bid price of β will be accepted by the seller. If $\beta = 0.00$, then $P(0.00) = 0$; meanwhile, there must exists a positive number M such that $P(M) = 1$.

The optimal quotations can be computed based on the seller's and buyer's confidence functions. Let $C_i^k \leq zp$ be the cost of the k-th power quantity that seller i plans to sell. Then, the seller can find the optimal quotation a^* in $a \leq (0, zp)$, such as to maximize the expected profit $E\left[\pi_{s,i}^k, (a, C_i^k), p(\alpha)\right]$. In actual transaction, the offer price a^* is not always acceptable to the buyer. Thus, the maximum profit of the seller through selling the k-th power quantity can be obtained by:

$$S_{s,i}^k = \max\left\{\max_{a\in(a^*, zp)} E\left[\pi_{s,i}^k(a, C_i^k), p(\alpha)\right], 0\right\} \tag{8}$$

Let $V_h^j \geq zy$ be the valuation of the h-th power quantity that buyer j plans to buy from the market. Then, the buyer can find the optimal quotation b^* in $b \leq (zy, \infty)$, such as to maximize the expected profit $E\left[\pi_{b,j}^h, (b, V_j^h), q(\beta)\right]$. However, the bid price b^* is not always acceptable to the seller. Thus, the maximum profit of the buyer through buying the h-th power quantity can be obtained as:

$$S_{b,j}^h = \max\left\{\max_{b\in(b^*, zp)} E\left[\pi_{b,j}^h, (b, V_j^h), q(\beta)\right], 0\right\} \tag{9}$$

(3) Quotation strategy

If the two parties quote prices solely based on their desired profit margins, it is possible that no transaction will take place in the market. To solve the problem, the two parties should adjust their prices gradually according to the current optimal bid and offer prices before each round of transaction until concluding a transaction.

The buyer's quotation strategy can be defined as:

$$P_b(t) = \begin{cases} P_{ave} + \eta\,[P_{ask}(t) - P_{bid}(t)] \\ P_{ave} + \delta\,[P_{ask}(t) - P_{bid}(t)] \end{cases}, \quad t \geq 1 \tag{10}$$

The seller's quotation strategy can be defined as:

$$Q_b(t) = \begin{cases} P_{ave} + \theta\,[P_{ask}(t) - P_{bid}(t)] \\ P_{ave} + \lambda\,[P_{ask}(t) - P_{bid}(t)] \end{cases}, \quad t \geq 1 \tag{11}$$

where $\eta \in (0, 1]$ is the increase rate of the bid price to energize the inactive market and boost the transaction quantity; $\delta \in [-1, 0)$ is the decrease rate of the bid price to reduce the cost under an active market; $\theta \in [-1, 0)$ is the decrease rate of the offer price to energize the inactive market and boost the transaction quantity; $\lambda \in (0, 1]$ is the increase rate of the offer price to improve the profit margin under in active market; P_{ave} is the benchmark price of the power market; $P_{ask}(t)$ and $P_{bid}(t)$ are the optimal prices quoted by the optimal buyer and the optimal seller in round t, respectively.

(4) Balance mechanism

Considering the prediction accuracy of DP output and load, the DPGC and the user should settle the power shortage or surplus caused by the prediction error with the grid company after the transaction is closed.

The DPGC should sell the excess power to the grid company if it generates more power than the transaction quantity, and buy power from the grid company to make up for the power shortage if it generates fewer power than the transaction quantity. Taking account of the prediction error, the actual profit G_{act} of the DPGC can be expressed as:

$$G_{act} = \begin{cases} p_a \cdot q + p_{s\text{-grid}} \cdot \Delta q, & \Delta q > 0 \\ p_a \cdot q + p_{b\text{-grid}} \cdot \Delta q, & \Delta q < 0 \end{cases} \tag{12}$$

where p_a is the mean selling price of power in the market; q is the total transaction quantity in the market; Δq is the prediction error ($\Delta q > 0$ means the DPGC generates more power than the transaction quantity; $\Delta q < 0$ means the DPGC generates fewer power than the transaction quantity); $p_{s\text{-grid}}$ is the price to sell power to the grid company; $p_{b\text{-grid}}$ is the price to buy power from the grid company.

The user should receive a refund and sell its excess power to the grid company if it consumes fewer power than the transaction quantity, and buy power from the grid company to make up for the power shortage if it consumes more power than the transaction quantity. Taking account of the prediction error, the actual cost T_{act} of the user can be expressed as:

$$T_{act} = \begin{cases} p_b \cdot w + a \cdot p_{s\text{-grid}} \cdot \Delta w, & \Delta w < 0 \\ p_b \cdot w + p_{b\text{-grid}} \cdot \Delta w, & \Delta w > 0 \end{cases} \tag{13}$$

where p_b is the mean buying price of power in the market; w is the total transaction quantity in the market; $a \in (0, 1)$ is the weight coefficient depending on the on-grid price and power loss; Δw is the prediction error ($\Delta w < 0$ means the user consumes fewer power than the transaction quantity; $\Delta w > 0$ means the user consumes more power than the transaction quantity); $p_{s\text{-grid}}$ is the price to sell power to the grid company; $p_{b\text{-grid}}$ is the price to buy power from the grid company.

4.3 Overall Structure

During DP transactions, the power quantities and prices of the buyers and sellers were matched through the continuous auction market. The transaction information was transmitted and the transaction was settled on the technical basis of energy blockchain. In this way, a blockchain-based distributed power mobile information system transaction mechanism was established. As shown in Fig. 3, the mechanism contains three blockchains, namely, the scheduling chain DU1, the transaction chain JY1 and the arbitration chain ZC1.

(1) The scheduling chain DU1 is a private chain, in which all nodes are of the same status. The chain generates the transaction power quantity for the specified duration of 2 h at a fixed cycle, and broadcasts the power quantity to all nodes in the transaction chain JY1. After the transaction chain reaches the preliminary transaction plan, the scheduling chain will verify the feasibility of the plan. If the plan is feasible, it will distribute the transaction power quantity to the designated user(s) at the specified time.

(2) The transaction chain JY1 is a public chain. Upon receiving the transaction power quantity for the corresponding duration at the same time, the sellers and buyers exchange the power quantities to be sold and bought and the bid and offer prices within the transaction duration. During the matching process, the transaction chain JY1 continuously publicize the transaction information to the sellers and buyers, including the transaction prices, the current optimal buyer and the current optimal seller. The chain also prepares the transaction plan through continuous double auction and submit the plan to the scheduling chain for verification.

(3) The arbitration chain ZC1 is an independently formed alliance chain. On this chain, the nodes only save the message digests generated from the transaction blocks in the transaction chain, and generate the directory tree of message digests to record the real-time transactions in the transaction chain, laying the basis for post-supervision. The arbitrary chain will arbitrate the possible disputes and protect the interests of both parties.

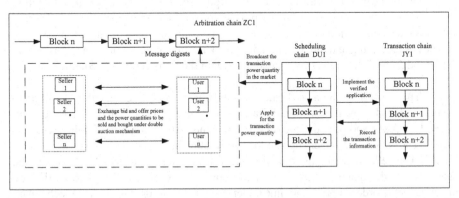

Fig. 3. Direct transaction model for energy blockchain mobile information system based on hybrid quotation strategy

It can be seen from Fig. 3 that the DP transaction hinges on the coordinated operation between the scheduling chain DU1, the transaction chain JY1 and the continuous double auction mechanism. Therefore, it is necessary to clarify the matching mechanism of the transaction chain JY1 and the logic control between the scheduling chain DU1 and the transaction chain JY1, under the auction mechanism defined by the scheduling chain DU1. The specific flow of energy blockchain-based transaction is illustrated in Fig. 4 below.

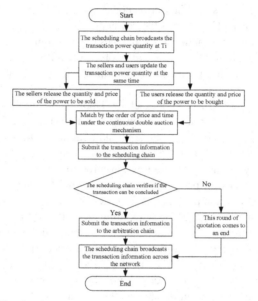

Fig. 4. The transaction flow based on energy blockchain

In light of the prediction accuracy of DP output and load, each node on the scheduling chain DU1 was required to negotiate the transaction power quantity in the specified period within a fixed transaction duration ($\Delta t = 1$ h), considering the fixed duration (10 min) of consensus-making and block-generation mechanism in blockchain technology. Then, the period from T_i to $T_i + \Delta t$ was cited to explain the transaction procedure:

Step 1: The scheduling chain DU1 calculates the transaction power quantity according to the planned load of the lines within the target area in the target period (effective moment: $T_{te} = T_i + 3\Delta t$), and provides the transmission and distribution price for the area.

Step 2: The sellers and buyers update the information at the same time.

Step 3: The sellers release the quantity and price of the power to be sold, while the users release the quantity and price of the power to be bought. The two parties are matched by the order of price and time under the continuous double auction mechanism. The scheduling chain DU1 checks whether the matching is successful, and records the matching result. The transaction chain JY1 executes the transaction and record the transaction information.

Step 4: Before the moment of ($T_i + 2\Delta t$), the scheduling chain DU1 generates the power transaction block based on the negotiated results, forms the point-to-point smart contract, and broadcasts the consensus across the network. In addition, the scheduling chain integrates the actual transaction information in the previous period into a block, and saves the message digest of the transaction block into the arbitration chain ZC1.

Step 5: The expected transaction information generated at $T_i + 2\Delta t$ is reported to the scheduling chain DU1 for verification, laying the basis for the transaction in the next period.

In the direct transaction model for energy blockchain based on hybrid quotation strategy [19], all DP nodes are of the same status, eliminating the fully centralized node. These nodes work together through the consensus mechanism to maintain the normal transaction. Under the blockchain mobile information system architecture, all DP nodes and users exchange power quantities and prices through continuous double auction, and complete market transactions by the order of price and time, leading to fair and effective real-time transactions. Through the distributed data storage and traceability, the blockchain technology maintains the completeness and prevents tampering of the transactions information in the power market [20, 21], and fully guarantees the storage of terminal transaction data.

5   Case Study

5.1   Parameter Settings

During the direct transaction in the energy blockchain mobile information system under the hybrid quotation strategy, all DPGCs and users have the same competitiveness. Following the hybrid quotation strategy, once the transaction market is opened, the users and DPGCs will quote their prices and conclude transactions through continuous double auction. It is assumed that the transaction market has ten users and six DPGCs. The transaction quantities of the two parties are listed in Tables 1 and 2 below.

Table 1. Transaction parameters of the users

Name	User 1	User 2	User 3	User 4	User 5	User 6	User 7	User 8	User 9	User 10
Transaction quantity/kWh	40	20	30	50	30	70	60	20	40	30

Table 2. Transaction parameters of the DPGCs

Name	DPGC1	DPGC2	DPGC3	DPGC4	DPGC5	DPGC6
Transaction quantity/kWh	80	70	50	90	70	60

5.2 Analysis on Transaction Results

During the simulation, the two parties were assumed to quote their prices at an interval of 0–2 s (the prices are quoted rapidly by agents in the continuous double auction market). The variations in transaction price and quantity are recorded in Fig. 5 below.

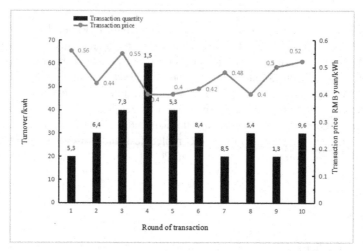

Fig. 5. The variations in transaction price and quantity of the market. *Note:* The two figures above each column are the serial number of the user and that of the DPGC concluding a transaction.

Through the transaction duration, the two parties concluded ten transactions in the first round. In this round, users 1, 5, 6, 7, 8 and 9 and DPGCs 3, 4, 5 and 6 were involved in the transactions. In general, these users had relatively high valuations and quoted relatively high prices, while these DPGCs quoted relatively low prices thanks to their low costs. These factors are conducive to the transaction under the continuous auction mechanism.

In the continuous double auction market, the two parties can make several rounds of quotations in a transaction duration, and conclude a transaction once the bid price meets the offer price. The matching speed is constrained by the quotation interval and the quoted prices. Figure 6 presents the quotation intervals and quoted prices of the two parties in the first transaction duration. As shown in Fig. 6(a), user 5, with the highest bid price, completed the transaction earlier than any other users, while users 2, 3, 4 and 10 did not conclude any transaction due to the low bid prices. During the transaction, user 1 made quotation earlier than user 5, and thus concluded the transaction with DPGC5.

Next, the transaction process of user 2 was cited to further illustrate how the two parties adjust their quotations. Figures 7, 8 and 9 respectively show the results of each round of transaction under profit-based equilibrium price, quotation strategy and confidence function-based profit analysis.

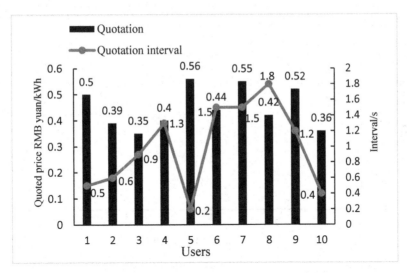

(a) . Quotation intervals and quoted prices of users

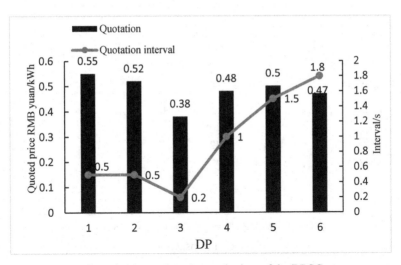

(b) . Quotation intervals and quoted prices of the DPGCs

Fig. 6. (a) Quotation intervals and quoted prices of users. (b) Quotation intervals and quoted prices of the DPGCs

From Figs. 5, 7 and 8, it can be seen that user 2 failed to match any DPGC in the first round, and did not enter into any transaction. Starting from the second round, the bid price was increased slightly and η was up-regulated to promote the success rate of transaction.

According to Figs. 7, 8 and 9, the transaction price gradually stabilized under the hybrid information quotation strategy, and the two parties both received satisfactory profits. In actual transaction, however, there might be an error in the prediction of DP

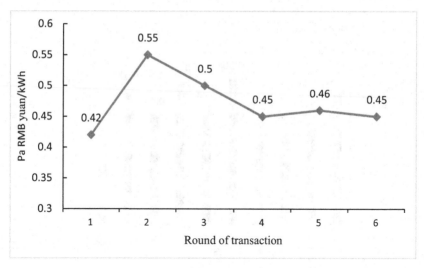

Fig. 7. Results under profit-based equilibrium price

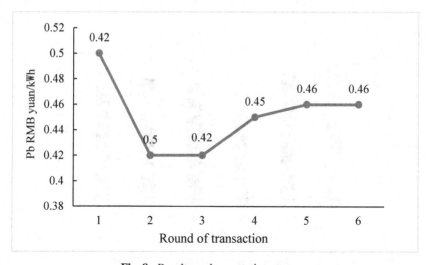

Fig. 8. Results under quotation strategy

output and load. It is necessary to analyze the effects of the error on the users' actual cost and the DPGC's profit. Here, DPGC 3 and user 3 are cited to disclose the effects. Without considering the error, the mean transaction prices of DPGC 3 and user 3 were respectively $p_a =$ RMB 0.45 yuan/kWh and $p_b =$ RMB 0.462 yuan/kWh. Meanwhile, $p_{s\text{-}grid} =$ RMB 0.412 yuan/kWh and $p_{b\text{-}grid} =$ RMB 0.495 yuan/kWh. Tables 3 and 4 show the actual cost of the user and the actual profit of the DPGC under the prediction error of ± 5 kWh.

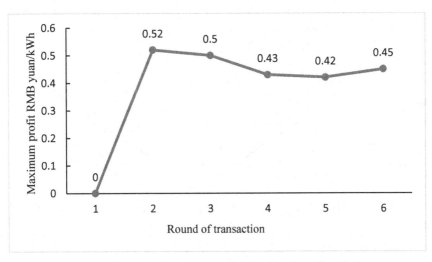

Fig. 9. Results under confidence function-based profit analysis

Table 3. The actual cost of the user considering prediction error

Type	Prediction error/kWh	Theoretical cost/RMB yuan	Actual cost/RMB yuan	a	Economic loss/RMB yuan
User	5	13.86	16.335	0	2.475
	−5	13.86	16.0215	0.6	2.1615

Table 4. The actual profit of the DPGC considering prediction error

Type	Prediction error/kWh	Theoretical profit/RMB yuan	Actual profit/RMB yuan	Economic loss/RMB yuan
DPGC	5	15.75	14.56	1.19
	−5	11.25	10.025	1.225

Tables 3 and 4 show that the transaction price between the user and the DPGC was below that with the grid company. When the user consumed fewer power than the transaction quantity, he/she could sell the excess power to the grid company at the cost of a certain amount of on-grid fee. When the user consumed more power than the transaction quantity, he/she should purchase power from the grid company to make up for the gap. Since the on-grid price is higher than the transaction price between the user and the DPGC, the user suffered economic loss under the prediction error. Similar to the user, the DPGC did not receive the expected profit in full amount. The specific economic losses of the two parties were measured under different prediction errors (Fig. 10), aiming to disclose how much the error affects the user cost and the DPGC profit.

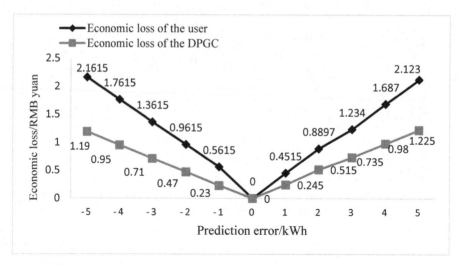

Fig. 10. Economic losses of the two parties under different prediction errors

As shown in Fig. 10, the economic losses of the user and the DPGC are positively correlated with the absolute value of the prediction error. The actual power consumption of the user and the actual DP output should be predicted accurately, to make the transaction profitable to both parties.

6 Conclusions

This paper explores the operation mode of energy blockchain mobile information system in the power market. The power market was modelled as a blockchain and integrated with continuous double auction mechanism, laying the basis for reliable transaction and real-time accurate transmission of transaction information. The proposed mobile information system transaction model enables the direct transaction between the DPGCs and users. Specifically, the continuous auction mechanism was introduced, allowing the two parties to adjust the bid and offer prices in real time, and jointly energize the market. In the blockchain system, the serial number of the transaction script was marked with a special label to prove the power quantity being transacted, such that the two parties can exchange the digital proof of transaction power and the transaction fee. In this way, the transaction between the DPGC and the user becomes more efficient, as no centralized agent is involved in the settlement. In addition, the hybrid information quotation strategy was adopted to analyze the transaction information in the market in an adaptive manner, and look for the optimal bid and offer prices according to the current transaction price, providing a guarantee to the profits of both parties. The case study shows that our model can satisfy the demand for decentralized, many-to-many transaction of small power information quantities. It effectively ensures the security of transaction information and secure storage of terminal privacy data.

With the gradual opening of China's power market, the future research will try to optimize the power price information game between the transaction parties with smart contrast, and further improve the direct transaction model for energy blockchain mobile information system under hybrid quotation strategy, providing a reference for the application of blockchain technology in DP mobile information transactions.

References

1. Paschen, M.: Dynamic analysis of the German day-ahead electricity spot market. Energy Econ. **59**, 118–128 (2016)
2. Ruoti, S., et al.: Blockchain technology: what is it good for? Commun. ACM **63**(1), 46–53 (2019)
3. Frade, P., Vieira-Costa, J., Osório, G., et al.: Influence of wind power on intraday electricity spot market: a comparative study based on real data. Energies **11**(11), 29–74 (2018)
4. Li, B., Zhang, J., Chi, B., et al.: Blockchain: support technology for demand side resources to participate in grid interaction. Power Constr. **38**(3), 1–8 (2017)
5. Ou, Y.X., Zhu, X.Q., Ye, L., et al.: Application of block chain technology in direct power purchase by large users. Chin. J. Electr. Eng. **37**(13), 3737–3745 (2017)
6. Yang, H., Pan, H., Luo, F., et al.: Operational planning of electric vehicles for balancing wind power and load fluctuations in a microgrid. IEEE Trans. Sustain. Energy **8**(2), 592–604 (2017)
7. Xu, C., Wang, K., Guo, M.: Intelligent resource management in blockchain-based cloud datacenters. IEEE Cloud Comput. **4**(6), 50–59 (2017)
8. Nosouhi, M.R., et al.: Blockchain for secure location verification. J. Parallel Distrib. Comput. **136**, 40–51 (2020)
9. Zhang, N., Wang, Y., Kang, C.Q., et al.: Block chain technology in energy Internet: research framework and typical applications. Chin. J. Electr. Eng. **36**(15), 4011–4022 (2016)
10. Wu, G., Zeng, B., Li, R., et al.: Application model research of block chain technology in integrated demand side response resource transaction. Chin. J. Electr. Eng. **37**(13), 3717–3728 (2017)
11. Shi, Q.S., Liu, K., Wen, M.: Inter-provincial power generation rights trading model based on block chain technology. Power Constr. **38**(9), 15–23 (2017)
12. Peck, M.E., Moore, S.K.: The blossoming of the blockchain. IEEE Spectrum **54**(10), 24–25 (2017)
13. Mengelkamp, E., Gärttner, J., Rock, K., et al.: Designing microgrid energy markets: a case study: the Brooklyn Microgrid. Appl. Energy **210**, 870–880 (2018)
14. Vytelingum, P., Cliff, D., Jennings, N.R.: Strategic bidding in continuous double auctions. Artif. Intell. **172**(14), 1700–1729 (2008)
15. Rong, J., Qin, T., An, B.: Competitive Cloud pricing for long-term revenue maximization. J. Comput. Sci. Technol. **34**(3), 645–656 (2019). https://doi.org/10.1007/s11390-019-1933-9
16. Fairley, P.: Blockchain world-feeding the blockchain beast if bitcoin ever does go mainstream, the electricity needed to sustain it will be enormous. IEEE Spectr. **54**(10), 36–59 (2017)
17. Cong, L.W., Zhi, G.H.: Blockchain disruption and smart contracts. Rev. Financ. Stud. **32**(5), 1754–1797 (2019)
18. Kang, J., Yu, R., Huang, X., et al.: Enabling localized peer-to-peer electricity trading among plug-in hybrid electric vehicles using consortium blockchains. IEEE Trans. Industr. Inf. **13**(6), 3154–3164 (2017)
19. Zeng, M., Cheng, J., Wang, Y.Q.: A preliminary study on multi-module collaborative autonomy model of energy Internet under the framework of blockchain. Chin. J. Electr. Eng. **37**(13), 3672–3681 (2017)
20. Wu, F.F., Varaiya, P.P., Hui, R.S.Y.: Smart grids with intelligent periphery: an architecture for the energy internet. Engineering **1**(4), 436–446 (2015)
21. Zhou, K., Yang, S., Shao, Z.: Energy internet: the business perspective. Appl. Energy **178**, 212–222 (2016)

Factors Influencing Mobile Tourism Recommender Systems Adoption by Smart Travellers: Perceived Value and Parasocial Interaction Perspectives

Dedi I. Inan[1], Zaenal Abidin[2], Achmad Nizar Hidayanto[3(✉)],
Muhammad Erlangga Rianto[3], Fadhlan Zakiri[3], Muhammad Dimas Praharsa[3],
and Kongkiti Phusavat[4]

[1] The University of Papua, Manokwari, West Papua 98314, Indonesia
d.inan@unipa.ac.id
[2] Universitas Negeri Semarang, Gunungpati, Semarang, Jawa Tengah 50229, Indonesia
z.abidin@mail.unnes.ac.id
[3] Universitas Indonesia, Depok, Jawa Barat 16424, Indonesia
nizar@cs.ui.ac.id
[4] Kasetsart University, Bangkok, Thailand
fengkkp@ku.ac.th

Abstract. This study aims to investigate the role of perceived value and parasocial interaction that encourages smart travellers in adopting mobile tourism recommendation systems (MTRS). This research is conducted by distributing an online questionnaire and obtained 172 respondents. The results show that functional, hedonic, and social value affect the perceived usefulness of the tourism recommendation system. While social interaction is only influenced by social value, both perceived usefulness and parasocial interaction affect the smart traveller's intention to use and recommend MTRS. Thus, this research contributes both on practices and theory, in particular revealing the perceived values of MTRS and their impact on parasocial interaction and adoption intention, which is rarely explored in the literature.

Keywords: Smart tourism · Mobile tourism recommender systems · Perceived value · Parasocial interaction · Technology adoption

1 Introduction

The trend of tourism in Indonesia in the past few years is growing fast. Indonesia ranks ninth in the list of countries with the fastest growing tourism in the world based on a list released by the World Travel & Tourism Council [1]. One of the triggers behind this is the advancement of Internet technologies that drive the emergence of social media, various smart tourism applications, online tour & travel services, startups engaged in tourism, etc.

© Springer Nature Switzerland AG 2020
G. Salvendy and J. Wei (Eds.): HCII 2020, LNCS 12216, pp. 52–62, 2020.
https://doi.org/10.1007/978-3-030-50350-5_5

Social media as one of the triggers for this development enables information sharing related to tourism among travellers. The use of social media through mobile devices, in fact, has been part of everyday human life, including by smart travellers, those who frequently seek recommendations related to tourism products. TripAdvisor, for example, as one of the global tourism recommendation sites, has an average of 455 million unique visitors each month. While in Indonesia, Instagram is still the most popular media for searching the tourism-related recommendations. Of its 56 million users in Indonesia, Instagram has a travel menu that users can use to see posts from others who share their experiences in tourism. The use of mobile devices to obtain recommendations for tourism products, we refer this to as mobile tourism recommender systems (MTRS).

Through MTRS, travellers obtain various benefits, for example, they can search for information related to tourist attractions, obtain various information on tourism products that suit their needs, including discussions with other travellers related their experiences in using these tourism products. The mobile device allows intense interaction between users and the MTRS, which certainly can open opportunities for travellers to establish parasocial interaction, a theory that was originally used on television and films to describe a one-sided feeling of intimacy [2].

Unfortunately, how the role of the value-based adoption model (VAM) [3] and parasocial interaction are still rarely explored in the context of MTRS adoption. Previous studies were mostly focused on the credibility and trust of the electronic word-of-mouth (e-wom) as the main sources of the recommendations [4–12]. Other studies used theories such as the Technology Acceptance Model [13, 14], and Theory of Planned Behavior [15]. As such, there are still plenty of opportunities to contribute in particular theory to see the role of perceived value and social interaction in encouraging travellers to use tourism products, which is becoming the main gap that we want to address in this study.

The rest of this paper is organized as follows. In the second section, we will discuss the key theories that underlie this research as well as our research hypotheses. Next, we present our research methodology followed by our results, discussion, and implications. Lastly, we provide the conclusions of this study.

2   Theoretical Background and Hypotheses Development

2.1   Perceived Usefulness

Perceived usefulness is a perception from a user that the system he/she uses can provide benefits to him/her, for example in efficiency and productivity. In the context of technology adoption, perceived usefulness is one of the biggest drivers of technology use, as evidenced in the Technology Acceptance Model (TAM) theory [16]. The results of that study show that this factor is empirically proven and able to explain the reasons for end users in using information systems. In addition, it can also define that the new systems that were being developed were accepted by end users. Later, this is also reinforced by Thompson, Higgins, & Howell [17] who showed that the usefulness of information technology is the expected effect by users of information technology in carrying out their duties. Perceived usefulness has been proven in many studies to have a major impact on technology adoption, including in the context of the use of social media [18].

2.2 Parasocial Interaction

Parasocial Interaction is a theory of communication that was first introduced by Horton & Wohl [2]. Parasocial interaction allows the audience to establish pseudo interactions in mass media such as television. Parasocial Interaction is widely used in television shows, such as talk shows, news, quizzes, and so on by engaging the audiences to communicate. Although it is actually a one-way communication through a particular mechanism, the host creates a pseudo interaction between him/her and the audiences. The audiences involve in that activities as they consider media personalities as friends, despite having limited interactions with. This communication or interaction is known as the Parasocial Interaction. Parasocial interaction is now widely used to model interactions in social media, and is proven to have an impact, for example on celebrity and follower relationships [19–21], intention to buy goods [22, 23], and so on.

2.3 Perceived Value

In business theory, perceived value is the trade-off between perceived benefits and perceived sacrifice (or trade-off between positive and negative consequences) [24]. The perception of benefits is the result of consumer evaluations of products, both physical attributes, service attributes, and technical support obtained when buying or using the product. While the perception of sacrifice is the cost or effort spent by consumers when buying or using a product, perceived value is the overall consumer assessment of product benefits based on what they receive and what they spend [25]. The proposed research model in this study can be seen in Fig. 1.

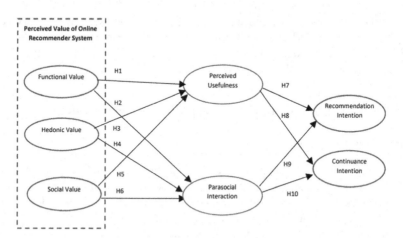

Fig. 1. Proposed research model.

In social network perspective, customer value includes three dimensions: functional, hedonic, and social values [26]. Functional value is based on the assumption that individuals are rational problem-solvers [26]. From an MTRS perspective, functional value reflects the ability of the system to provide tourism product recommendations that meet users' needs. By providing information and recommendations related to tourism products, users can optimise their time in finding the tourism products they need.

Hedonic values represent the feelings and emotions of pleasure obtained by customers from their community involvement [27]. While hedonic value illustrates the enjoyment felt by travellers in using MTRS which will ultimately lead to fun and pleasure, social values describe user status and self-esteem for the communities they follow [28]. MTRS allows a traveller to share information related to his/her experience in using tourism products, which can later be used by other travellers. Travellers who often contributes to MTRS will definitely obtain a higher social status compared to others.

When a traveller perceives the benefits of MTRS, then surely travellers can feel the usefulness of the MTRS. MTRS allows travellers to obtain information related to tourism, discuss with other travellers in the community, and include having fun by seeing various tourism information provided by travellers with various multimedia formats. Thus, travellers will feel the usefulness of MTRS, especially related to the ease of making decisions associated to tourism products. This is confirmed by the findings of Chen & Lu [29] and Rafique et al. [30] which shows the role of perceived value in influencing perceived usefulness. From these, we draw hypotheses as follows:

H1: The functional value of MTRS positively affects the perceived usefulness of MTRS
H2: Hedonic value of MTRS positively affects the perceived usefulness of MTRS
H3: The social value of MTRS positively affects the perceived usefulness of MTRS

The perceived value obtained from MTRS also encourages travellers to experience parasocial interaction. The travellers can feel the interaction provided by MTRS through various tourism recommendations, both given by travellers who are members of MTRS, as well as by MTRS itself that can learn the behaviour of its users. Study of Zheng et al. [31] shows how task, physical and social attraction affect parasocial interaction. Thus, the following hypothesis can be formulated:

H4: Functional value of MTRS positively influences parasocial interaction with MTRS
H5: Hedonic value of MTRS positively influences parasocial interaction with MTRS
H6: Social value of MTRS positively influences parasocial interaction with MTRS

Parasocial interaction with MTRS causes MTRS to be seen as a friend by the travellers. This makes it easier for travellers to accept the recommendations given by MTRS. Thus, it is easier for travellers to continue using MTRS by considering their closeness to MTRS [31]. This close relationship certainly also makes it easier for travellers to recommend MTRS to other travellers. Perceived usefulness has also been shown in previous studies to influence behavioural intention in technology [16]. Thus, the perceived usefulness of MTRS will encourage the use of MTRS and their intention to recommend MTRS to other travellers. Thus, the following hypothesis can be formulated:

H7: Perceived usefulness of MTRS affects the intention to continue using MTRS again
H8: Perceived usefulness of MTRS influences intention to recommend MTRS
H9: Parasocial interaction with MTRS affects the intention to continue using MTRS
H10: Parasocial interaction with MTRS affects the intention to recommend MTRS.

3 Research Methodology

This research is conducted by distributing an online questionnaire to users of MTRS. The users of MTRS are those who use a recommender system such as TripAdvisor or Instagram travel through their mobile devices. We posted our request to social media such as Facebook, Instagram, and Twitter which have the largest users base in Indonesia. The questionnaire consists of 21 questions representing seven variables in the proposed model and developed using five points Likert scale (1-strongly disagree, 5-strongly agree). The functional, hedonic, social value, continuance intention, and recommendation intention constructs were adapted from Ukpabi et al. [32]. Perceived usefulness and parasocial interaction constructs are adapted from Xiang et al. [22]. All questions in the questionnaire have experienced a readability testing to avoid ambiguity. The collected data is then processed using Partial Least Square (PLS) technique with the help of SmartPLS 3.0 software. The PLS procedures follow the recommendation from Hair, Ringle, & Sarstedt [33] which comprises two main stages: measurement model testing and structural model testing.

4 Results and Discussion

After collecting data for two weeks, we obtained 172 respondents. The majority of respondents aged 18–25 years or amounted to 83.7%. From their job, 74.6% are students, 20.7% are workers and the rest are others. From their educational level, 66.9% are undergraduate, 4.1% are diploma, and the rest are high school or below. From the frequency use of MTRS in a day, 45.3% use 1 - <3 h, and 32.6% 3 - <5 h. The data is then processed with SmartPLS 3.0 and the results are presented in the following section.

4.1 Measurement Model Evaluation

Measurement model evaluation is carried out to evaluate the validity and reliability of research instruments. The suitability of the measurement model is done by looking at the value of convergent validity, discriminant validity, and reliability. Evaluation of convergent validity is done by looking at the values of the loading factor. The loading factor value should be above 0.7 according to the recommendations of Hair, Ringle, & Sarstedt [33]. As such, there is one indicator (CI3) that must be removed from the model. After deletion it, all loading factor values are above 0.7.

The average variance extracted (AVE) is also entirely above 0.5 according to recommendations from Hair, Ringle, & Sarstedt [33]. For reliability, the evaluated value is composite reliability (CR), all of which are above 0.7 and meet recommendation from Hair, Ringle, & Sarstedt [33]. The value of loading factor, CR and AVE can be seen in Table 1. The results of the discriminant validity test in Table 2 have also shown no correlation between variables, the square root of the AVE value is already higher than the correlation between each construct [33]. Thus, the discriminant validity criteria have also been reached.

Table 1. The values of loading factor, composite reliability, average variance extracted.

Variable	Indicator	Loading factor	CR	AVE
Functional value	FV1	0.867	0.888	0.726
	FV3	0.798		
	FV4	0.887		
Hedonic value	HV1	0.893	0.844	0.731
	HV2	0.815		
Social value	SV1	0.897	0.932	0.819
	SV2	0.943		
	SV3	0.875		
Perceived usefulness	USEF1	0.894	0.910	0.771
	USEF2	0.869		
	USEF3	0.870		
Parasocial interaction	PSI1	0.790	0.885	0.721
	PSI4	0.889		
	PSI5	0.865		
Recommendation intention	RI1	0.904	0.931	0.817
	RI3	0.924		
	RI4	0.885		
Continuance intention	CI1	0.800	0.766	0.53
	CI2	0.877		
	CI3*	−0.035		
	CI4	0.842		

*Deleted

Table 2. Fornell-Larcker testing results.

Variable	CI	FV	HV	PSI	USEF	RI	SV
CI	0.728						
FV	0.510	0.852					
HV	0.437	0.658	0.855				
PSI	0.479	0.244	0.165	0.849			
USEF	0.486	0.455	0.394	0.336	0.878		
RI	0.634	0.490	0.537	0.453	0.451	0.904	
SV	0.562	0.328	0.231	0.668	0.288	0.460	0.905

4.2 Structural Model Evaluation

Structural test is then performed using bootstrapping with a subsample of 5000. Evaluation of structural tests was carried out by looking at the value of R2, as well as the p-value of all hypothesis relationships (one-tailed with alpha 0.05). The overall results of the hypothesis test can be seen in Table 3. While the R2 values for all endogenous variables can be seen in Table 4.

Table 3. Structural model testing results.

	Hypothesis	t-value	p-value	Conclusion*
H1	Functional value → perceived usefulness	2.850	0.002	Accepted
H2	Hedonic value → perceived usefulness	1.738	0.041	Accepted
H3	Social value → perceived usefulness	2.304	0.021	Accepted
H4	Functional value → parasocial interaction	0.403	0.344	Rejected
H5	Hedonic value → parasocial interaction	0.102	0.459	Rejected
H6	Social value → parasocial interaction	12.521	0.000	Accepted
H7	Perceived usefulness → Recommendation intention	4.002	0.000	Accepted
H8	Perceived usefulness → Continuance intention	5.250	0.000	Accepted
H9	Parasocial interaction → Recommendation intention	3.581	0.000	Accepted
H10	Parasocial interaction → Continuance intention	4.071	0.000	Accepted

*We accept the hypothesis with 95% level of confidence.

Table 4. The values of R^2.

Endogenous variable	R-square
Continuance intention	0.349
Parasocial interaction	0.446
Perceived usefulness	0.244
Recommendation intention	0.306

The results showed that 8 out of 10 hypotheses were accepted in this study. Functional value, hedonic value, and social value affect the perceived usefulness of MTRS. While parasocial interaction is only influenced by social value. Both perceived usefulness and parasocial interaction influence the travellers' intention to use and recommend MTRS. The R2 values of perceived usefulness, parasocial interaction, continuance intention, and recommendation intention were 0.244, 0.446, 0.349, and 0.306 respectively.

4.3 Discussion and Implications

The results of this study indicate the important role of perceived value in encouraging intentions to adopt MTRS. The three dimensions of perceived value namely functional value, hedonic value, and social value were proven to influence the perceived usefulness of MTRS. Of the three dimensions of perceived value investigated, the dimension that influences perceived usefulness the most is functional value, followed by social value, and finally is hedonic value. The main function of the MTRS is to provide tourism product recommendations to travellers through their mobile devices. This makes the travellers to carry out their travel planning easier. Therefore, the functional value is considered as the biggest driver of perceived value compared to the other dimensions. This is in line with [34] which also emphasizes the importance functional value or utilitarian value that drives the perceived usefulness of mobile reading. As the purpose of MTRS is for travel planning, thus the travellers feel that the functional value of MTRS is the most essential dimension that should be considered by MTRS developers.

Furthermore, our findings also showed that the parasocial interaction of MTRS is only influenced by social value. Parasocial interaction is a pseudo interaction in a media, so that through social value travellers certainly feel themselves to be friends of MTRS who always provide tourism recommendations for them. Through the recommendations given at any time by the MTRS, the apparent interaction occurs. These results support the findings of Zheng et al. [31] that showed the role of social attraction (or we refer to as social value) as the highest driver of parasocial interaction in the social commerce website. On the other hand, our results did not support the findings of Zheng et al. [31] that highlighted the importance of task attraction (or we refer to as functional value) as the determinant of parasocial interaction.

The results also showed that both perceived usefulness and parasocial interaction had an impact on adoption and intention to recommend MTRS. Both variables are almost equally powerful in giving an impact on adoption and recommendation intentions, although perceived usefulness contributes a little more. Our results confirm the findings from [35] that shows the role of parasocial interaction and perceived usefulness in driving use intention of online games. However, our results are slightly different with the results from Zheng et al. [31] in that the significant relationship between parasocial interaction and use intention but not for the path between perceived usefulness and use intention.

These results show the important role of perceived value and social interaction that drives the adoption of MTRS by smart travellers. For MTRS providers, the results of this research give important directions in MTRS design focus, that are required to pay attention to functionality, hedonic features, and especially social features that drive both perceived usefulness and parasocial interaction. MTRS providers can strengthen social features possessed by MTRS, for example by providing discussion features among travellers, messaging features that are more personal, and group feature to accommodate travellers with the same interests. In addition, related to functionality, MTRS providers must strengthen recommendation features that adjust to the preferences of the traveller, and include the reputation functions to assist travellers in evaluating e-wom created by the others. From a theoretical perspective, this research contributes a new perspective on MTRS adoption theory, which is currently more focused on the e-wom context (dominated by credibility and trust theory). This research opens insights related to the important role of perceived value and social interaction in MTRS adoption.

5   Conclusions

This research was conducted to investigate the role of MTRS perceived value and its impact on perceived usefulness and parasocial interaction. The results showed that the three dimensions of perceived value (functional value, hedonic value, and social value) had an impact on perceived value and parasocial interaction. The three dimensions of perceived value indicate an influence on perceived usefulness, whereas social interaction is only influenced by social value. Both perceived value and parasocial interaction affect continuance intention and recommendation intention. These results open an important role of perceived value and social interaction in the adoption of MTRS. This research also has limitations. The small sampling size is one of the potential problems in the generalization of the results of this study. Similarly, demographics are still dominated by students. For further research, other researchers can explore more on MTRS characteristics, for example by looking at the quality of the recommendation and personalization, to see their role in the adoption of MTRS. Besides, we also can explore the role of perceived enjoyment in driving MTRS adoption.

Acknowledgement. This research has been supported by PDUPT as part of the project entitled "Pengembangan Konsep Tourism Information Service Untuk Smart Experience Pariwisata di Indonesia". It also has been supported by Ministry of Research, Technology and Higher Education of the Republic of Indonesia through a "Penelitian Kompetitif Nasional – Penelitian Pasca Doktor".

References

1. WTTC: Travel and Tourism: Economic Impact 2019 Top 20 Countries (2019). https://www.wttc.org/economic-impact/country-analysis/league-table-summaries/. Accessed 15 Jan 2020
2. Horton, D., Wohl, R.: Mass communication and para-social interaction: observations on intimacy at a distance. Psychiatry **19**(3), 215–229 (1956)
3. Kim, H.W., Chan, H.C., Gupta, S.: Value-based adoption of mobile internet: an empirical investigation. Decis. Support Syst. **43**(1), 111–126 (2007)
4. Ayeh, J.K.: Travellers' acceptance of consumer-generated media: an integrated model of technology acceptance and source credibility theories. Comput. Hum. Behav. **48**, 173–180 (2015)
5. Filieri, F., Alguezaui, S., McLeay, F.: Why do travellers trust TripAdvisor? Antecedents of trust towards consumer-generated media and its influence on recommendation adoption and word of mouth. Tour. Manag. **51**, 174–185 (2015)
6. Goh, T.T., Yang, B., Dai, X., Jin, D.: A study of purchase influence and behavioral intention on the adoption of electronic word of mouth (eWOM) systems. J. Electron. Commer. Organ. (JECO) **15**(3), 14–32 (2017)
7. Alhabsyi, S., Mardhiyah, D.: The influence of website trust on recommendation adoption and word-of-mouth communication: study on TripAdvisor website. KnE Soc. Sci. **3**(10), 1–10 (2018)
8. Chong, A.Y.L., Khong, K.W., Ma, T., McCabe, S., Wang, Y.: Analyzing key influences of tourists' acceptance of online reviews in travel decisions. Internet Res. **28**(3), 564–586 (2018)
9. Assaker, G.: Age and gender differences in online travel reviews and user-generated-content (UGC) adoption: extending the technology acceptance model (TAM) with credibility theory. J. Hosp. Mark. Manag. **28**, 1–22 (2019)

10. Corkindale, D., Chen, H., Ram, J.: Empirically analysing factors influencing users' adoption of online information services (OISs): a case of a travel business in Taiwan. Electron. J. Inf. Syst. Eval. **22**(1), 38–53 (2019)
11. Lee, J., Hong, I.B.: Consumer's electronic word-of-mouth adoption: the trust transfer perspective. Int. J. Electron. Commer. **23**(4), 595–627 (2019)
12. Reyes-Menendez, A., Saura, J.R., Martinez-Navalon, J.G.: The impact of e-WOM on hotels management reputation: exploring TripAdvisor review credibility with the ELM model. IEEE Access **7**, 68868–68877 (2019)
13. Muñoz-Leiva, F., Hernandez-Mendez, J., Sanchez-Fernandez, J.: Generalizing user behavior in online travel sites through the travel 2.0 website acceptance model. Online Inf. Rev. **36**(6), 879–902 (2012)
14. Kuo, T.S., Huang, K.C., Nguyen, T.Q., Nguyen, P.H.: Adoption of mobile applications for identifying tourism destinations by travellers: an integrative approach. J. Bus. Econ. Manag. **20**(5), 860–877 (2019)
15. Ku, E.C.S.: Recommendations from a virtual community as a catalytic agent of travel decisions. Internet Res. **21**(3), 282–303 (2011)
16. Davis, F.D.: Perceived usefulness, perceived ease of use, and user acceptance of information technology. MIS Q. **13**, 319–340 (1989)
17. Thompson, R.L., Higgins, C.A., Howell, J.M.: Personal computing: toward a conceptual model of utilization. MIS Q. **15**(1), 125–143 (1991)
18. Siamagka, N.T., Christodoulides, G., Michaelidou, N., Valvi, A.: Determinants of social media adoption by B2B organizations. Ind. Mark. Manag. **51**, 89–99 (2015)
19. Thorson, K.S., Rodgers, S.: Relationships between blogs as EWOM and interactivity, perceived interactivity, and parasocial interaction. J. Interact. Advert. **6**(2), 5–44 (2006)
20. Frederick, E.L., Lim, C.H., Clavio, G., Walsh, P.: Why we follow: an examination of parasocial interaction and fan motivations for following athlete archetypes on Twitter. Int. J. Sport Commun. **5**(4), 481–502 (2012)
21. Kim, J., Song, H.: Celebrity's self-disclosure on Twitter and parasocial relationships: a mediating role of social presence. Comput. Hum. Behav. **62**, 570–577 (2016)
22. Xiang, L., Zheng, X., Lee, M.K.O., Zhao, D.: Exploring consumers' impulse buying behavior on social commerce platform: the role of parasocial interaction. Int. J. Inf. Manag. **36**(3), 333–347 (2016)
23. Sokolova, K., Kefi, H.: Instagram and YouTube bloggers promote it, why should I buy? How credibility and parasocial interaction influence purchase intentions. J. Retail. Consum. Serv. **53** (2020)
24. Payne, A., Holt, S.: Diagnosing customer value: integrating the value process and relationship marketing. Br. J. Manag. **12**, 159–182 (2001)
25. Lai, T.L.: Service quality and perceived value's impact on satisfaction, intention and usage of short message service (SMS). Inf. Syst. Front. **6**(4), 353–368 (2004). https://doi.org/10.1023/B:ISFI.0000046377.32617.3d
26. Zhang, M., Guo, L., Hu, M., Liu, W.: Influence of customer engagement with company social networks on stickiness: mediating effect of customer value creation. Int J. Inf. Manag. **37**(3), 229–240 (2017)
27. Karjaluoto, H., Shaikh, A., Saarijärvi, H., Saraniemi, S.: How perceived value drives the use of mobile financial services apps? Int. J. Inf. Manag. **47**, 252–261 (2019)
28. Rintamäki, T., Kanto, A., Kuusela, H., Spence, M.T.: Decomposing the value of department store shopping into utilitarian, hedonic and social dimensions: evidence from Finland. Int. J. Retail. Distrib. Manag. **34**(1), 6–24 (2006)
29. Chen, S.Y., Lu, C.C.: Exploring the relationships of green perceived value, the diffusion of innovations, and the technology acceptance model of green transportation. Transp. J. **55**(1), 51–77 (2016)

30. Rafique, H., Anwer, F., Shamim, A., Minaei-Bidgoli, B., Qureshi, M.A., Shamshirband, S.: Factors affecting acceptance of mobile library applications: structural equation model. Libri **68**(2), 99–112 (2018)
31. Zheng, X., Men, J., Xiang, L., Yang, F.: Role of technology attraction and parasocial interaction in social shopping websites. Int. J. Inf. Manag. **51**, 102043 (2020)
32. Ukpabi, D., Karjaluoto, H., Olaleye, S., Mogaji, E.: Influence of offline activities and customer value creation on online travel community continuance usage intention. In: Pesonen, J., Neidhardt, J. (eds.) Information and Communication Technologies in Tourism 2019, pp. 450–460. Springer, Cham (2019). https://doi.org/10.1007/978-3-030-05940-8_35
33. Hair, J.F., Ringle, C.M., Sarstedt, M.: Partial least squares structural equation modeling: rigorous applications, better results and higher acceptance. Long Range Plan. **46**(1–2), 1–12 (2013)
34. Wang, Q., Zhou, X., Zhang, X.: Study of how experience involvement affects users' continuance intention to use mobile reading. J. Syst. Sci. Inf. **2**(6), 532–542 (2014)
35. Lin, H.Y., Chiang, C.H.: Analyzing behaviors influencing the adoption of online games from the perspective of virtual contact. Soc. Behav. Pers. Int. J. **41**(1), 113–122 (2013)

The Impact of Mobile IT on the Performance of Manufacturing Enterprise

Caihong Liu[1]([✉]) and June Wei[2]

[1] School of Business, Jiaxing University, Jiaxing 314001, China
liuch0001@163.com
[2] College of Business, University of West Florida, Pensacola, FL 32514, USA

Abstract. With the rapid development of wireless network and mobile communication technology, the research on business value of mobile information technology represented by Internet of things, cloud computing and mobile Internet has become the focus of people's attention. Especially with the development of intelligent manufacturing industry, mobile information technology is more and more widely used in enterprises. However, some enterprises blindly adopt mobile information technology, which makes the operation performance of enterprises not obvious. The reason lies in people's insufficient understanding of the factors and evaluation indicators of the impact of mobile information technology on enterprise performance. Therefore, on the basis of relevant theoretical analysis, this paper takes China's manufacturing industry as the research object, and carries out questionnaire survey through questionnaire design and measurement index design. From the four dimensions of enterprise finance, customer, management and employee, this paper studies the impact on enterprise performance, and constructs the evaluation index system of enterprise management information system on enterprise performance by using AHP, in order to provide reference for enterprises to correctly understand the impact of mobile information technology on enterprise informatization process and enterprise manufacturing capacity, so as to promote the competitiveness of China's manufacturing industry to be strengthened.

Keywords: Mobile information technology (abbr. MIT) · Performance · Manufacturing enterprise

1 Introduction

With the development of computer and network technology, human beings have entered the era of information explosion. Therefore, the technology of information transmission and information management is changing with each passing day. The continuous development and upgrading of mobile communication equipment, wireless networks, advanced management concepts and big data processing capabilities makes our socio-economic model more dependent on mobile information technology (abbr. MIT). Furthermore, enterprises, especially manufacturing companies, have gradually put mobile

© Springer Nature Switzerland AG 2020
G. Salvendy and J. Wei (Eds.): HCII 2020, LNCS 12216, pp. 63–72, 2020.
https://doi.org/10.1007/978-3-030-50350-5_6

informationization strategies on the agenda to establish competitive advantages for enterprises. As a large manufacturing country, China's emerging MIT industry has not only driven the development of the manufacturing industry, but also further promoted the transformation and upgrading of the real economy. It makes the whole manufacturing industry of China more digital, intelligent, mobile and green. To do it, enterprises need to have a full understanding of the value of MIT. However, there may be some deviation in the cognition of MIT value from enterprise decision-makers, and the cognition angle is also different, which will affect the effective investment and adoption of MIT. Mobile technology has changed the internal and external environment of enterprises, and changed the competition rules of products, processes and even industries [1]. Business managers began to strengthen the adoption and application of MIT in production and management. MIT is no longer just an improvement or extension of traditional IT technology, but also a disruptive new technology. It is triggering changes in organizational structure, thinking, and behavioral patterns, and it is changing the meaning of "quality" and "quantity" in corporate IT values [2]. Whether the expected value of MIT can be realized is both an opportunity and a challenge for enterprises [3].

Although business managers recognize that the reasonable use of MIT will establish a competitive advantage for enterprises, there are also many cases of spending huge sums of money to set up mobile information systems that lead to failure or that the input and output are not proportional. MIT is a double-edged sword. It brings us changes in information management and information use. At the same time, because of its characteristics of decentralization, heterogeneity, diversity, sensibility and democracy [4], it makes the environment of enterprises more and more complex and uncertain. Compared with traditional IT, what are the main aspects of the utility of MIT to enterprises? How to organize MIT resources reasonably to better play its utility? These problems are the puzzles faced by enterprises. Therefore, from the perspective of management control and information support, this paper conducts a questionnaire survey on some manufacturing enterprises in China, and through statistical analysis, discusses the impact factors of MIT on the operation performance of manufacturing enterprises.

2 Literature Review

2.1 Research on the Commercial Value of MIT

Managers' perceptions and thinking about IT are advancing with the times. The discussion of MIT value is focused on how to generate value, not whether it has value. **From the research object**, the research on MIT mostly starts from the role of user in the user's situation [5], revealing the value of MIT at the personal level. For example, the impact of MIT on consumer value perception based on Technology Acceptance Model (TAM). However, few researchers have explored the strategic value of MIT for enterprises at the enterprise or organizational level [6, 7]. **In terms the scope of research**. Firstly, MIT belongs to the category of IT, and its application in enterprises is also part of IT investment, so the value of MIT and IT value have a certain correlation. The measurement of IT business value is mainly measured at the individual level, process orientation, company level, and industry and macroeconomic levels. The value data of IT is mainly divided into two types [8], one is derived from financial objective data, such as ROI, ROA, market share, productivity, etc.; the other is subjective perception data and recognition in the fields of behavior, psychology, and sociology. Cognitive Constructs, such as user satisfaction, perceived net benefits, awareness of increased efficiency, improved managerial management, and perceived quality [9, 10]. **In view of the fact that the financial** data mainly comes from various financial reports released publicly, the reliability is high, but the validity is not high. The perception data is mainly derived from the subjective perception data of various stakeholders (such as senior managers, IT managers, technical staff, etc.), which is mainly based on the true knowledge and ideas of previous experience levels, so it has a high level of Validity is considered to be low because of its subjectivity (MJ Davern and Wilkin, 2010). The reliability and validity of cognitive indicators can meet research needs [11]. Although the former is more objective, the data is lagging behind, and the multiple constructs contained in the latter have rich value connotations. Although there are prejudices and flaws in perceived data, studying the business value of IT from a cognitive perspective to a certain extent Indicator reliability and validity are acceptable.

It can be seen that this study can use questionnaire surveys to obtain some cognitive and perceptual data for research.

2.2   Research on the Impact of IT on Enterprise Performance

Chen Yun (2010) believes that the current performance management of most companies does not match their own development strategies. With the role of management information systems becoming more and more significant, more and more scholars have analyzed the relationship between management information systems and enterprise performance according to the actual situation of enterprises [12]. Lou Runping (2011) believes that the use of IT technology has a statistically significant positive impact on the profit performance of enterprises [13]. Yang et al. (2008) proposed that IT has a significant effect on the improvement of corporate sales, labor demand, turnover rate of current assets and turnover rate of accounts receivable [14]. Lucas et al. (1999) also studied the impact of management information systems on corporate earnings performance, and proposed that management information systems have significantly improved the return on net assets and return on investment, especially in the interest rate monetization [15]. Of course, there are some scholars who believe that management information systems have no effect on corporate profitability. These scholars mainly use the two indicators of return on net assets and return on assets to measure, and have concluded that management information systems and corporate profitability are not direct relationship.

In general, foreign countries mainly include management information system and enterprise value, management information system and enterprise asset management performance, management information system and enterprise operation capability, relationship between management information system and enterprise profit performance, and the impact on these four aspects. Among them, in terms of impact on profit performance, different scholars hold different opinions and opinions; in terms of impact on asset management performance, it can be seen that the reasonable use of management information systems can greatly help asset management performance. As for the research on management information system and enterprise value, there is currently no related research in China. Although foreign research in this field is relatively rich, it should be noted that

China's national conditions and economic conditions are significantly different from other countries, so the results of foreign scholars' research cannot be directly applied. In this regard, it can be seen that it is necessary to evaluate the impact of domestic enterprise management information systems on corporate performance. Only in this way can the optimization of IT be achieved, and finally the goal of maximizing the role of management information systems can be achieved.

3   Analysis of MIT's Impact on Enterprise Performance Based on Survey Data

3.1   Survey Design

In this study, the questionnaire items shown in Table 1 were summarized mainly through literature reading methods.

A questionnaire survey was conducted on the information departments of 150 manufacturing enterprises in Zhejiang Province. Most of the variables involved in this study are difficult to quantify. The Likert seven-point scale was used to measure the variables. The score of each measurable item is measured on five levels of 5, 4, 3, 2, 1 points respectively. The larger the number is, the higher the score of the item is. Then, survey data based, SPSS17.0 software will be used to analyze the survey results.

3.2   Reliability and Validity

The information management departments of 150 companies were surveyed by telephone. After data compilation, 4 unqualified questionnaire data were eliminated, and 146 actual valid data were obtained.

The value of the scale depends mainly on reliability and validity. Reliability mainly reflects the stability and consistency of the measured variables. Only a high consistency index (Cronbach Alpha) can ensure that the measurement of the variables meets the reliability requirements. When the Cronbach Alpha value is greater than 0.70, the reliability of the variable measure is stronger, and then it can be further analyzed. Validity reflects whether the content measured in the scale meets the specific characteristics of the variable to be measured. This paper uses the Cronbach Alpha coefficient and Composite Reliability (CR) to calculate the reliability level of the scale; factor analysis and Average Variance Extracted (AVE) are used to evaluate the validity of the questionnaire. The reliability analysis of the variables is shown in Table 2.

The overall 'a' value is 0.929. The credibility of each variable is shown in Table 2. Except that IN1 is slightly less than 0.7, the 'a' value of each construct is greater than 0.7, so each variable has better reliability. Overall, the variables have good internal consistency and stability, and the research data are more reliable.

The overall validity is shown in Table 3.

The test results show that the KMO and B test meet the requirements and have strong statistical significance at the level of $P < 0.001$. The questionnaire data meets the validity requirements, and factor analysis can be performed.

Table 1. Questionnaire measurement.

Variable	Sub-conception	Problem item
Information Capabilities of MIT (IN)	IT application environment (IN1)	Whether the mobile communication equipment and network meet the needs?
		Is the enterprise's informatization high?
	Ease of use (IN2)	Is it convenient to transfer and share information?
		Is mobile device easy to learn and use?
	Usefulness (IN3)	Is the information obtained relatively new?
		Is MIT a great help to business management and employees?
Performance of manufacturing companies (JX)	Network business processing capabilities (JX1)	Can work remotely or process business online?
		Does the company have strong intelligent production capacity?
	Product quality inspection capability (JX2)	Can companies automatically monitor product quality?
		Does MIT help improve product qualification rates?
	Customer service quality (JX3)	Can you make full use of the Internet to provide customers with instant services?
		Is there a big improvement in service satisfaction?
	Reduced production costs (JX4)	Are production materials and auxiliary resources dispatched fast?
		Does MIT help reduce procurement and sales costs?
	Business process integration (JX5)	Was the previous business link driving the decision-making of the next business link?
		Is the information sharing between different businesses high?

Table 2. Reliability of variables.

Sub-conception	Cronbach Alpha
IN1	0.688
IN2	0.887
IN3	0.754
JX1	0.727
JX2	0.844
JX3	0.776

Table 3. KMO and Bartlett test[a].

KMO measure		.904
Bartlett test	Chi-Square	1119.633
	df	66
	Sig.	.000

3.3 Factor Analysis

Pearson Correlation Coefficient (abbr. P) is used to measure the correlation between variables. The close strength of the relationship between the measurable variables can be shown in Table 4 through correlation analysis.

It can be seen that the significance of other variables are all <0.05, and the P value is >0.4. The variables were moderately related.

3.4 Influencing Factor Analysis

In order to explore the influence factors of MIT on the business performance and the relationship between these factors, the principal component analysis of the factors is shown by the maximum variation method with Kaiser Normalization in Table 5.

The factor composition table is reduced to two dimensions by factor rotation, which is consistent with the impact dimension of the original theory. That is, the impact of MIT on the performance of manufacturing enterprises is mainly reflected in two aspects: information support and enterprise manufacturing management capabilities. Therefore, considering the meaning of the above questionnaire indicators and the dimensions of the questionnaire indicators, the first and second major components are the management performance (It is represented by f1) and information support performance of the manufacturing enterprise (It is represented by f2), respectively. Based on this, the regression equation formed is as follows:

$$f1 = IN11 * 0.47 + IN22 * (-0.93) + IN32 * 0.36 + JX11 * 0.395 + JX12 * 0.221$$
$$+ JX21 * 0.288 + JX22 * 0.31 + JX31 * 0.270 + JX32 * 0.086$$

Table 4. Correlation of measurable variables.

		IN11	IN12	IN21	IN22	IN31	IN32	JX11	JX12	JX21
IN11	P	1								
	Sig.	0								
IN12	P	$.525^{**}$	1							
	Sig.	0	0							
IN21	P	$.531^{**}$	$.583^{**}$	1						
	Sig.	0	0	0						
IN22	P	$.557^{**}$	$.537^{**}$	$.796^{**}$	1					
	Sig.	0	0	0	0					
IN31	P	$.586^{**}$	$.649^{**}$	$.678^{**}$	$.668^{**}$	1				
	Sig.	0	0	0	0	0				
IN32	P	$.421^{**}$	$.559^{**}$	$.494^{**}$	$.599^{**}$	$.592^{**}$	1			
	Sig.	0	0	0	0	0	0			
JX11	P	$.438^{**}$	$.437^{**}$	$.453^{**}$	$.492^{**}$	$.485^{**}$	$.528^{**}$	1		
	Sig.	0	0	0	0	0	0	0		
JX12	P	$.510^{**}$	$.478^{**}$	$.494^{**}$	$.521^{**}$	$.464^{**}$	$.528^{**}$	$.522^{**}$	1	
	Sig.	0	0	0	0	0	0	0	0	
JX21	P	$.457^{**}$	$.435^{**}$	$.493^{**}$	$.579^{**}$	$.496^{**}$	$.488^{**}$	$.520^{**}$	$.674^{**}$	1
	Sig.	0	0	0	0	0	0	0	0	0
JX22	P	$.615^{**}$	$.431^{**}$	$.516^{**}$	$.610^{**}$	$.500^{**}$	$.433^{**}$	$.561^{**}$	$.623^{**}$	$.730^{**}$
	Sig.	0	0	0	0	0	0	0	0	0

$$f2 = IN12 * 0.310 + IN21 * 0.415 + IN31 * 0.378$$

We can see the composition of each influencing dimension and the coefficients of the composition factors. These coefficients explain the degree of influence on the corresponding elements. Enterprises can adjust according to this MIT informationization strategy. Among them, the index with a larger influence coefficient is more in line with common sense, that is, the degree of enterprise informatization, the convenience of information transmission, and the renewability of information are the keys to determine the enterprise's information capabilities, while the informationzed hardware environment and online business processing capabilities. And the improvement of the qualified rate of finished products is a key factor affecting the manufacturing management capabilities of enterprises. The impact scope and factors of MIT on the performance of manufacturing enterprises can be inflected from the two main components from the two dimensions of information ability and manufacturing management ability of MIT manufacturing enterprises.

Table 5. Factor score matrix.

	Components	
	1	2
IN11	.047	.122
IN12	−.153	.310
IN21	−.220	.415
IN22	−.093	.280
IN31	−.193	.378
IN32	.036	.106
JX11	.395	−.211
JX12	.221	−.102
JX21	.288	−.146
JX22	.313	−.159
JX31	.270	−.103
JX32	.086	−.024

3.5   The Importance of the Indicators in IN to the Possible Impact of JX

In view of the impact of MIT (IN) on enterprise performance (JX), to clarify the influence of IN on JX in a dynamic environment, we can take the information ability of MIT as an independent variable and corporate performance as a dependent variable, so as to further explore the importance of independent variables in the possible impact. In this paper, the neural network function in SPSS software is used to predict the importance of the indicators in IN to JX. The results show that the importance of the independent variables is shown in Table 6.

Table 6. The significance of independent variables.

	Significance	The standardized significance
IN11	.326	100.0%
IN12	.055	16.9%
IN21	.113	34.7%
IN22	.293	90.0%
IN31	.019	5.7%
IN32	.195	59.8%

Obviously, in the possible dynamic environment, the force of IN' indexes on JX are different. Among them, the more adequate the hardware foundation of MIT is, the stronger the information support capabilities of manufacturing companies, and the higher their performance. Enterprises should pay attention to the construction of mobile information hardware facilities, which is the first condition. The Second more important factor is the ease of operation and use of MIT mobile devices. However, as can be seen from Table 5, this effect is negative. In other words, as far as the manufacturing management capability of an enterprise is concerned, the easier it is to use MIT equipment, the more easily it will cause confusion in production management. This may be a reduction in the professional requirements of the operation, and anyone can also intervene. On the contrary, it will not be conducive to ensuring the quality of production and the uniform coordination of business processes. At some extent, this finding may be new and should be paid more attention for business managers. In general, the higher the information quality and real-time business support of MIT is, the higher the manufacturing performance of enterprises is.

4 Conclusion

Based on the information ability of MIT, taking providing information support and intelligent management support for manufacturing enterprises as the research dimension, a questionnaire was designed to investigate more than 100 manufacturing enterprises in Zhejiang Province. Through SPSS statistical analysis, the constructed variables have the reliability and validity that meet the research requirements, which can reflect the consistency and accuracy of the research issues. Through factor principal component analysis and factor importance analysis based on neural network, it is clear that MIT is an important strategic tool and resource in modern manufacturing enterprises. The higher the quality of MIT is, the stronger the impact on the information ability and intelligent management ability of enterprises. Compared with traditional IT technology, mobile information technology has the characteristics of anytime and anywhere, which improves the availability and timeliness of information. In addition, mobile information technology integrates information communication channels, monitors business processes anytime and anywhere, can find problems in business processes in real time and provide accurate and complete information in time, making the implementation of business processes more efficient and business processes more efficient Smooth. Finally, in terms of enterprise performance, managers should invest less in simple and easy-to-use MIT equipment. In a word, MIT can provide enterprises with more advanced business technology and information support to maintain their long-term competitive advantage.

Funding. This research was supported by the Natural Science Foundation of Zhejiang Province in China (Grant No. LY18G010011).

References

1. Wood, K.R.: Leaders' perceptions of mobile technology in the workplace. Proquest LLC, p. 196 (2012)
2. Buhalis, D.: eAirlines: strategic and tactical use of ICTS in the airline industry. Inf. Manag. **41**(7), 805–825 (2004). https://doi.org/10.1016/j.im.2003.08.015

3. Scheepers, R., Middleton, C.: Personal ICT ensembles and ubiquitous information systems environments: key issues and research implications. Commun. Assoc. Inf. Syst. **33**(1), 381–392 (2013). https://doi.org/10.17705/1CAIS.03322
4. Xiang, J.B., Cai, H., Liu, R.J.: What is Internet thinking in the end. Electronic Industry Press, Beijing (2014)
5. Middleton, C.A., Scheepers, R., Tuunainen, V.K.: When mobile is the norm: researching mobile information systems and mobility as post-adoption phenomena. EJIS **23**(5), 503–512 (2014)
6. Donner, J., Escobari, M.X.: A review of evidence on mobile use by micro and small enterprises in developing countries. J. Int. Dev. **22**(5), 641–658 (2010)
7. Sheng, H., Nah, F.F.H., Siau, K.: Strategic implications of mobile technology: a case study using value-focused thinking. J. Strateg. Inf. Syst. **14**(3), 269–290 (2005)
8. Zhang, Y.: Research on business value of mobile information technology from the perspective of management cognition. Master's thesis, Shantou University (2017)
9. Tan, F.B., Hunter, M.G.: The repertory grid technique: a method for the study of cognition in information systems. MIS Q. **26**(1), 39–57 (2002)
10. Vincent, C., Wright, R.: Exploring the evaluation framework of strategic information systems using repertory grid technique: a cognitive perspective from chief information officers. Behav. Inf. Technol. **29**(5), 447–457 (2010)
11. Ketokivi, M.A., Schroeder, R.G.: Perceptual measures of performance: fact or fiction? J. Oper. Manag. **22**(3), 247–264 (2004)
12. Chen, Y.: Discussion on performance management of state-owned enterprises. Mod. Enterp. Cult. **23**, 45–46 (2010)
13. Lou, R.P., Xue, Sh.G.: ERP and corporate profit performance: empirical evidence from listed companies in Shanghai and Shenzhen. Syst. Eng. Theory Pract. **31**(08), 1460–1469 (2011)
14. Yang, H.D., Kang, H.R., Mason, R.M.: An exploratory study on meta skills in software development teams: antecedent cooperation skills and personality for shared mental models. Eur. J. Inf. Syst. **17**(1), 47–61 (2008)
15. Lucas, H.C., Spitler, V.K.: Technology use and performance: a field study of broker workstations. Decis. Sci. **30**(2), 291–311 (1999)

The Impact of Block-Chain on Collaborative Product Innovation of Manufacturing Supply Chain

Caihong Liu[1]([✉]), Hannah Ji[2], and June Wei[3]

[1] School of Business, Jiaxing University, Jiaxing 314001, China
rainbowliu@zjxu.edu.cn
[2] Hannah Ji, Carey Business School, Johns Hopkins University, Baltimore, MD 20723, USA
[3] College of Business, University of West Florida, Pensacola, FL 32514, USA

Abstract. In view of the collaborative innovation and development of enterprises' products. It is an effective measure to improve the innovation efficiency of the manufacturing industry of China and promote the steady development of enterprises. More and more enterprises attach importance to collaborative product innovation based on resource sharing among supply chain nodes. As a decentralized data collection and sharing technology, the block-chain can provide support for resource sharing and business collaboration among enterprises in supply chain. As a trust guarantee system, the block-chain can provide support for resource sharing and business collaboration among supply chain enterprises. However, as a new technology, the use of block-chain by enterprises is still in a wait-and-see state. In order to help enterprises effectively understand the impact of block-chain on the collaborative product innovation of manufacturing supply chain, this paper will study the influencing factors of collaborative product innovation of supply chain on the basis of characteristics and actual situation of collaborative product innovation of Chinese manufacturing enterprises. First of all, we will make an empirical analysis on the current situation and existing problems of supply chain collaborative product innovation in China's manufacturing industry through questionnaire survey, so as to study the problems in detail. Secondly, through the literature analysis of supply chain collaborative product innovation, this paper puts forward some measurement indicators, some research hypotheses, and then constructs a conceptual model of the influence factors of supply chain collaborative product innovation. Finally, based on the empirical study of the proposed model, some suggestions are put forward to improve the efficiency of supply chain collaborative product innovation.

Keywords: Supply chain (abbr.Sc) · Block-chain · Collaborative product innovation · Impact factors

1 Introduction

In the increasingly competitive manufacturing market, production technology innovation and product innovation have become one of the most dependent ways for the economic

G. Salvendy and J. Wei (Eds.): HCII 2020, LNCS 12216, pp. 73–83, 2020.
https://doi.org/10.1007/978-3-030-50350-5_7

growth of manufacturing enterprises. It can not only promote the development of the industry, but also make the enterprise become the controller of the industry value chain and form its own core competitiveness. Industrial innovation is the coordination of product innovation, technology innovation, organization innovation and market innovation. New product innovation is the source of industrial innovation, which is the most important innovation. It is worth attention and investment. At the same time, on the basis of new product innovation, the growth and development of emerging industries are realized through the re innovation of other three links of industrialization innovation. Product innovation and technological innovation will oppress the relevant cooperative enterprises through the original or reformed cooperation network and industrial chain value chain to carry out relevant re innovation and achieve the chain effect of innovation. Therefore, the product innovation of the enterprise must be transferred from the original enterprise to the product collaborative innovation based on the value chain. This is not only the key to common promotion under the environment of cooperative network, but also an effective way to meet the needs of customer differentiation and stratification and reduce the risk of product innovation. In recent years, China has attached great importance to collaborative innovate on the industrial chain. Various collaboration methods such as production collaboration, resource sharing, and open platforms are promoted to drive the common development of upstream and downstream enterprises. But rather the supply chain based collaboration product innovation is the key of collaborative innovation for the industry chain. Supply chain based collaborative product innovation, as a new way of product innovation, provides a new choice for enterprise. It can effectively integrate the resources between supply chain node enterprises, realize complementary advantages, fully promote the upgrading of enterprise innovation ability, and at the same time can realize the supply chain node enterprise benefit sharing, risk sharing, so as to reduce the risk of enterprise innovation, shorten the product innovation cycle, and effectively promote the process of enterprise product innovation [1]. However, due to the looseness of each subject, link and activity in the supply chain, there is no effective way of coordinating constraints and driven by the nature of capital's profit-seeking, it will be difficult to effectively implement the collaboration between the main bodies based on the supply chain. Fortunately, block-chain can provide effective guarantee for collaborative innovation. Block-chain is a database composed of various blocks (the collection of information and data), which has the characteristics of decentralization, smart contract, security transparency and verifiability [2]. As a structure of data storage in cryptography, block chain has many core characteristics, such as multi-party maintenance, non-tampering data, data traceability, etc. These characteristics are consistent with the characteristics of multi-party cooperation in the operation and management of SC and the demand for enhancing information sharing and transparency [3, 4]. Therefore, they are considered as the key technology to solve the problems of SC management. The use of block-chain in SC can track all aspects of SC and improve the overall security of SC [5]. Meanwhile, the block-chain can break the information islands in SC, strengthen the information links between the members of SC, and improve the efficiency of collaboration between participants. The consistency of the node information of the block-chain can also make information traceability and supervision easier [6]. The supply chain is a network structure composed of suppliers, manufacturers, warehouses, distribution centers, and channel vendors based on trust and task coordination. In the supply chain, capital flow, for the more difficult interaction and coordination between capital flow, information flow, logistics, etc., the traditional coordination model of relying on single-chain master-core enterprises cannot meet the diversified and rapid development of market demand. The use of emerging technologies such as block-chain to establish a supply chain-based collaborative product innovation mechanism and method is a powerful measure to further promote the healthy development of SC and enhance the competitiveness of enterprises.

In order to further clarify the value of block-chain in the application of collaborative innovation of supply chain products, so that enterprises can make strategic decisions on technology investment, this paper will study the impact of block-chain on Collaborative Innovation of supply chain products on the basis of questionnaire research.

2 Literature Review

2.1 Application Research of Block-Chain

After ten years of development, block-chain has entered the stage of 3.0 [2] full access to areas of social life. Zhang Bo (2016) proposed that the block-chain has four major technical characteristics: low cost, high security, strong transparency, and strong scalability, which provides technical possibilities for the formation of new business models [7]. The application research of block-chain has involved many fields, such as identity authentication, notarization, audit, logistics control, medical medicine, voting statistics and so on [8]. For the application of block-chain in SC, some research and practice have been done at home and abroad. Huckle et al. (2016) proposed to integrate block-chain and the Internet of Things to build a secure, real-time information sharing decentralized application, and to automatic payment, international travel and other three scenarios as an example to demonstrate the feasibility of the scheme [9]. From the macro level, block-chain can change the execution process, docking speed, operation cost and operation environment of transaction activities; from the micro level, it can affect the internal information management, incentive and restraint mechanism, technological progress and environmental governance of enterprises [10]. In supply chain transactions, digital currency is used to effectively reduce transaction links and save transaction costs among members of the supply chain [11]. A quality management tracking method has been designed for the Indian rice industry using block-chain [12]. Reference [13] proposed a framework reconstruction plan for a fresh food mobile traceability platform based on block-chain. Generally, its application mainly focuses on the field of product tracing. As for the true value of the block-chain, there is less research. This is not conducive to the research and application of targeted block-chains.

2.2 The Collaboration on Supply Chain

Simatupang and Sridharan (2005) proposed that the supply chain collaboration model should include three major parts: information sharing, decision coordination, and effective incentive mechanisms [14]. Ramanathan (2017) divides enterprises into two types: "smart planning" and "traditional planning". Through comparative analysis, it is found that intelligent data management is critical to the maintenance of supply chain enterprise partnerships and the optimization of supply chain synergies [15]. Research by Zhong (2016) et al. points out that how to effectively process and analyze big data has become the main way for supply chains to obtain demand information in a timely manner, improve the science of demand forecasting, and gain competitive advantage, but relying solely on existing database management tools or traditional processing applications is challenging [16]. Lu Shan (2008) pointed out that the supply chain synergy can be realized from the following three aspects: cultivating corporate philosophy with information sharing as the core, building trust-restriction relationships, and establishing an integrated collaborative information management system for the supply chain [17]. Liang Jing and Cai Shuqin (2007) proposed that the improvement of supply chain collaboration requires the coordination of three major sections, namely: human-machine, technology and management, of which human-machine collaboration plays a decisive role. Technical collaboration is the underlying support and management of collaboration. Synergy is the foundation [18]. Fu Pengbo et al. (2007) pointed out that the key to supply chain collaborative management is mutual trust and data coordination. The lack of these two aspects has caused problems such as slow market demand response in traditional supply chains, lack of trust among member companies, and poor overall efficiency [19]. Liaono et al. (2014) takes supply chain coordination as the intermediate variable, uses the structural equation to construct an indirect theoretical model that affects the performance of the enterprise, and the empirical research shows that the quality and content of information sharing will affect the performance of the enterprise [20].

In short, the importance of supply chain collaboration has been unanimously recognized. The research content is mainly focused on the research of the conceptual framework and theoretical model. The content of supply chain information collaboration is mainly reflected in the factors affecting the supply chain information collaboration and its impact on supply chain performance. However, the influence of blockchain on supply chain synergy, and even on supply chain co-innovation, is less. This is a topic worth studying.

3   The Conceptual Models and Research Hypotheses

3.1 Conceptual Model

Technology Acceptance Model (TAM) is the most profound theoretical model in the field of information systems. TAM is based on cognitive usefulness and cognitive ease of use as independent variables, and user attitudes, behavioral intentions and behavior as dependent variables. It is argued that cognitive usefulness and ease of use affect the attitude of using technology, and thus the specific behavior performance, and that the use of IT by people is influenced by their behavior intention [21]. This model can be widely used to interpret or predict the influence factors of information technology use. Therefore, this paper will give a research model based on TAM. In this paper, a more instructive IDT-TAM integrated model is adopted at the acceptance level of block-chain [22, 23]. Based on the theory of product life cycle, with reference to Zhang Jing et al. [24], the performance measurement of supply chain collaborative product innovation is divided into development cycle, development cost and irreplaceability dimensions.

Based on the above analysis, the characteristics of mobile supply chain and the technical characteristics of block chain, a theoretical model of the block chain-based impact on the collaborative product innovation in supply chain is proposed, as shown in Fig. 1.

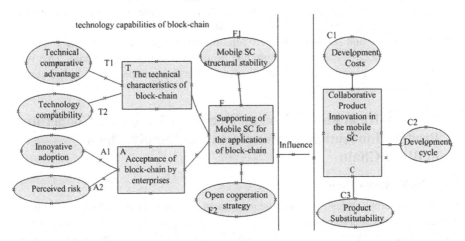

Fig. 1. The conceptual model.

In this paper, the ease of use and perceived usefulness of technology are reflected in the three aspects of the technical characteristics of block-chain, the adoption attitude of enterprises and the supporting of SC to block-chain. Then the application capability index of block-chain technology can be formed to play its role in supply chain collaborative product innovation impact.

3.2 Research Hypothesis

The new technology features are the basic driving force for its promotion [25]. Among them, "technical comparative advantage" and "technology compatibility" are its core characteristics. Xie Xuemei [26] studied the main supporting factors positively affecting the enterprise through empirical analysis The effect of collaborative innovation, and the main supporting factors include the environment and culture that encourages innovation and collaboration, the company's own research and development capabilities and innovation capabilities, organizational structure, the importance of senior leaders, and the experience of collaborative cooperation. Hilletofth and Eriksson [27] and others based on qualitative research and used case study methods to study the close cooperation between supply chain members to help product innovation. Based on the perspective of user innovation, Wang Bingfu et al. [28] studied the impact of platform interaction and resource sharing on corporate collaborative innovation, and pointed out that the platform construction is an influential factor of collaborative innovation. In summary, we propose the following hypothesis:

H1: The essential technical characteristics of the block-chain positively affect the collaborative capability of the supply chain.

H2: The acceptability of enterprises to block-chain affects the collaborative capability of their supply chain.

H3: Supply chain enterprises have a positive impact on the innovation acceptance of block-chain on the collaborative product innovation in supply chain.

H4: The technical characteristics of block-chain have a positive impact on the innovation performance of supply chain collaborative products.

H5: The dynamic and stable cooperative relationship between enterprises is positively related to the effect of collaborative product innovation in the supply chain. That is to say, the collaborative capability of supply chain has a direct impact on its collaborative product innovation performance.

4   The Empirical Research on the Factors Affecting the Cooperative Product Innovation of Manufacturing Supply Chain in Block-Chain

4.1   The Research Design

Based on literature review, taking some manufacturing enterprises in Zhejiang Province of China as the research object, considering the characteristics of manufacturing enterprises in Zhejiang Province, specific sub-variables were determined, and a questionnaire was constructed. As the application of block-chain in Chinese manufacturing enterprises is not yet widespread, this survey, as far as possible, obtained 86 valid questionnaires through telephone interviews.

4.2   Exploratory Factor Analysis

4.2.1   Reliability Analysis

The overall reliability of the questionnaire data is shown in Table 1 by SPSS 17 software.

Table 1. Reliability.

Cronbach's alpha	Items
0.903	9

As shown in Table 1, it can be seen that the questionnaire data in this article is greater than 0.9, which belongs to a high level of acceptance. The questionnaire has good reliability and can be used for subsequent research.

4.2.2   The Validity Analysis of Sample

Factor analysis was carried out after orthogonal rotation of the maximum variance of SPSS17.0 software. The KMO and Bartlett test results of the class validation questionnaire were shown in Table 2.

As shown in Table 2, the KMO value is 0.806, and the Bartlett sphere chi-square test value is 512.474, which is significant at the level of $p < 0.001$. So, the factor analysis can be performed.

Table 2. The KMO and Bartlett test.

Kaiser Meyer Olkin measure of sampling adequacy		0.806
Bartlett's spherical test	Approximate chi-square	512.474
	df	36
	Sig.	0

4.2.3 The Common Factor ANOVA

The specific conditions of the common factor variance are shown in Table 3:

Table 3. The common factor variance.

Variable	Initial value	Extraction
T1	1.000	.827
T2	1.000	.787
A1	1.000	.784
A2	1.000	.798
F1	1.000	.591
F2	1.000	.640
C1	1.000	.834
C2	1.000	.628
C3	1.000	.465

From Table 3, in addition to C3 close to 0.5 which will be deleted, the variance of the common factors of all terms is greater than 0.5, indicating that the measured variables have a significant impact on the innovation of the supply chain collaborative products, which can well explain the effect of the factors on the innovation of the supply chain collaborative products.

After the exploratory factor analysis described above, this paper concludes that the total explanatory contrast of the initial variables is 70.854%, which meets the conditions of greater than 50%. It shows that the extracted variables can better represent most of the information of the measured variables.

5 The Confirmatory Factor Analysis

5.1 Hypothesis Testing

According to Fig. 1, the paper uses the maximum likelihood method in the AMOS structural equation software to analyze the influence path of the model by the AMOS.22 software. The regression coefficient of model is shown in Table 4.

Table 4. The regression coefficient of model.

X	→	Y	Non standardized path coefficient	z	SE	p	Standardized path coefficient
T	→	F	−0.419	−1.097	0.382	0.273	−0.496
A	→	F	1.125	2.597	0.433	0.009	1.214
F	→	C	0.933	6.493	0.144	0	0.748

It can be seen from Table 4 that this path does not show significant (z = − 1.097, P = 0.273 > 0.05) when testing the impact of T on F, so it shows that t does not have an impact on f. Considering the influence of a and F, their normalized path coefficient value is 1.214 > 0, and this path shows a significant level of 0.01 (z = 2.597, P = 0.009 < 0.01), which indicates that a will have a significant positive influence on f. The influence of F on C can be attributed to their standardized path coefficient values of 0.748 > 0, and the path shows a significant level of 0.01 (z = 6.493, P = 0.000 < 0.01), which indicates that f will have a significant positive impact on C.

Therefore, the three hypotheses of H1, H2 and H5 are valid, while H3 and H4 are not. It also shows that the influence of block-chain on collaborative product innovation of supply chain is realized through the intermediary variable - the collaborative ability of supply chain. Only the organic integration of block-chain and supply chain can truly promote collaborative product innovation.

5.2 The Structural Equation Model

The influence relationship between the factors and the path coefficient can be obtained from the structural equation model shown in Fig. 2.

This figure also further illustrates that block-chain promotes collaborative product innovation through the functional carrier of supply chain. It also shows that the new technology can not directly produce performance to the enterprise, but should improve certain management mode through the new technology, and then promote the enterprise effect or performance. New technology can play a role only through certain functional carriers. In addition, unexpectedly, a positive correlation between T and A was also found in the study for their normalized path coefficient with 0.910, which was a result that was not expected before. This also confirms that the characteristics of new technologies determine the attitude of adopting for an enterprise.

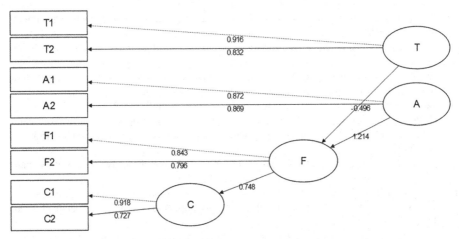

Fig. 2. The structural equation model.

6 Conclusion

In view of people's fuzzy attitude towards the use of new technology, it affects the management strategy decision of enterprises. According to the characteristics of block-chain technology, this paper puts forward its application value in supply chain collaborative product innovation. Based on the TAM theory and the collaborative characteristics of supply chain, we propose a theoretical model of the impact of block-chain on collaborative product innovation in supply chain. Then through the questionnaire data empirical research hypothesis, and gives the structural equation model, influence path and influence coefficient more detailed. This study can provide a reference for enterprises to reasonably apply block-chain, and also provide a new way for collaborative innovation of products in the supply chain environment.

Funding. This research was supported by the Natural Science Foundation of Zhejiang Province in China (Grant No. LY18G010011) and the Natural Science Foundation of Zhejiang Province in China (Grant No. LY13G010005).

References

1. Yingxiu, L.: Study on the Influential Factors of Collaborative Product Innovation in Manufacturing Supply Chain of Shanxi Province. Doctoral dissertation, Taiyuan University of Technology (2018)
2. Swan, M.: Block-chain: Blue Print for a New Economy. O' Reilly, Sebastopol (2015)
3. Feng, C.: Block-chain driven supply chain innovation. China Logist. Purch. **15**, 33–35 (2017)
4. Francisco, K., Swanson, D.: The supply chain has no clothes: technology adoption of block-chain for supply chain transparency. Logistics **2**(1), 2 (2018)
5. Wang, Y., Hongshan, W.: Application and development of block-chain technology in supply chain. Fin. Expo **4**, 54–55 (2018)
6. Liu, Y.: Design and implementation of supply chain information platform based on block-chain. Master's thesis of Inner Mongolia University (2019)

7. Bo, Z.: Application of foreign blockchain technology and related enlightenments. Age Fintech **5**, 35–38 (2016)
8. Changjiang, D.: Application and development prospect of blockchain. Inf. Technol. Stand. **12**, 12–15 (2017)
9. Huckle, S., Bhattacharya, R., White, M., et al.: Internet of Things, blockchain and shared economy applications. Proc. Comput. Sci. **98**(2), 461–466 (2016)
10. Tao, Y., Bin, W.: Decentralized finance and block-chain. Fin. Expo **12**, 18–19 (2016)
11. Huanwen, Z., Xuegong, L.: Application imagination and development path of blockchain in the field of cold chain logistics of agricultural products. Taiwan Agric. Explor. **153**(04), 70–73 (2018)
12. Kumar, M.V., Iyengar, N.C.S.: A framework for blockchain technology in rice supply chain management. Adv. Sci. Technol. Lett. **146**, 125–130 (2017)
13. Zhao, L., Bi, X., Zhao, A.: Reconstruction of the fresh food mobile traceability platform framework based on block-chain. Food Sci. (2019). http://kns.cnki.net/kcms/detail/11.2206.TS.20190110.1258.010.html
14. Simatupang, T.M., Sridharan, R.: The collaboration index: a measure for supply chain collaboration. Int. J. Phys. Distrib. Logist. Manage. **35**(1), 44–62 (2005)
15. Ramanathan, U.: How smart operations help better planning and replenishment?: Empirical study–supply chain collaboration for smart operations. In: Supply Chain Management in the Big Data Era, pp. 25–49. IGI Global (2017)
16. Zhong, R.Y., Newman, S.T., Huang, G.Q., et al.: Big data for supply chain management in the service and manufacturing sectors: challenges, opportunities, and future perspectives. Comput. Ind. Eng. **101**(5), 572–591 (2016)
17. Shan, L.: Supply chain collaboration: an analysis based on the core competence theory. Enterp. Econ. **11**, 56–58 (2008)
18. Shuqin, C., Jing, L.: Research on the relationship between supply chain collaboration and information sharing. Chin. J. Manage. **4**(2), 157–162 (2007)
19. Fu Pengbo, L., Yongbo, R.Y., et al.: Research on information sharing mechanism under supply chain collaborative management mode. Logist. Technol. **26**(6), 88–90 (2007)
20. Nuo, L., Wei, D., Weilang, Z., et al.: Research on the mechanism of indirect impact of information sharing on enterprise performance – taking supply chain collaboration as an intermediary variable. J. Guangdong Univ. Technol. **31**(4), 31–35 (2014)
21. Davis, F.D.: A Technology Acceptance Model for Empirically Testing New End-User Information Systems: Theory and Results. MIT, Cambridge (1986)
22. Nan, Z., Xunhua, G., Guoqing, C.: IDT-TAM integrated model for IT adoption. Tsinghua Sci. Technol. **03**, 306–311 (2008)
23. Jinyang, H.: Decision model of technology innovation diffusion: comprehensive review and construction of new model. Sci. Technol. Prog. Pol. **32**(05), 5–10 (2015)
24. Jing, Z., Yanling, D.: Empirical research on the impact of market-oriented equilibrium on product innovation performance of manufacturing enterprises. World Manage. **12**, 119–130 (2010)
25. Amara, N., Landry, R.: Sources of information as determinants of novelty of innovation in manufacturing firms: evidence from the 1999 statistics Canada innovation survey. Technovation **25**(3), 245–259 (2005)

26. Xuemei, X.: An empirical study on the multi-dimensional relationship between the influencing factors and the degree of collaborative innovation of enterprises. Sci. Res. Manag. **02**, 69–78 (2015)
27. Hilletofth, P., Eriksson, D.: Coordinating new product development with supply chain management. Ind. Manage. Data Syst. **111**(2), 264–281 (2011)
28. Bingfu, W., Zhun, Z.: Construction of the framework of the theory of factors affecting user innovation from the perspective of cooperative innovation. Sci. Technol. Prog. Countermeas. **33**(17), 14–19 (2016)

Research on the Impact Factors of Quality Risk in the Mobile Supply Chain of Intelligent Manufacturing

Caihong Liu[1]([⊠]) and June Wei[2]

[1] School of Business, Jiaxing University, Jiaxing 314001, China
liuch0001@163.com
[2] College of Business, University of West Florida, Pensacola, FL 32514, USA

Abstract. The formation of global market pattern makes the market competition develop from the traditional competition among enterprises to the competition among supply chains. With the transformation of China's manufacturing industry to intelligent manufacturing and the development of supply chain mobile application, the mobile supply chain (SC) facing intelligent manufacturing is endowed with more market elements, technical elements and innovative management elements. Therefore, mobile supply chain operation also faces some new potential quality risk factors. According to the characteristics of dynamic and complex supply chain environment, large loss of quality risk and wide range, this paper puts forward the research topic of mobile supply chain risk factor identification under intelligent manufacturing. Based on the application status of mobile supply chain in China's manufacturing industry, this paper analyzes the quality risk path of mobile supply chain, discusses the measurement factors of supply chain quality risk, and designs the corresponding questionnaire. Then, a questionnaire survey was conducted in Zhejiang Province. SPSS software was used for correlation analysis, cluster analysis and principal component analysis. The evaluation model of supply chain quality risk factors in the "intelligent manufacturing" environment is established. This study can provide theoretical support for manufacturing enterprises to prevent and deal with supply chain quality risk, so as to promote the healthy development of intelligent manufacturing mobile supply chains.

Keywords: Intelligent manufacturing · Mobile supply chain · Quality risk factors

1 Introduction

To become a manufacturing power for China, it is a key strategy to improve the importance of "made in China" in the global manufacturing industry and get rid of "made in China". China has put forward the development strategy of "made in China 2025", which focuses on the transformation of Chinese manufacturing enterprises to intelligent manufacturing characterized by digitalization, networking and intelligence. The proposal of intelligent manufacturing is to get rid of the dilemma of high loss and low

© Springer Nature Switzerland AG 2020
G. Salvendy and J. Wei (Eds.): HCII 2020, LNCS 12216, pp. 84–93, 2020.
https://doi.org/10.1007/978-3-030-50350-5_8

efficiency in China's manufacturing industry, and to improve the competitiveness of manufacturing industry is the only way to become a "manufacturing power". In the intelligent manufacturing environment, how to use intelligent communication devices, such as smart phones, wireless information sensing technology, such as the Internet of things, wireless networks, some mobile phone apps with certain business functions and information integration technology, etc., to promote the smooth implementation of intelligent manufacturing by enterprises, which is an effective way for China's manufacturing to transform into "intelligent manufacturing". In view of the formation and application of smart supply chain, which is relied on by smart manufacturing, is not mature and popular enough, this paper proposes to use the concept of mobile supply chain to assist the "smart manufacturing" of Chinese manufacturing enterprises with mobile supply chain as the transition form of smart supply chain. Mobile supply chain [1] is proposed because the global mobile communication market has entered a mature period in recent years, and mobile data service has become an important driving force to promote market share and revenue growth. Because of the heterogeneity and diversity of mobile data service, mobile operators cannot provide data service alone, Supply Chain Management (SCM) is exactly in line with the requirements of this trend. Its core is cooperation and integration, but for a long time, the application of supply chain is mainly concentrated in manufacturing and circulation service industry, and the application in mobile communication industry is still a relatively new field. Its purpose is to improve the management ability of mobile data service with the help of supply chain management theory. In short, the combination of mobile data service and supply chain brings about the concept of mobile supply chain. Since this concept was put forward, the relevant research is to discuss some mobile supply chain problems for mobile services. There is little consideration of reverse application of mobile data and mobile supply chain to other fields, such as manufacturing. This paper argues that in the new era of Internet plus, the reverse utility of mobile supply chain should have some value. With the help of mobile information technology, mobile supply chain can be an effective way to solve the problems of information flow and logistics mismatch, real-time information of supply chain is difficult to obtain, intermediate state uncertainty and overall decision-making under information sharing. Based on this, in order to make up for the lack of intelligence in manufacturing supply chain with mobile supply chain, this paper tries to think about the application of mobile supply chain in China's intelligent manufacturing environment, and at the same time studies the possible quality risks in the application of mobile supply chain in intelligent manufacturing.

2   Literature Review

2.1   Mobile Supply Chain for Manufacturing Enterprise

The introduction of mobile information technologies, such as RFID and GPS, has triggered unprecedented levels of vitality in the supply chain operation layer, and has brought about a dramatic increase in the efficiency of all aspects of the supply chain [2]. The concept of Mobile SC has been proposed, and it has quickly become an emerging area of concern for the supply chain academia [3, 4]. With the development of Internet technology, the supply chain is also developing towards digital networked supply. The integration of industry supply chains through mobile information platforms has become a development trend. The mobile supply chain has promoted intensive use of enterprise resources and leaned cooperation in the industrial chain. Digital supply network and high-precision data analysis capabilities are the embryonic form of agile, flexible and intelligent supply chains. The goal of Henan Mobile's supply chain capability evolution is to effectively combine massive data with big data analysis capabilities to make the supply network covered All levels of managers and participants can get comprehensive and customized decision-making guidance services [5]. The traditional supply chain is represented by the SCOR (Supply-Chain Operations Reference-model) model, which has five basic processes: Make, Plan, Deliver, Source and Return. This model summarizes the supply chain process. However, the management mode of mobile supply chain is different. It is not the management mode of the whole process of supply chain, but the abstract mode of using the local process of mobile supply chain management. The mobile supply chain management mode is divided to three levels, including user, network, and system platform levels. They jointly realize the specific functions of mobile SC and conduct management in the whole mobile supply chain management system [6]. According to the research of domestic and foreign scholars such as Rulke (2002) [7] and Yuan Yufei (2003) [8], the value chain for the third generation mobile commerce mainly includes service providers of portal and access, service providers of contents and applications, service providers of supports, operators of wireless networks, terminal platforms, and users, etc. Zhu Weiping [9] mainly describes how to use RFID technology in logistics distribution from two aspects of transportation and receiving. And it gives the solution of middleware and monitoring equipment. Ziqi Liao [10] et al. studied the taxi service management of vehicle automatic location distribution system based on global positioning system (GPS).

It can be seen that mobile supply chain research has become a research hotspot in the fields of commerce and information. The theory and method of mobile supply chain have not formed a complete system. The topics of most articles focus on the impact and significance of mobile technology on business models, consumer acceptance behaviors, as well as wireless/mobile technologies and network-based technical articles. As a mature research field, how the mobile supply chain needs to improve the efficiency of business operations and the integration of specific industry applications and mobile commerce are at the exploratory stage. Both the amount of research and the content of the research are insufficient [2].

2.2 The Development of Supply Chain for Intelligent Manufacturing

With the deep integration of the new artificial intelligence and artificial technology, a new generation of intelligent manufacturing has emerged at the historic moment and has become the core technology of a new round of industrial revolution. It will lead to major changes in the development concept and production mode of the manufacturing industry, and reshape the development path, technology system and industrial format of the manufacturing industry. Huang Junjun (2018) [11] proposed that Intelligent Manufacturing IM refers to the use of intelligent machines to interact with humans and ultimately achieve human-machine integration. Throughout the system, computer can be used for efficient prediction, analysis, and decision making, which is more advanced and accurate. Zhang Jiangpeng et al. (2018) [12] pointed out that the development of intelligent manufacturing is also continuously affecting the economic development of enterprises. With the development of the supply chain model and the deepening of practice, suppliers face greater credit risk when selling on credit. Zhao Yabo (2002) [13] believes that intelligent manufacturing technology refers to the technology that uses computers to simulate the analysis, evaluation, reasoning, design and decision-making of human experts in manufacturing industry. It combines these intelligent activities with intelligent machines. Intelligent assembly system is formed by the deep integration of advanced manufacturing technology, information technology and intelligent technology to form equipment systems with sensing, analysis, reasoning, decision making and control functions. These smart devices have become a basic capability to improve manufacturing transformation [14].

2.3 Supply Chain Quality Risk

Supply chain quality risk is the sum of the quality of the supply chain of various risks, and all the parties to all risks. High quality risk refers to the probability that a negative event will occur or not occur in the future, and the event is responsible for the event Quality does not want to occur which may cause quality loss or other negative effects [15]. Manufacturing enterprises should reorient themselves through promotion, adjust production methods and management modes, and reduce supply chain quality risk, which is the prerequisite for manufacturing enterprises to win [16]. Supply chain quality risk management is a large and complex systematic project. Like supply chain risk management, current research mainly focuses on quality risk identification, assessment, and control. At present, most related research focuses on traditional quality process management, Qualitative research such as systematic risk identification and estimation, few literatures consider product quality risk issues from the perspective of supply chain [17]. Li Yan et al. [18] studied the issue of outsourcing quality risk control and incentive mechanism by designing a menu-type contract mechanism based on the principal-agent theory, considering risk preference. Wang Wenshan proposed corresponding quality risk control mechanisms for the generation and transmission effects of product quality risks in the supply chain [19]. Chen Nan [20] divided the supply chain quality risk into quality credit risk and quality technology risk, and studied the control methods of these two quality risks from the perspective of supply and demand cooperation. Zhou Huijun et al. [21] aimed at the problem of insufficient supplier quality risk control (quality effort) in the cross-border e-commerce supply chain and the lack of promotion efforts of the retailer's products, through the Nash negotiation model to achieve supply chain prevention. Zhu Fan [22] believes that the occurrence of supply chain quality risks is not only the responsibility of a single company, but it should start from the three aspects of supply chain upstream and downstream enterprises, Ik, downstream enterprises and government departments to achieve supply chain quality risk control.

Supply chain quality risk has attracted everyone's attention, but the research on the quality risk problem of mobile supply chain has not been basically done. Therefore, related research is urgent.

3 The Reliability and Validity of the Questionnaire

3.1 Survey Design

Based on the understanding of the status quo of quality risks in the intelligent manufacturing supply chain and the characteristics of quality risks, a questionnaire was designed. The most direct investigative target of the factors affecting the quality risk of the intelligent manufacturing supply chain we investigated is intelligent manufacturing related companies. We can get the most critical data from the enterprise. Therefore, the questionnaires are selected by employees of the relevant departments of smart manufacturing enterprises. We use intelligent manufacturing companies in Jiangsu and Zhejiang to issue questionnaires and collect data. We distributed 200 questionnaires. 176 questionnaires and 157 valid questionnaires were recovered. The effective utilization rate reached 89.2%. Data analysis was performed using SPSS statistical software. The setting of survey indicators is firstly a survey of the nature of the company. Mastery of the nature of the company helps us analyze whether different types of smart manufacturing companies have an impact on the quality of the supply chain; secondly, the survey of the personal data of the respondents, Focus on investigating his working life, his department position and understanding of the quality risk of intelligent manufacturing supply, so as to judge the feasibility of the questionnaire he filled out; finally, the assessment of the factors affecting the supply chain quality risk in the intelligent manufacturing environment of the enterprise, From the perspective of suppliers that the enterprise cooperates with, the stability of the intelligent manufacturing supply chain of the enterprise, the perspective of the production chain of the intelligent manufacturing supply chain of the enterprise, the perspective of the enterprise's management of the intelligent supply chain production product, and the perspective of the enterprise's grasp of the relevant intelligent manufacturing technology give survey indicators.

3.2 Reliability Analysis

Reliability is to test the reliability of questionnaire data collection, and the main internal consistency of test results is stability. Through SPSS software, the reliability analysis by SPSS software is as follows.

It can be seen from Table 1 that the whole Cronbach' Alpha are within the reliable range, indicating that the reliability of the whole questionnaire is relatively satisfactory.

Table 1. Questionnaire measurement.

Cronbach's Alpha	Items
0.785	15

3.3 Validity

Factor analysis was used to verify the validity of the questionnaire. Using factor analysis, we can find that some questions of the questionnaire may be merged into other factors, so as to evaluate the validity of the questionnaire. Validity analysis by SPSS software has been given as Table 2.

Table 2. The structural validity of the questionnaire.

Variable	Item number	KMO	Total variance of cumulative interpretation
The basic information of the surveyed	Q1.2 Q2.5 Q2.6 QA1	0.815	81.547
Mobile supplier quality (V1)	QA2 QA3 QA4	0.778	75.455
Chain structure stability (V2)	QB1 QB2 QC1	0.65	80.726
Production process quality (V3)	QC2 QC3 QC4 QD1	0.703	85.703
Colloborative risk of mobile commerce (V4)	QD2 QD3 QE1	0.765	69.07
Intelligent production risk	QE2 QE3	0.66	73.289
Mobile information technology application capabilities	QF1 QF2	0.755	76.253

From Table 2, it can be seen that the KMO value is above 0.9, indicating that it is very suitable for factor analysis; 0.8–0.9: very suitable; 0.7–0.8 suitable; 0.6–0.7 is acceptable; 0.5–0.6 means very poor; 0.45 Following: should be abandoned. In the above table, the KOM values of all variables are greater than 0.6, and factor analysis can be performed with good validity. The total variance of the cumulative explanation is around 70 and above. Considering the factors of the actual questionnaire, this data is still within the acceptable range.

4 The Factors Influencing the Quality Risk of Mobile Supply for Intelligent Manufacturing

4.1 Correlation Analysis

In order to measure the correlation among the six indicators in the questionnaire, factor correlation analysis was carried out, and the results are shown in Table 3.

Table 3. The correlation of variables.

V6	1					
V1	.248**	1				
V2	.359**	.325**	1			
V3	.256**	0.178	.553**	1		
V4	.379**	.400*	.548**	.561**	1	
V5	.169*	0.395	.316**	.340**	.614**	1

We can see that these six variables have influence on each other.

4.2 The Principal Component Analysis

The analysis results of common factor variance of six variables are as follows through the extraction method of principal component analysis.

As can be seen from Table 4 that the extraction of the common factors of the six indicators is greater than 0.5. This means that the information contained in each variable can be represented by the extracted common factor.

Table 4. The variance of common factor.

	Initial value	Extraction
V6	1	0.848
V1	1	0.64
V2	1	0.595
V3	1	0.616
V4	1	0.757
V5	1	0.525

4.3 Factor Analysis

In order to bring together highly relevant variables, thereby reducing the number of variables that need to be analyzed, and reducing the complexity of problem analysis. We use the principal component extraction method to reduce the dimensions of the factors shown as Table 5.

Table 5. Components

	Components	
	1	2
V6	0.267	0.881
V1	0.667	0.442
V2	0.747	−0.189
V3	0.752	−0.227
V4	0.835	−0.245
V5	0.725	−0.019

It shows in Table 5 that most indicator information is concentrated in factor 1, indicating that they are highly correlated with the first factor, but the correlation between the other factor and the original variable is relatively small, which is not conducive to the definition of factor attributes. At the same time, 2 ingredients have been extracted.

In order to make a better distinction between the indicators of each factor, the rotation method of Kaiser standardized maximum variance is used for rotation, and the maximum convergence iteration times are 3 times. The factor score matrix after rotation is shown in Table 6.

Table 6. Factor score matrix

	Components	
	1	2
V6	−0.187	0.77
V1	0.081	0.451
V2	0.304	−0.067
V3	0.317	−0.098
V4	0.35	−0.104
V5	0.243	0.072

It can be seen that the two main components are more appropriately explained by mobile technology risks and risks brought by the results of the supply chain system, and they are more in line with the two risk dimensions of the technology and chain structure of mobile supply chain quality risks. Then, according to the score coefficient matrix, the regression equation of each principal component is given.

Technical risk of mobile commerce = V6 * 0.77 + V1 * 0.451

Quality risk of supply chain = V2 * 0.304 + V3 * 0.317 + V4 * 0.350 + V5 * 0.243

Therefore, the composition of the quality risk factors for mobile supply chain can be represented by Fig. 1.

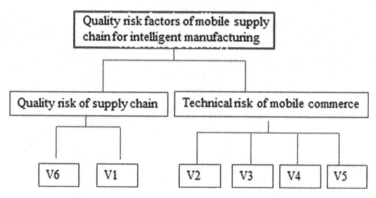

Fig. 1. The compositional structure of risk factors.

At present, the mobile supply chain in China's intelligent manufacturing environment is still in the primary stage of development. Under the environment of intelligent manufacturing market, supply chain emphasizes more on intelligent technology and efficient integrated business processing capability. This will also bring some new risks to the supply chain. Mobile supply chain is the aggregation of mobile technology and supply chain. From these two aspects, it is common practice to think about some factors that may make it face risks. This paper also discusses these potential risks and the relationship between the factors through empirical methods.

5 Conclusion

Considering that the combination of mobile information technology and supply chain is still limited to low-level business operation activities, the research on the risk of mobile supply chain is still lagging behind. From the perspective of mobile quality, this paper empirically studies the influencing factors of quality risk of mobile supply chain for intelligent manufacturing and the importance of these factors. There are still some deficiencies in the study, which will be further deepened in the future. This study is not only to attract people's attention, but also to provide some theoretical reference for enterprises and related research.

Funding. This research was supported by the Natural Science Foundation of Zhejiang Province in China (Grant No. LY18G010011) and the Natural Science Foundation of Zhejiang Province in China (Grant No. LY13G010005).

References

1. Li, H.: Supply chain management of mobile data services. Master's thesis, Beijing University of Posts and Telecommunications (2004)
2. Wang, L.: Research on the theory and method of mobile supply chain collaboration. Doctoral dissertation, Harbin University of Technology (2009)
3. Yuan, Q., Xiaokang, Z., Qiong, Z.: Key technology and system design in mobile supply chain management. In: 2008 International Symposium Electronic Commerce and Security, vol. 5, no. 1, pp. 258–262 (2008)
4. Eng, T.-Y.: Mobile supply chain management: challenges for implementation. Technovation 26(5), 682–686 (2006)
5. Creating a Comprehensive Intelligent Digital Supply Network Introduction of Henan Mobile's Supply Chain Management Innovation Practices. Tendr. Procure. Manage. (2), 47–49 (2018)
6. Miao, L., et al.: Research on the construction of mobile supply chain for manufacturing enterprises. Logist. Technol. 30(9), 104–106 (2007)
7. Rulke, E.A., Iyer, A., Chiasson, G.: The ecology of mobile commerce: charting a course for success using value chain analysis. In: Mobile Commerce: Technology, Theory, and Applications, pp. 534–535. Idea Group Publishing, Hershey (2002). Selected chapter in M.E. Brain and S.J. Troy
8. Yuan, Y.F., Zhang, J.: Towards an appropriate business model For M-commerce. Int. J. Mob. Commun. 1(12), 35–56 (2003)
9. Zhu, W., Wang, D., Sheng, H.: Mobile RFID technology for improving M-commerce. Proc. ICEBE 12(4), 125–132 (2005)
10. Liao, Z.: Real-time taxi dispatching using global positioning systems. Commun. ACM 5(46), 81–83 (2003)
11. Huang, J.: Key technologies and implementation in intelligent manufacturing. Electron. Technol. Softw. Eng. (15), 65 (2018)
12. Jiangpeng, Z., et al.: The formation of accounts receivable risks of core enterprises under the supply chain model—taking manufacturing industry in the undeveloped regions of Western China as an example. China Fin. Account. Monthly 17, 23–31 (2018)
13. Yabo, Z.: Intelligent manufacturing. Ind. Control Comput. 15(3), 1–4 (2002)
14. Intelligent manufacturing—main attack direction of 2025 made in China. Lifting Transp. Mach. (1), 44–45 (2018)
15. Jiang, J., Zhao, Y., Feng, Y.: Study on the forms and characteristics of quality risk in supply Chain. J. Manage. (z1), 17–23 (2007)
16. Zhuo, Y., Ke, Y., Weidong, T.: Research on supply chain quality risk management model. Sci. Fortune 10, 5–6 (2013)
17. Zhang, Yu., Shouyang, W.: Supply Chain Quality Risk Management. Science Press, Beijing (2013)
18. Li, Y., Song, H., Xu, Q., et al.: Research on outsourcing quality risk control and incentive mechanism considering risk preference. China Manage. Sci. (s1), 190–197 (2013)
19. Wang, W.: Research on Product Quality Risk Control in Supply Chain. Master's Degree Thesis of Nankai University (2008)
20. Chen, N.: Research on supply chain quality risk control based on supply and demand cooperation. Master's Degree Thesis of Harbin Institute of Technology (2008)
21. Huijun, Z., Wei, Y., Lang, X.: Decision and coordination of cross-border e-commerce supply chain under quality risk control and promotion. J. Shanghai Marit. Univ. 38(3), 67–71 (2017)
22. Fan, Z.: Control and prevention of quality risk in supply chain. China Sci. Technol. Expo 21, 112–113 (2009)

Research on the Issues and Countermeasures of VAT Legislation for China Mobile Business Users

Yun Ruan[1(✉)] and Wanyu Li[2]

[1] The People's Bank of China Nanyang Central Sub-branch, Nanyang, China
1663766256@qq.com
[2] International College of Zhengzhou University, Zhengzhou, China
1413659882@qq.com

Abstract. Mobile commerce has become a new trend in e-commerce in recent years and a new engine of economic growth in the digital economy. However, the rapid development of this new business activity has brought about a series of tax problems while promoting economic growth. Firstly, this paper analyzes whether China's current VAT-related regulations can adapt to the mobile commerce environment. Secondly, it sorts out the relevant measures of the international society on the digital economy and e-commerce environment, and analyzes the reasons for taking these measures. Finally, appropriate recommendations of Chinese mobile commerce VAT legislation are proposed in consideration of China's specific national conditions, national interests and characteristics of mobile commerce.

Keywords: Mobile commerce · E-Commerce · Digital economy · Value-added tax · Legislation

1 Introduction

With the emergence of mobile terminals and the popularity of wireless and mobile networks, mobile commerce has shown strong development potential. Mobile commerce breaks the limitations of time and place in business activities so that people can carry out business activities anytime and anywhere. According to data from the International Telecommunication Union in 2018, 96% of the world's population have an access to mobile networks. In addition, according to *2018 (I) China Online Retail Market Data Monitoring Report* released by the China Electronic Commerce Research Center, China's mobile online shopping in the first half of 2018 totaled 2.737 trillion yuan, accounting for 67.1% of the online shopping. Mobile commerce shows strong development potential.

Currently, the tax system applied by International community follows the basic framework of the 1920s. It appears somewhat stretched in the current digital economy. Zhu Jun (2015) used the average tax burden method and the attrition rate method to find out that China's tax losses were caused by e-commerce. Due to the development of the digital economy, tax losses in various countries have been exacerbated. According

G. Salvendy and J. Wei (Eds.): HCII 2020, LNCS 12216, pp. 94–106, 2020.
https://doi.org/10.1007/978-3-030-50350-5_9

to researches of scholars at home and abroad, mobile commerce is the latest extension of the digital economy and e-commerce. In 2015, the OECD released Tackling the Tax Challenges of the Digital Economy which states that e-commerce is one of the business models of the digital economy. Liu Bailing, Lei Chao, Li Yanhui (2016), Bi Juan, Zhou Lingqiang, Sun Gaojian (2017), Chen Zhigang, Fang Hui (2018), Xiang Mengeng, Guo Shunli, Zhang Xiangxian (2018) and other scholars have found that mobile commerce is the extension of e-commerce. As the latest extension of the digital economy and e-commerce, mobile commerce not only has common features with the digital economy and e-commerce, but also has its own unique characteristics. If we just study the digital economy and e-commerce taxation issues, we cant not solve the problem of mobile commerce's taxation. Thus, we need to specialize in mobile commerce taxation. However, domestic and foreign scholars are relatively weak in this aspect, and China's current tax system is difficult to adapt to the mobile commerce environment.

At present, international research on the tax management of the digital economy and e-commerce is in full swing. Income tax and value-added tax are the two major types of tax revenue in China. Therefore, this article starts with whether China's current VAT law can deal with mobile commerce and international VAT legislation or not. Finally, we propose countermeasures for China Mobile Commerce VAT. On the one hand, this article improves theoretically relevant research on digital economy, e-commerce and mobile commerce; on the other hand, it follows the international trend by contributing to… and reducing to the improvement of China's current VAT laws and can reduce the loss of China's VAT taxes.

2 Features of Mobile Commerce

2.1 The Concept and Characteristics of Digital Economy

The OECD believes that with the development of modern information and communication technology, data has become increasingly prominent in the economy, and the digital economy emerge as the times require. Shen Yali, Beixin Lin, and Liao Weimin (2015) defined the digital economy and believed that it promoted economic development through digital products and digital methods on the basis of the Internet and modern information technology. It can be seen that the digital economy is an economic activity that uses data as one of production inputs and is based on the development of modern information technology.

According to the characteristics of digitalization in the definition of the digital economy, Chen Yongsheng, Pan Guozhong, and Wang Wenlai (2016) found that the digital economy has two characteristics: it can exist without a entity and needs the cooperation between sellers and buyers. Ma Huateng (2017) also summarized the characteristics of the digital economy in the book: (1) Data is regarded as a factor of production.; (2) Digital infrastructure is considered as an infrastructure for economic activity; (3) Sellers and buyers need to have some digital knowledge; (4) Because the digital economy requires sellers and buyers to cooperate with each other, the boundaries between the two sides will gradually blur; (5) People's lives are more closely connected with the Internet. Li Helin (2018) explored the difference between digital economy and traditional economy, and believed that when cross-border digital economic activities occurred, the economic scale could not be easily identified. Based on the OECD's relevant explanations on the digital economy, this article believes that digital economy is featured with liquidity, concealment, reduced entityization, blurred boundaries between buyers and sellers, and regarding data as factors of production input and so on.

2.2 The Concept and Characteristics of E-Commerce

The World Conference on Electronic Commerce was held in France in 1997. Scholars explained the definition of electronic commerce that electronic commerce is a business activity that digitizes traditional trading activities on the basis of modern information technology and computer networks. He Feiyun (2002) researches that e-commerce mainly depends on network media. Two key aspects of e-commerce are identity verification and payment. Ding Weirong and Zhang Fan (2015) defined e-commerce. They believe that on the one hand e-commerce is different from traditional business activities in terms of sales channels; on the other hand, goods or services can be electronicized and then transmitted online. Cai Chang (2017) researched that e-commerce converts capital flow, logistics and the like into information flow through modern network technology. Based on the above, scholars have basically reached a consensus on the concept of e-commerce. E-commerce uses modern communications and network technologies to turn traditional offline business activities into electronic online activities. Therefore, the definition of electronic commerce in this article is the combination of "electronic" and "commerce". "Electronic" is the method meaning Internet transaction system, and "commerce" is the purpose.

E-commerce is embodied as a combination of "electronic" and "commerce", which means that components of e-commerce add the "electronic" compared with traditional business activities. Ouyang Zeyu and Wang Kehan (2014) thought that the components of e-commerce include buyers, sellers, payment centers and sales centers. Yang Bo and Xu Lijuan (2017) researched that the "electronic" nature of e-commerce adds network, payment centers, logistics providers, buyer and seller identity authentication parts to e-commerce. Wang Zhiwen and Yu Yong (2017) researched that e-commerce has added authentication centers and payment centers to traditional business activities. In summary, the elements of e-commerce include buyers, sellers, networks, intermediary platforms, financial service providers, logistics and so on. The intermediary platform is responsible for the identity verification of buyers and sellers, as shown in Fig. 1.

Zhang Ying (2006) believed that e-commerce has the characteristics of being free from geographical restrictions, liquidity, digitization, and concealment. Yang Xiangying and Yang Hui (2009) researched that e-commerce has the characteristics of being free from geographical restrictions, strong interaction between buyers and sellers, and low cost. Liu Ye (2014) believed that e-commerce has the characteristics of liquidity, digitization, and concealment. Ma Xiuling (2015) believed that e-commerce has changed the habit of traditional business activities which require face-to-face contact in order to conduct transactions. Buyers and sellers can conduct transactions electronically, so e-commerce has the characteristic of being free of geographical restrictions. Guo Weiqi (2016) believed that e-commerce has the characteristics of being free from geographical restrictions, liquidity, digitization, concealment, and blurred source of goods. Wang Zhiwen and Yu Yong (2017) believed that e-commerce has the characteristics of

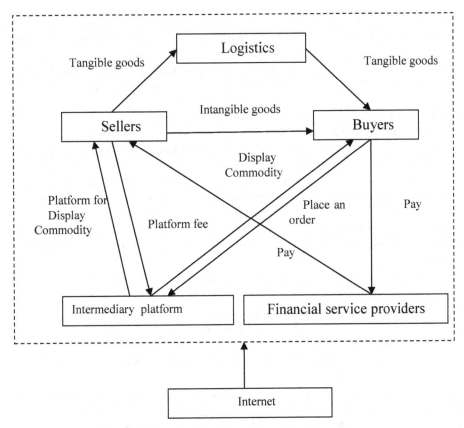

Fig. 1. Pattern diagram of the components of e-commerce

strong interaction, convenience, security and comprehensiveness of buyers and sellers. It can be seen that scholars generally believe that e-commerce has the characteristics of being free from geographical restrictions, liquidity, digitalization, strong interaction and concealment between buyers and sellers.

2.3   The Concept and Characteristics of M-Commerce

Gai Jianhua (2009) believed that mobile commerce is an extension of e-commerce, and network application activities have expanded from wired to wireless. Ren Tinghai and Zhang Xumei (2015) also believed that mobile commerce is an extension of e-commerce. Liu Bailing, Lei Chao, and Li Yanhui (2016) believed that mobile commerce is an activity that uses mobile terminals to achieve information and business interaction. Ye Fengyun (2017) simply defined the concept of mobile commerce as mobile shopping. Xu Chaoyi and Wang Jianguo (2017) believed that mobile commerce enables people to use mobile terminals to complete various business activities anytime and anywhere. When defining mobile commerce, Bi Juan, Zhou Lingqiang, Sun Gaojian (2017) emphasized that mobile commerce is an extension of e-commerce on the one hand and on the other hand pointed out that mobile commerce activities can take place anywhere and anytime. Chen Zhigang, Fang Hui (2018), Xiang Mengmeng, Guo Shunli, and Zhang Xiangxian (2018) emphasized that mobile commerce is a combination of e-commerce and mobile terminals. Therefore, this article defines mobile commerce as the combination of "mobile" and "terminal". "Mobile" is a means to expand from wired to wireless and "commerce" is the purpose.

Liu Yujun (2012) emphasized the importance of mobile operators in the research of the elements of mobile commerce. Zhang Runtong (2017) researched that mobile commerce has two more components——mobile terminal and mobile operator, compared with e-commerce. Therefore, the constituent elements for of mobile commerce in this article are shown in Fig. 2. Mobile terminal providers and mobile operators are the foundation of the entire mobile commerce activities and support the occurrence of mobile commerce activities. The product provider and the consumer reach a transaction through an intermediary platform, and then the financial service provider realizes the transfer of the loan. If the purchased product is tangible, then the logistics provider is required to transport it.

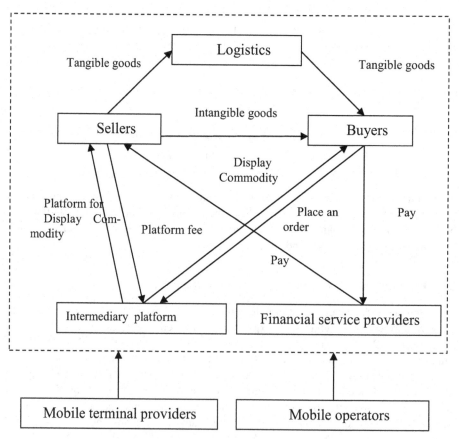

Fig. 2. Pattern diagram of mobile commerce components

According to the relevant literatures, scholars generally believe that mobile commerce has the characteristics of breaking geographical restrictions, customization, mobility, location relevance, convenience and so on. Wu Xiaobo and Chen Xiaoling (2010) researched that mobile commerce has the characteristics of breaking geographical restrictions, customization and flexibility. Yang Xuecheng (2017) believed that mobile commerce has the characteristics of breaking geographical restrictions, customization, mobility, location relevance, and more timely access to information. Zhang Runtong (2017) believed that mobile commerce has the characteristics of breaking geographical restrictions, customization, location relevance, convenience, more timely access to information, and recognizability. Wang Zhiwen and Yu Yong (2017) believed that mobile commerce has the characteristics of breaking geographical restrictions, customization, recognizability and innovation. Dai Junmin, Lu Yake, and Song Fangwei (2017) believed that mobile commerce has the characteristics of breaking geographical restrictions, customization, location relevance, convenience, more timely and recognizable information. Among them, breaking the geographical restrictions, customization, mobility, and location correlation are mainly due to the combination of mobile commerce and mobile terminals. Because mobile commerce is an extension of e-commerce, mobile commerce also has the characteristic of concealment like e-commerce.

3   Challenges to China's VAT from Mobile Commerce

In the mobile commerce environment, the traditional tax system seems not enough. Therefore, this part analyzes whether China's current VAT-related laws can adapt to the environment of mobile commerce from four aspects: the taxpayer, the object of taxation and the tax rate, the location of the taxation and the method of collecting imported goods tax.

3.1   The Taxpayer

According to the *Interim Regulation of the People's Republic of China on Value Added Tax (2017 Revision)*, units and individuals that sell goods, services, intangible assets and real estate within the territory of People's Republic of China are taxpayers of VAT. According to regulations, individuals or businesses engaged in mobile commerce activities are required to pay VAT if they meet the requirements for sales activities in China. If a foreign company conducts cross-border sales activities, its domestic agent is required as the withholding agent; if there is no agent, the buyer will be the withholding agent. It can be seen that enterprises or individuals engaged in mobile commerce to achieve sales are also within the current VAT-related regulations.

3.2   The Taxpayer and the Tax Rate

The tax rates applicable to mobile business activities are the same as those applicable to traditional business activities. If you are engaged in domestic mobile commerce activities, different tax rates apply depending on the type of goods sold. If you are engaged in imported mobile commerce, audio-visual products, electronic publications and the like are applicable to the value-added tax rate of 9%; otherwise the tax rate is 13%. It can be seen that China's value-added tax laws has relevant provisions on the applicable tax rates for goods sold by mobile commerce.

3.3 The Location of the Tax

Judgment on the place where VAT is paid can be roughly divided into two cases. One type is fixed business households, which generally make tax declaration at the location of the organization. The other type is non-fixed business households, which generally make tax declaration at the place of sale or labor service. In the digital economy and mobile commerce environment, consumers can purchase goods across regions and goods can come from all over the world. If the goods are services or intangible goods that can be used by multiple parties, it is difficult to judge where they are sold or where the labor service occurs. With the development of network technology, this situation is more prominent in the mobile commerce environment. From this, it can be seen that the current relevant regulations on VAT taxation locations cannot fully be applied to the environment of mobile commerce, and the judgment of VAT taxation locations needs to be more detailed in order to adapt to the mobile commerce environment and reduce tax loss.

3.4 The Method of Collecting Imported Goods Tax

According to the current relevant VAT regulations, the consignee of imported goods or the units and individuals who handle customs declaration procedures are the taxpayers of import VAT. China's VAT collection method belongs to the buyer's collection model. According to the relevant provisions of the General Administration of Customs' announcement No. 194 of 2018, e-commerce platform companies, logistics companies or list declaration companies are the tax collection and payment obligors. This regulation in China is aimed at the increasing number of cross-border transactions in the mobile commerce environment, and the consignees are mostly individuals. If the original VAT collection method is followed, tax costs may increase. Therefore, relevant regulations will Platforms, logistics companies, or list-declaration companies serve as tax collection and payment obligors. *The Opinions of the General Office of the State Council on Promoting the Coordinated Development of E-commerce and Express Logistics* was released in 2018, the opinion encourages e-commerce platforms and logistics companies to exchange and share data with tax authorities on the basis of ensuring consumer information security. This is also to deal with the hidden characteristics of related transaction activities in the mobile commerce environment. It can be seen that China is actively exploring the collection of VAT on imported goods.

4   OECD VAT Related Tax Management Practices

In OECD's *Addressing the Tax Challenges of the Digital Economy* published in 2015, the value-added tax collection model and the location of value-added tax for imported goods have been analyzed. In this part, we will analyze the OECD's tax management related to the digital economy in detail.

4.1 VAT Collection Model for Imported Tangible Goods

The levy models of tangible goods import VAT are: the traditional collection model, the purchaser collection model, the vendor collection model and the intermediary collection model. It is courier carriers and postal transportation that collect tax through traditional model. Buyer model is used by the buyer of the product to pay taxes. The seller model requires the seller to pay VAT in the importing country, but this will increase the burden on non-resident enterprises in the importing country. The intermediary model is mainly to collect VAT through postal operators, courier operators, e-commerce platforms, financial intermediaries and so on. Specific evaluations of the four VAT collection models are shown in Table 1.

Table 1. Evaluation of import VAT collection model

Collection mode	Evaluation
Traditional collection model	On the one hand, because low-value goods may be exempt from VAT, domestic consumers will tend to purchase foreign low-value goods, which will distort competition at home and abroad. One the other hand, When tax authorities levy value-added tax through postal operators, they mainly rely on paper materials for information transmission, which results in low efficiency in value-added tax collection
Purchaser collection model	The success of the purchaser collection model mainly depends on the buyer's tax compliance. On the one hand, the buyer needs to pay taxes, which will increase the burden on the buyer and distort competition at home and abroad. On the other hand, the buyer needs to learn the relevant tax knowledge
Vendor collection model	The vendor collection model will increase the burden on the sellers of non-resident enterprises. The core of this collection model is to improve the tax compliance of non-resident sellers. In order to improve the tax compliance of non-resident enterprises and reduce the burden on sellers of non-resident enterprises, it is recommended to simplify the corresponding VAT registration and compliance system
Intermediary collection model	The e-commerce platform intermediary collection model requires some adjustments to the customs system, but this model will increase tax neutrality

According to the relevant statements of OECD, the intermediary collection model will increase tax neutrality compared with the traditional collection model, the purchaser collection model and the vendor collection model. However, if the tax authorities adopt the intermediary collection model, this will require some adjustments to customs procedures, which will increase the tax costs of the tax authorities. Therefore, whether the country adopts the intermediary collection model needs careful consideration. In the past, China's VAT was mainly based on the purchaser collection model, which would increase the buyer's tax burden and then affect the neutrality of taxation. Therefore, China is gradually accepting the intermediary collection model in related regulations to increase the neutrality of taxation. To sum up, in this respect, China's VAT regulations continue to adapt to the environment of mobile commerce.

4.2   The Judgment of VAT Location

If the goods are tangible, the taxable location can be judged based on the "tangible" characteristics of the goods. When the goods are intangible goods or services, the judgment of the tax location is not very clear. In the mobile commerce environment, due to the continuous improvement of online degree, this situation is more prominent. At the same time, when conducting cross-border transactions, tax authorities generally use the principle of destination to determine the place of tax payment. In order to promote international tax coordination, the OECD also uses destination rules as a principle for judging the place where VAT is paid.

When the purchaser is an enterprise, it will cause trouble to the judgment of the VAT tax payment location for the enterprise may have more than one place of business. Therefore, OECD recommends using direct use approach, direct delivery approach, recharge method as the basis for judging the location of VAT tax payment. The direct use approach is applicable to cases that the use of service or intangible assets is very obvious. The direct delivery approach is applicable to cases that the service or the goods need to be provided by the seller on the site. The recharge method is applicable to cases that the use of service or intangible assets will have subsequent costs happening. When the purchaser is an individual, the OECD recommends the following two methods to determine the tax location: (1) the location where the service is consumed or intangible assets are used, and both the buyer and the seller are present; (2) the buyer's usual residence.

5   Suggestions on China Mobile Business VAT Legislation

5.1   The Principles of China Mobile Commerce Tax

At present, the e-commerce taxation principles generally accepted by the international community are the principles of *E-commerce: Tax Framework Conditions* proposed in 1998. In 2015, the OECD supplemented the principles correspondingly in *Addressing the Tax Challenges of the Digital Economy*. Therefore, we integrate these tax principles to analyze China's mobile business environment.

1. Neutrality. Neutrality of domestic and foreign competition and neutrality of traditional business activities and mobile business activities.
2. Efficiency. Reduce tax costs and improve tax efficiency.

3. Certainty and simplicity. Relevant tax regulations cannot be ambiguous, and the corresponding institutional processes must be simplified.
4. Effectiveness and fairness. Failure to pay taxes in accordance with regulations will be punished accordingly. Fairness includes horizontal justice and vertical justice.
5. Flexibility. Ability to adapt to changes in the environment, rather than rigidity.
6. Equity. Equity has two main elements: horizontal equity and vertical equity.

5.2 The Goals of China Mobile Business VAT Legislation

On the one hand, China Mobile Commerce taxation needs to safeguard national interests and defend national tax jurisdiction. On the other hand, it needs to conform to government policy goals that at present China advocates tax reduction and burden reduction. Therefore, specifically, the legislative objectives of China Mobile Commerce VAT are: (1) to fill in China's current VAT-related tax loopholes and reduce country-related VAT tax losses; (2) to protect national interests and improve the relevant VAT regulations and at the same time not discourage the development enthusiasm of large e-commerce platforms such as Alibaba, Jingdong in China. (3) to reduce tax burden on the basis of improving relevant VAT regulations, the state should try not to increase the tax burden on taxpayers.

5.3 Specific Recommendations

According to the previous analysis, it is found that the relevant provisions of China's value-added tax are mainly weak in the judgment of the tax location. When the purchaser of intangible assets or services is an enterprise and the enterprise has more than one business location, the tax location cannot be accurately and consistently judged. When the purchaser of intangible assets or services is an individual due to the mobility of mobile terminals and people, the tax payment locations can not be judged accurately. Therefore, this article draws on the relevant provisions of the OECD VAT taxation location judgment in the digital economy environment, and judges its applicability to China's mobile business environment. The specific analysis is shown in Table 2.

In the digital economy environment, most of the judgments of OECD value-added tax payment sites are applicable to China Mobile Commerce. However, in the mobile commerce environment, when the buyer is an individual, it is recommended not to use the place of usual residence as the tax location, but to use the big data platform. Besides, it is recommended to use the mobile terminal, mobile network frequently, receiving address, payment address and so on as the basis for judging the place where VAT is paid.

Table 2. Applicability analysis of VAT tax location determination

Purchaser	Method	Applicability
Enterprise	Direct use approach	In the context of mobile commerce, the combination of enterprises and "mobile terminals" is not very distinctive. Therefore, this method can be used as the basis for judging the location of China Mobile's business value-added tax (the enterprise has more than one place of business)
	Direct delivery approach	Same as above
	Recharge method	Same as above
Individual	The location where the service is consumed or intangible assets are used, and both the buyer and the seller are present.	This method is applicable when the service or intangible assets, the buyer, and the seller move at the same time. When the three conditions are met at the same time, the tax location can be judged
	The buyer's usual residence	The place of usual residence does not mean where the mobile commerce sales activity takes place. Consumers may not purchase in places of usual residence. It is recommended to use the location of the mobile terminal, the location where the mobile network is often used, the delivery address, the payment address and so on to make judgments

6 Conclusions

No matter from the indirect data such as the number of mobile phone users and the number of mobile broadband subscriptions, or the direct data such as the number of consumers shopping on the mobile terminal and the proportion of mobile payments, they all show that mobile commerce has become a new growth point for e-commerce. The rapid development of mobile commerce, while driving economic growth, also brings great challenges to tax management. VAT accounts for a large proportion of China's tax revenue, so it is necessary to focus on whether the current VAT-related regulations can adapt to the mobile commerce environment. Through analysis, it is found that China's current value-added tax is basically able to adapt to the mobile business environment in terms of taxpayers, tax rates, and imported goods collection modes, but it is slightly weak in judging the location of VAT taxes. Therefore, it is recommended that the determination of the VAT taxation location of intangible assets or services should be more detailed, which is different when the purchaser is an individual or a business.

Due to my limited ability, on the one hand, there may be insufficient understanding in the analysis of OECD VAT related management practices; on the other hand, the analysis of China's current VAT related regulations may be incomplete. It is expected that follow-up scholars will continue to conduct in-depth research to improve China's VAT related regulations.

References

Ballard, C.L., Lee, J.: Internet purchases, cross-border Shopping, and sales taxes. Nat. Tax J. **60**(4), 711–725 (2007)

Einav, L., Knoepfle, D.T., Levin, J., et al.: Sales taxes and internet commerce. Soc. Sci. Electron. Publishing **104**(1), 1–26 (2014)

Fox, W.F., Luna, L.A., Murray, M.N.: The SSTP and technology: implications for the future of the sales tax. Nat. Tax J. **61**(4), 823–841 (2008)

Hoopes, J.L., et al.: Does use tax evasion provide a competitive advantage to E-Tailers? Nat. Tax J. **69**(1), 133–168 (2016). https://doi.org/10.17310/ntj.2016.1.05. EBSCOhost

Jones, R., Basu, S.: Taxation of electronic commerce: a developing problem. Int. Rev. Law Comput. Technol. **16**(1), 35–51 (2002)

Meharia, P.: E-commerce and taxation: past, present and future. IUP J. Account. Res. Audit Pract. **11**(4), 25–33 (2012)

OECD: Addressing the Tax Challenges of the Digital Economy, Action 1 - 2015 Final Report, OECD/G20 Base Erosion and Profit Shifting Project. OECD Publishing, Paris (2015). https://doi.org/10.1787/9789264241046-en

OECD: Additional Guidance on the Attribution of Profits to Permanent Establishments, BEPS Action 7 (2018).www.oecd.org/tax/beps/additional-guidance-attribution-of-profits-to-a-permanent-establishment-under-bepsaction7.htm

Redpath Esq, I.J., Redpath, E.M., Ryan, K.: Sales and use taxation in E-commerce: where we are and what needs to be done. J. Inf. Syst. Manage. **24**(3), 239–245 (2007)

毕娟, 周玲强, 孙高建. 游客使用景区移动商务的关键影响因素研究[J]. 浙江大学学报(理学版), 2017, 44(5):616-622.

崔晓静, 何朔. "美国微软公司避税案"评析及启示[J]. 法学, 2015(12):92-102.

陈咏升, 潘国忠, 王文来. 应对跨境数字产品交易的税收方案[J]. 税务研究, 2016(10):100-102.

蔡昌. 电商税收流失测算与治理研究[J]. 会计之友, 2017(8):2-13.

陈志刚, 方卉. 国内移动商务用户行为研究综述[J]. 情报科学, 2018, V36(1):164-171.

丁玮蓉, 张帆. 韩国电子商务税制研究及对中国的启示[J]. 经济问题探索, 2015(9):45-50.

代俊敏, 芦亚柯, 宋方伟主编. 电子商务理论与实务[M]. 2017.

盖建华. 端到端的移动商务安全框架[J]. 现代管理科学, 2009, 2009(4):44-45.

郭伟奇. 电子商务环境下的茶叶贸易策略研究[J]. 福建茶叶, 2016(5):56-57.

刘铮. 电子商务背景下的税收问题[J]. 宏观经济管理, 2014(11):55-58.

雷晴. 论电子商务的征税影响[J]. 税务研究, 2015(3):88-94.

刘百灵, 雷超, 李延晖. 移动商务环境中基于交易票据的自动信任协商协议[J]. 计算机科学, 2016, 43(10):160-165.

马秀玲. 从税法角度看电子商务发展问题及对策[J]. 人民论坛, 2015(A12):74-76.

欧阳泽宇, 王科涵. 加强电子商务征税途径的探讨[J]. 价格理论与实践, 2014(6):113-115.

任廷海, 张旭梅. 移动互联网环境下制造企业的移动商务模式及策略研究[J]. 科技管理研究, 2015, 35(21):107-110.

沈娅莉, Beixin, 廖伟民. 数字经济下跨国企业在中国逃避税现状、途径及防治策略研究[J]. 云南财经大学学报, 2015(6):135-142.

吴晓波, 陈小玲. 移动商务与电子商务的比较研究———基于价值创造视角[J]. 情报杂志, 2010, 29(8):19-21.

王志文, 于泳主编. 电子商务理论与实务[M]. 2017.

徐超毅, 王建国. 双视角下移动商务用户满意度实证研究[J]. 中国流通经济, 2017, 31(6):89-96.

相甍甍, 郭顺利, 张向先. 面向用户信息需求的移动商务在线评论效用评价研究[J]. 情报科学, 2018, V36(2):132-138.

杨向英, 杨慧. 电子商务的税收问题研究[J]. 江苏商论, 2009(1):41-42.

杨波, 许丽娟. 电子商务概论[M]. 北京邮电大学出版社, 2014.

叶凤云. 移动商务用户信息质量感知对粘性倾向的影响研究[J]. 现代情报, 2017, 37(4):72-81.

杨学成. 移动商务管理[M]. 经济管理出版社, 2017.

张迎. 电子商务税收问题探讨[J]. 工业技术经济, 2006, 25(4):157-159.

Features of Mobile Tracking Apps: A Review of Literature and Analysis of Current Apps Compared Against Travel Agency Requirements

Wing Ging Too, Chee Ling Thong[✉], Su Mon Chit, Lee Yen Chaw, and Chiw Yi Lee

Faculty of Business and Information Science, UCSI University, Kuala Lumpur, Malaysia
felixtoo@gmail.com, {chloethong,chitsm,chawly,
leecy}@ucsiuniversity.edu.my

Abstract. Nowadays tourists have high expectations on the service quality provided by travel agencies. In order to increase service quality, there is a growth of using mobile apps by travel agencies which enables tourists to navigate places of interest, traveling information and plan trips ahead time. Although travel agencies are willing to invest in mobile apps for customer experience enhancement, the potential of mobile tracking apps for manager is largely unexplored. In the provision of transportation services, travel agencies must obtain real-time, relevant trip status from the transportation service providers and relay the information to the tourist. This paper aims to review relevant literature in mobile vehicle tracking applications by searching online vendor markets (online store for Apple and Google Android) and journal database. Findings of literature review show there is a lack of mobile vehicle tracking apps which enables managers in travel agencies to obtain location-based information. In order to gather desired features of mobile vehicles tracking apps for travel agencies and issues faced by them, interviews were conducted with director and project manager of a reputable travel agency namely NCR Travel and Tours located in Kuala Lumpur, Malaysia. Interview findings show the issues identified are poor communication and time coordination between the manager, driver and tour guide due to lack of real time location-based information of the driver. Based on literature review and requirements provided by NCR, this study proposes key features of mobile vehicles tracking apps for travel agencies. The proposed mobile apps possess trip scheduling feature and it enables the manager to track location of the driver in real time based on pre-determined route. Google Maps Direction API is used to determine the best route and Firebase Realtime Database is used to communicate the trip status between manager and driver. A prototype is proposed, and user acceptance test are conducted in future work.

Keywords: Mobile tracking apps · Travel agency · GPS · GSM

1 Introduction

Nowadays tourists expect quality of service provided by travel agencies. In the event of any service failures in terms of delay and unexpected events, it affects the service

© Springer Nature Switzerland AG 2020
G. Salvendy and J. Wei (Eds.): HCII 2020, LNCS 12216, pp. 107–120, 2020.
https://doi.org/10.1007/978-3-030-50350-5_10

quality provided by travel agencies. According to a review study conducted by Ennew, Schoefer, Tourism and Institute (2003), service failures such as unavailability, delays and unexpected events are inevitable. Transportation services as an integral part of Tourism Supply Chain (TSC) is usually planned and estimated by travel agency before commencement of trips, but nevertheless a journey plan is likely to be disrupted and delayed by unexpected circumstances such as road transportation delays from traffic conditions or accidents [1, 2]. Tourists place their sense of trust to travel agencies and the tourists expect prompt feedback on their emergent information needs. As such, the competency and efficiency of the travel agencies in crisis management are measured by their service recovery level, that is, how quick information and alternatives can be provided to assure the tourists with a sense that the journey is under control [2]. The close link between quality of service recovery with tolerance of service failure and tourists' satisfaction is supported in several researches, which if leave unremedied leads to negative complaints, discontinuity of service and negative perception on the service provider [1, 3].

In order to provide an effective service recovery, the service provider is required to acknowledge the issue, followed by detailed and accurate explanation of failure and recovery methods [1]. However, it is difficult to satisfy such information needs in transportation services when accurate real-time information such as current whereabouts of assigned transportations and its estimated time of arrival (ETA) from destination is unavailable. Tourists values more on position-dependent information, for instance, information on how far away the destination or transportation service is [4]. To effectively satisfy tourists' transportation related information needs, travel agencies first need to acquire real-time transportation data such as exact location of assigned transportation vehicle and its ETA to tourist's destination at any specific time of inquiry by tourists. Hence, the question here is what are the tools and features that may assist manager in travel agency in acquiring and providing useful position-dependent information to the tourists upon inquiry? On that note, the potentials of mobile tracking apps as a mediator to touristic services and service recovery in transportation services is investigated.

To further understand what features in mobile tracking apps are important to travel agency, requirements in provision of transportation services and how these features assist travel agency in bettering their service quality, this paper aims to review relevant literature in mobile vehicle tracking applications by searching online vendor markets (online store for Apple and Google Android) and journal database. We included mobile apps that track location of vehicles using GPS and excluded apps that do not use GPS. Travel agency requirements are also gathered in this study. The following section presents the features of existing mobile vehicle tracking apps in online vendor markets such as Google Playstore.

2   Literature Review

Various designs of intelligent transportation systems (ITS) have been studied by researchers with the coverage of vehicle anti-theft tracking systems, vehicle position tracking systems, and fleet management systems [5]. From these researches, it is found that one of the most widely used approach for vehicle tracking system are vehicle tracking system with GPS-GSM modules [5, 6]. The vehicle tracking system comprises 2 major components which are the transmitting/tracking unit which tracks location information using GPS modules and transmitted by the GSM module to the ends users and the monitoring unit, which is the application interface between the transmitting/tracking unit and the end users [7].

GPS is used to provide accurate location information. Originated from U.S in 1973 which was then used for military purposes, GPS uses constellations of earth orbit satellites and permits GPS receiver to calculate latitude and longitude of a location by computing radio signals received from at least 3 satellites [5–7]. Using the 3 satellites transmissions, location can be obtained through triangulation, and altitude tracking is possible if more than 3 satellites are available. The information receivable by a GPS module are location, latitude and longitude, altitude and speed [5]. Although GLONASS and GALILEO provides better accuracy than GPS, GPS is still widely used due to its affordability and standardized built-in GPS receiver in Android smart phones [7]. On the other hand, GSM (Global System for Mobile Communications) is a mobile communication standard developed by European Telecommunication Standard Institute (ETSI) in 1982 used for establishing communication between two devices using radio waves. With the help of GSM module, SMS messages and voice calls are possible given that SIM (Subscriber Identity Module) is provided [5, 6].

The tracking/transmitting devices which comprises of the GPS receiver and GSM modules are usually installed in vehicles. The GPS receiver periodically request for its location information from the GPS satellite. The information is then sent via GSM modules to the server which stores location information [7]. The transmitting device is usually a microcontroller or on-board unit (OBU) with simple application that interfaces between the GPS receiver and GSM module. The monitoring unit refers to application, which can be either a web or mobile application which requests for location information such as latitude and longitude of the tracking object from the server database, which can then be mapped into map applications such as Google Maps for visual representation of the tracking process [7].

There numerous existing commercial mobile vehicles tracking, and navigation solutions from online vendor market such as Google Playstore and Google web search are reviewed and summarized below. Only mobile vehicle tracking applications that applies GPS location-based services are included in the review. The selected mobile vehicles tracking applications which are relevant in this study are iDispatch, Detrack, Moovit, GoFleet Mobile GPS and Waze.

iDispatch offers driver tracking services for transportation companies. The transportation company can use iDispatch for tracking its own drivers or drivers from other companies, and the transportation company can view the driver's location, speed limit and trip information via a live map. iDispatch has a notification alert feature for reporting driver's activities, and alarm feature which informs the company if a predefined route distance is not covered within a specified time period. One of the special features in iDispatch is that it allows the driver to communicate with the manager, or other drivers via the application (http://www.idispatch.com) (Fig. 1).

Detrack offers driver tracking for delivery services to the customers via a live map. The customers can track the vehicle's location, speed and distance and will be updated of the delivery progress via email updates. The customers can track more than one driver at

Fig. 1. User interface for idispatch tracking service (Source: http://www.idispatch.com)

a time, and the number of drivers trackable are scalable according to users' needs (http://www.detrack.com) (Fig. 2).

Fig. 2. User interface for detrack tracking service for delivery services (Souce: http://www.det rack.com/)

Moovit is a public transport tracking application which offers real time tracking of buses and transits via live map. The application contains detailed itineraries and trip schedules for public transits, and user can search for routes or stations nearby that may assist the user to reach his or her desired location. As compared to other tracking systems, Moovit tracks the users against fixed routes and schedules, which enables the application to inform the user when he or she should get off a station or bus stops. However, the ETA may not be accurate as the prediction is done based on transits frequency (https://company.moovit.com) (Fig. 3).

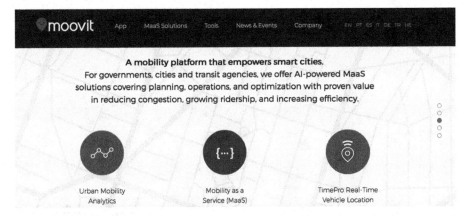

Fig. 3. User interface for Moovit (Source: https://company.moovit.com)

GoFleet Mobile GPS offers fleet management solution for the users which includes worker tracking, work logging, driver tracking and geofence alerting features. Users can track the driver's location from anywhere, anytime via a live map, and they can choose to receive notifications on drivers update from either email, text messages or popups. The fleet management suite is scalable to the users' tracking needs and allows add-ons for other fleet management software (https://www.gofleet.com) (Fig. 4).

Real-Time GPS Fleet Tracking

Some of our competitors claim to offer fleet vehicle tracking that is 'real-time' but in fact offer 1, 2, or 5 minute interval tracking. With GoFleet, even if your vehicle is parked indoors and underground, the technology will start tracking as soon as the vehicle moves. Our standard tracking is at about 15 second intervals, but our new active tracking is second-by-second. Our GPS vehicle tracking always provides you second-by-second data accuracy of ignition on, trip distance and time, as well as engine idling and speed.

Fig. 4. User interface for gofleet (Source: https://www.gofleet.com)

Waze is a GPS navigation application which serves to assist drivers in navigating to their desired locations with location information such as distance, traffic conditions, and ETA. Drivers can update traffic conditions on the map, enabling interactions between drivers. Waze also launched Waze Carpool, which is currently a regional feature that allows carpooling between different users (http://www.waze.com) (Fig. 5).

Based on these GPS tracking applications, it can be summarized that all these applications have real-live tracking features, most of which is shown visually through live maps. These applications usually come in either mobile or both web and mobile application for platform supports. Mobile applications are widely used due to its built-in GPS receiver and its portability. ETA and notification alerts are incorporated in these tracking applications and serves as the core features to these applications as it informs user on

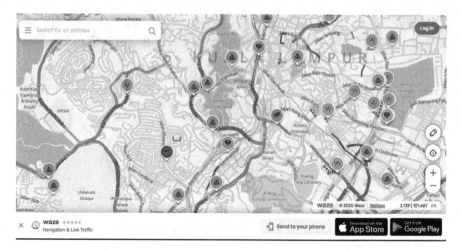

Fig. 5. User interface for waze (Source: https://www.waze.com)

the trip status. It is found that most of these potential mobile apps available are targeting either generic transit users of their intended key users (e.g. delivery drivers in Detrack). From the application reviewed from the online vendor market, there is little to none tracking application that is targeted at travel agency at managerial level. In order to provide better quality of service in tourism industry, mobile apps for manager is needed in assisting the decision making and conflict resolution process. The summary of features of selected mobile vehicle tracking application is presented in Table 1.

Table 1. Features comparison of selected mobile vehicle tracking application

Application	Mobile/Web	Real-time tracking	ETA	Map	Notification alerts
iDispatch	Both	Yes	Yes	Yes	Yes
Detrack	Both	Yes	Yes	Yes	Yes
Moovit	Both	Yes	Yes	Yes	Yes
GoFleet mobile GPS	Mobile	Yes	Yes	Yes	Yes
Waze	Both	Yes	Yes	Yes	Yes

3　Methodology

The methodology used to achieve the research objectives are: 1) literature review and analysis of current apps; 2) identify the issues faced by travel agency and at the same time gather user requirements from manager in travel agency (as a case) thorugh interview and 3) compared the analysis results of literature review against user requirements and a prototype is proposed with desired features.

Literature review and analysis of current apps is done through searching online vendor market such as Google Playstore and readily available mobile web apps. Key features in these applications are grouped by their similarities in terms of features in providing location-based information. The features are then summarized and tabulated.

Focus group interview is conducted to validate the actual issues and gather user requirements. Focus group interview is unstructured, free flowing interview with a small group of people, and it is conducted in a flexible format [8]. The focus group consists of the director of the travel agency and the manager who manages the trip and car drivers. The interviewees are selected based on purposive sampling. Each interview takes up to 60 min throughout a period of one month. Semi-structured interview is chosen for requirement gathering to acquire as many insights on transportation services management from a managerial perspective of the travel agency.

The design of interview questions are divided into two sections. The first section is to identify the current issued faced by the director and/or managers in travel agency addressing driver delay. The second section is to propose solution using ICT to resolve the issues faced by the travel agency at managerial level and core functionalities are gathered for travel agency requirements. At the same time, interview also find out tourists' feedback and complaints on their transportation services.

The interview results obtained are analyzed using thematic content analysis. Thematic content analysis or thematic analysis is an analysis method which categorizes the interview data into different themes of interest [9, 10]. Thematic analysis begins with familiarizing with data acquired by reading and understanding the data repeatedly, in this case, the interview recordings are first transcribed into full scripts. Based on the transcript codes, which are brief description of an interesting topic of data segments, are then generated from each interviewee response to the questions. The codes are then reviewed and categorized into themes, according to the interview questions sections [9, 10].

4   Results and Discussion

This section is divided into three sub-sections: 1) interview results and comparison of analysis results of literature review against user requirements, 2) discussions include implications of the study; and 3) the proposed prototype.

A. Interview Results

The interview questions are pilot tested. Pilot testing is important in ensuring validating of the interview questions. The interview questions are found to be well-structured and understandable by respondents. The process of interview is firstly, the respondents is asked about their business operations and roles within the organization. The respondents are then asked about issues faced within their daily work in general, and then specific in transportation services. The researcher asks follow-up questions and clarifications if the content is inline with the research objectives or if there are any ambiguity within the answer. The responses are recorded upon respondent's permission and transcribed into scripts for analysis (Table 2).

Table 2. Basic demographic of the respondents

Respondent	Job position	Job responsibilities
1	Director	- Manages company's business affairs - Oversees trip and coordinate communication between tour guide, driver and tourists
2	Project manager	- Plan and organize trips - Oversees trip and coordinate communication between tour guide, driver and tourists - Handle feedback from tour guide, driver and tourists

The interview generates insight into the situation surrounding car delay issues. In terms of transportation services, several issues are identified which complicates the trip scheduling process. The major issue identified is inadequate coordination between the travel agency operation manager, the tour guide and the driver. The role of managing tourists and drivers during the trip itself is commonly delegated to the tour guide, and the tour guide is not under any obligations to report the trip progress to the manager unless prompted. Similarly, driver is not under any obligations to report the trip progress to the manager unless prompted. This leads to difficulties in tracking the location of the tourists and drivers.

According to respondent 1, there are instances where the tour guide and driver is unreachable via phone calls due to signal loss or irresponsible behavior where they refuse to pick up calls. This issue is prevalent during peak seasons where activities stated in itinerary is prone to trip changes, and tour guide have to guide the tourists to another sightseeing site without informing the managers. Time coordination between the manager, tour guide and driver are difficult, especially in airport pickups due to customs check with variable queue size, and it have led to either long waiting time for the tourists or the drivers. As of the interview, the respondent responded that currently there are no immediate solution when there is a delay in schedule besides reassign or cancelling the transportation services after the trips.

From the tourist's perspective, respondent 2 suggested that the tourists generally comment on late transportation services and long waiting time, unhygienic bus condition, bad driver's behavior and irresponsive drivers where the driver did not pickup calls from the tour guide. For collaborating events or trips, the collaborating partner often questions and doubts the travel agency due to conflict in trip schedules when the specified trip itinerary is not followed strictly. These claims pose threats to the brand of the company, but however the travel agency manager does not have sufficient understanding and proof of past trip activities to reassure the collaborating partners of the trip situation. The issue worsens when the tour guide and driver both provided different feedback on what happened during the trip. Respondent 2 also mentioned that currently there are no metrics or tools for measuring the effectiveness of service recovery after tourist complaints, and the only basis for service improvement is the reduction in number of complaints from tourists.

Based on the interview results, it is found that the key functionalities that travel agency most desired is to allow the manager to understand the trip status by tracking the driver's location in real time and his or her estimated time of arrival (ETA) to trip destination points specified according to the trip itinerary. This feature is to allow the travel agency to be better informed about the trip status and be ready to communicate with the tour guides and tourists about changes and status of the trip itinerary.

Contrary to the mobile application reviewed from online vendor market, the key functionalities desired by the travel agency manager invests its focus on understanding the trip status itself rather than merely arriving the destination on time. From the managerial perspective of a travel agency, the accompanied risks are higher in a sense where the travel agency is required to coordinate all information needs of the tour guide, tourists and driver in detail. At the same time prepare for any unexpected trip changes. Notification alerts are one of the features reviewed among the mobile tracking apps and is intended to update the user on the tracking trip status. From a managerial perspective, the notification feature is needed, but the information needs differ from existing vehicle tracking market where the manager requires notification on all events happened within the trip with as much context as possible. This is important especially during a trip with multiple destinations. For instance, trip is delayed due to long queue in customs or driver is late because of a traffic accident.

B. Findings and Implications

From the analysis results, it is found that the common situation without using ICT to support a travel agency manager's information management role is that travel agency manager has no means of identifying, tracking and verifying a trip status after a planned trip commenced. Without ICT, the Tourism Supply Chain (TSC) is built on trust of each tour units, and information needs are fulfilled upon inquiry between TSC units. This indicates a potential risk to role delegation during service failure, and slow service recovery due to the lack of information on trip status. It is also implied there is no specific mobile apps used by travel agency manager to address the issues of transportation service delay, besides the generic real-time tracking application that is currently available in online vendor market. The demand in trip information for travel agency manager is required not only in real time, but also in context where it is easily understood by the travel agency manager and assist the manager in making decisions. Without these features in mobile tracking apps, several implications are identified. The implications are as follows:

Time-Consuming and Error-Prone

Besides organizing trips, the main role of a travel agency manager is to coordinate the information needs between all parties that constitute a trip, namely the tour guide, driver, tourists and any other service providers involved in the trip. When there is no communication channel for these parties to communicate their information needs, the only solution for the travel agency manager to coordinate these parties are via phone calls, which is time-consuming unreliable, disruptive to the trip and error prone. The manager is required to relay information from one party to another from time to time, and miscommunication may occur along the communication channel. Furthermore, the manager may not provide the best solution when an unexpected situation arises due to insufficient understand of the trip status.

Uncertainty

Without location-based services, the trip status can be only known via phone calls between the travel agency manager, the tour guide, driver and tourists. When one of the parties inquires for the location of the other, the travel agency manager is required to provide accurate location information to the inquirer's satisfaction. However, the ETA and exact location of the driver or the tourists are not known to the manager, and even if such information is provided, the information is uncertain as the basis of information is from driver's experience, without consideration on traffic conditions. If uncertain information is relayed from the travel agency manager to the tourists, it implies that the travel agency manager is unreliable and has no control of the trip.

In summary, the findings of the analysis results in comparison of literature review against travel agency requirements shows that although there are plenty of mobile tracking apps in current market, but not many mobile tracking apps is able to fulfill the requirements of the travel agency entirely. This result is in line with [5] research, where high customization is required for a vehicle tracking system targeted at specific users, and in this case, the travel agency manager. As such, a prototype of vehicle tracking system with the aim of assisting the travel agency manager in acquiring trip information is proposed.

C. The Proposed Prototype

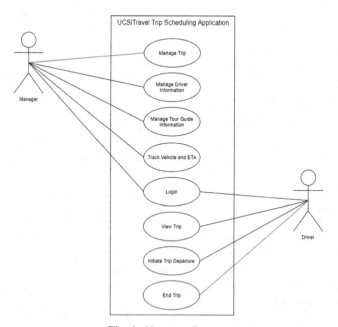

Fig. 6. Use case diagram

A prototype is proposed based on findings of literature review and analysis of current apps compared against requirements of travel agency. The key user for the prototype is manager in travel agency and Fig. 6 presents the use-case diagram. The proposed prototype is named as UCSITravel Trip Scheduling Application.

They are two main actors in the use case diagram: manager and driver. Manager is able to manage the entire trip by managing tourist, tour guide and driver information. Manager also able to track transportation service and view the location of driver and estimate arrival time (ETA) of said service to the next destination. Driver is playing key role in providing location-based information to the manager using mobile apps. Driver can read the trip information such as departure time and destinations in trip, initiate trip departure when he departs, and can end the tracking feature when he arrives the destination (Fig. 7).

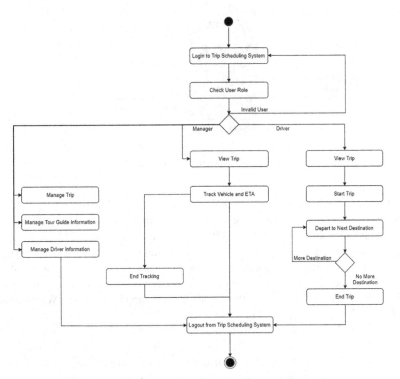

Fig. 7. Activity diagram

All users for the trip scheduling application is required to authenticate themselves before they can use the system. The users are first required to submit their credentials including the username and password to the system to authenticate their role. The application will then validate the username and password and redirect the user to their respective interface depending on their roles. The user is registered by the manager before a trip, hence self-registration is not possible except for the manager. The manager can perform managerial tasks in managing the trip, tour guide, and driver. The manager can view all trips and when a trip is initiated by the driver, the manager can track the location of the vehicle and its ETA to the next destination. Tracking can be ended as the manager wishes, and by default it ends when the driver ends the trip. The driver can view trip information including the trip destinations and the tour guide information. The drivers can initiate their upcoming trips when they depart from one destination to another. When the trip is not completed, that is, there are more destinations to go, the driver is required to initiate a new process of departing from one destination to another destination, until the final destination. Upon reaching the last destination, the driver ends the trip. The users can logout from the system when there are no more actions to be done to protect the system from unauthorized intruders. The overall system architecture of the proposed system is presented in Fig. 8.

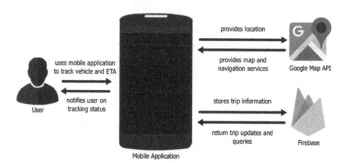

Fig. 8. System architecture

The manager uses the mobile application to track the vehicle and its ETA in a trip, and the mobile application notifies the manager regarding changes in the trip status. The mobile application uses Google Map API for map and Directions API for navigation services. Firebase Realtime Database for its cloud database service for storage and query of trip relevant information. Firebase Realtime Database allows the synchronization of data across devices, and any update in data will reflect immediately across all devices.

Figure 9 shows user interface of the mobile tracking app for manager. When manager is notified of an available trip tracking, they can track the driver by clicking on the "Track" button, which will then show the position of the driver, the route navigation and ETA to the next destination. The manager can stop the tracking anytime, or the tracking will be ended when the driver ends the trip. All trip information and trip status is shown within the draggable layout, and the manager will be notified about any trip status update.

In summary, this paper presents a comparison study of literature review on existing mobile tracking application against travel agency requirement is studied. Literature review on existing mobile tracking apps and their features are reviewed and summarized. In order to determine the travel agency needs of mobile tracking apps, a focus group interview is conducted with a travel agency as a case. Based on the interview findings, it is found that travel agency is facing the issue of not having proper channel of obtaining accurate, real-time, assistive information for their trip managing information needs. The apps features identified are then compared with the interview results. It is found that existing applications in the market focuses on solutions for obtaining real time location information for general public, or their targeted users such as delivery drivers, but none has been done for travel agency managers. As the results of reviewing literature and analysis of current apps compared against travel agency requirements, a mobile application is proposed. This mobile application allows the managers of travel agency to acquire real-time location information from the drivers hired for each trip and updates the trip status based on the travel agency manager needs. With this information, the managers can improve their service quality by responsively relaying trip status to the tourists upon inquiry on estimated waiting time. Using Google Maps Direction API, the mobile application identifies the best guess, shortest route to the next destination in a trip and through Firebase Realtime Database, display it in a visual map to both the driver and the manager. The manager can track the driver when the driver is on the move between destinations and is able to understand the trip status.

5 Conclusion

Issues identified in this study are able to overcome by using mobile vehicle tracking application. The proposed mobile application possesses features which enable manager to manage location-based information of drivers, which result in increasing service quality provided by travel agency to the customer (tourists). It is believed that the proposed mobile application is able to meet the requirements of travel agency, however user acceptance test only will be conducted in future study.

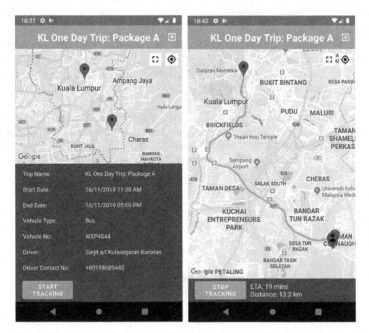

Fig. 9. User interface of proposed mobile vehicle tracking app (Manager)

Acknowledgement. This work is supported by UCSI University under the University Pioneer Scientist Incentive Fund (PSIF).

References

1. Ennew, C., Schoefer, K.: Service failure and service recovery in tourism: a review. Christel DeHaan Tourism and Travel Research Institute, Nottingham University Business School (2003). https://books.google.com.my/books?id=TQ4ZMwEACAAJ
2. Wang, D., Park, S., Fesenmaier, D.R.: The role of smartphones in mediating the touristic experience. J. Travel Res. **51**(4), 371–387 (2002). https://doi.org/10.1177/0047287511426341
3. Hess, R.L., Ganesan, S., Klein, N.M.: Service failure and recovery: the impact of relationship factors on customer satisfaction. J. Acad. Mark. Sci. **31**(2), 127–145 (2003). https://doi.org/10.1177/0092070302250898
4. Berger, S., Lehmann, H., Lehner, F.: Location-based services in tourist industry. J. Inf. Technol. Tour. **5**, 243–256 (2003). https://doi.org/10.3727/109830503108751171
5. Bojan, T., Kumar, U., Bojan, V.: Designing vehicle tracking system: an open source approach. In: 2014 IEEE International Conference on Vehicular Electronics and Safety, pp. 135–140. IEEE (2014). https://doi.org/10.1109/ICVES.2014.7063737
6. Wukkadada, B., Fernandes, A.: Vehicle tracking system using GSM and GPS technologies. IOSR J. Comput. Eng. (IOSR-JCE) 5–8 (2017). http://iosrjournals.org/iosr-jce/papers/Conf.16055/Volume-1/2.05-08.pdf?id=7557
7. Dhumal, A., Naikoji, A., Patwa, Y., Shilimkar, M., Nighot, M.K.: Survey paper on vehicle tracking system using GPS and Android. Int. J. Adv. Res. Comput. Eng. Technol. (IJARCET) **3**(11), 3762–3765 (2014). http://ijarcet.org/wp-content/uploads/IJARCET-VOL-3-ISSUE-11-3762-3765.pdf
8. Zikmund, W.: Business Research Methods, 7th edn. Thomson South-Western, Ohio (2003). http://www.sciepub.com/reference/6738
9. Maguire, M., Delahunt, B.: Doing a thematic analysis: a practical, step-by-step guide for learning and teaching scholars. Irel. J. High. Educ. **9**(3), 3352–3354 (2017). http://ojs.aishe.org/index.php/aishe-j/article/view/335
10. Mortensen, D.: How to do a thematic analysis of user interviews. Interaction Design Foundation (2019). https://www.interaction-design.org/literature/article/how-to-do-a-thematic-analysis-of-user-interviews

Enhancing E/M-Government Synergy in Kenya: Citizens' Perspectives on the Driving Factors for M-Government Diffusion

Sharon Mirella Wakhu[1]([✉]), Xu Fuyuan[1], and John O. Kakonge[2]

[1] University of Shanghai for Science and Technology, 516, Jungong Road, Shanghai 200093, China
sharon.mirella@gmail.com, xufy@usst.edu.cn
[2] Association of International Civil Servants-Kenya, P.O. Box 1736, Nairobi 00621, Kenya
john.o.kakonge@gmail.com

Abstract. This research investigated the driving factors of mobile government diffusion as antecedents that expand the specificity and explanatory power of traditional technology adoption models in mobile contexts. A robust conceptual model for evaluating the adoption of electronic and mobile government services is proposed. Focusing on the first component of the model, namely, the drivers of m-government diffusion, five innovation attributes that influence the decision to adopt m-government were examined. Following a qualitative approach based on grounded theory, 91 mobile phone users were interviewed using a questionnaire. Five attributes of diffusion of innovation were investigated: relative advantage, complexity, compatibility, trialability, and observability. The qualitative data obtained was coded and analyzed for theme frequency distribution. The driving factors that emerged from the themes were: accessibility, efficiency, connectivity and time-saving (dominant factors); convenience, user-friendly, features and service provider (moderate factors), and cost and security (minor factors). Future research should consider how the key driving factors for m-government diffusion can be leveraged to facilitate greater adoption of and synergy between e- and m-government. Empirical validation of the conceptual model is recommended to confirm its appropriateness in enhancing the adoption of electronic and mobile government services in Sub-Saharan Africa.

Keywords: Adoption of mobile technologies · M-government · E-government · Diffusion of innovations · Sub-Saharan Africa

1 Introduction

The potential for mobile technologies to enhance existing e-government services is high, therefore the synergy between electronic and mobile government (e/m-government) approaches continues to be a subject of debate among information system (IS) researchers in Africa [1–3]. In Sub-Saharan Africa (SSA), access to mobile platforms greatly surpasses access to traditional fixed terminals. In selected economies such as

© Springer Nature Switzerland AG 2020
G. Salvendy and J. Wei (Eds.): HCII 2020, LNCS 12216, pp. 121–137, 2020.
https://doi.org/10.1007/978-3-030-50350-5_11

South Africa, Mauritius, Kenya, Rwanda, Seychelles and Botswana, every household in both urban and rural areas has access to a mobile phone [4]. However, the significant growth witnessed in the mobile technology sector has not translated into synonymous gains in e/m-government adoption [5].

The telecommunications industry in Kenya is essentially driven by an aggressive private sector. Over the past 20 years, a large mobile (*Orange Telkom, Safaricom, Airtel,* and *Essar Telecom*) and data (*Jamii Telcom, Liquid Telecom, Access Kenya Group, Wananchi Group,* and *MTN*) infrastructure, has been deployed in both rural and urban areas of the country. Internet access and use statistics for Kenya show exponential growth in the internet and mobile markets, making the country one of the most vibrant mobile market economies in Africa [6, 7]. According to the *Communications Authority of Kenya* (CAK), of the approximately 47 million people comprising Kenya's population, as at September 2018, the mobile subscription was 46.6 million, with a mobile penetration of 100.1%, while the mobile data/internet subscriptions were 42.2 million [8].

Despite the extensive adoption of mobile technologies by the Kenyan people, e-governance in the region has not recorded a commensurate growth [9]. The *E-Government Development Index* (EGDI) measures the national capacity for e-government mobilization using information and communications technology (ICT) in delivering public services [4]. In Africa, Kenya is ranked ninth with an EGDI of 0.4541 which surpasses the continent's average of 0.3423. However, at position 122 out of 193 United Nations (UN) member countries, Kenya still falls short of the world average of 0.5491 and is classified among the medium-level EGDI countries [9].

The viability of an e/m-government synergy relies on the effectiveness of m-government as a platform for enhancing the uptake of e-government services [10]. This research investigates the diffusion of mobile technology in a developing country context, including citizens' technological requirements and individual expectations that boost the adoption of e/m-government services. By investigating and clarifying the factors relating to m-government diffusion, researchers will have a more holistic understanding of how the interaction between citizens and e-government initiatives can be enhanced using mobile technologies.

1.1 Problem Statement

Review of the literature shows that studies on the diffusion of m-government services in SSA are limited [6, 11, 12]. The focus of IS research has mainly been on identifying the opportunities and challenges facing the e/m-government sector, without adhering to a specific IS theoretical foundation [13–15]. Mpekoa and Dlamini [16] decried the lack of focus on m-government theory. This has led to a knowledge gap on the disparity between e-government and m-government synergy despite the continued exponential growth witnessed in the mobile technology sector. Crandall and Mutuku [17] undertook an m-government survey in Kenya which revealed that mobile devices are not the preferred means of communication between citizens and government. Although the potential for extensive interaction with citizens through mobile devices exists, the current e-government strategies do not explore these avenues sufficiently.

1.2   Research Question

The primary research question in this study was: *what are the driving factors for mobile and electronic government adoption in Kenya from the citizens' perspective?* In keeping with Rogers' [18] Diffusion of Innovation (DOI) theory, it was postulated that the rate at which individuals adopt e/m-government services is determined by their perceptions of five characteristics of mobile innovations, namely: relative advantage, complexity, compatibility, trialability, and observability. In this study, exploratory research was undertaken to uncover the underlying factors that influence the mobile technology adoption decision-making process based on the five DOI attributes.

The exploratory survey was based on five main questions. 1) *What are the advantages of using mobile phones to access e-government services?* 2) *Is the use of mobile phones for e-government services simple?* 3) *Are mobile phones well-suited for accessing e-government services? Explain* 4) *Have you tested e-government functions on a mobile phone?* 5) *What direct benefits have you observed when accessing e-government services using a mobile phone?* The findings from the exploratory survey questions respond to the main research question in this paper.

1.3   Significance of the Research

This study examined the mobile government innovation attributes in a SSA country. Contextual factors were uncovered and envisaged as antecedents that can expand the specificity and explanatory power of traditional technology adoption models in the e/m-government context. From the literature review, no research scrutinizes these factors to address the e/m-government gaps in SSA countries. A robust conceptual model for evaluating the adoption of electronic and mobile government services is proposed. The model amalgamates constructs from the diffusion of innovation and technology acceptance theoretical paradigms. By incorporating established information system (IS) theories such as the Technology Acceptance Model (TAM) [19] and Unified Theory of Acceptance and Use of Technology (UTAUT) [20], the conceptual model enables more in-depth empirical investigations commensurate to mobile technology contexts. For stakeholders in public and private practice, a more accurate understanding of citizens' interactions with mobile technology will enhance e/m-government service delivery strategies deployed in Kenya and Sub-Saharan Africa as a whole.

2   Literature Review

2.1   Adoption of Electronic and Mobile Government Services

The constructs of the traditional information technology (IT) adoption models such as TAM, UTAUT, and DOI, are each intended to be universal to every instance of IS adoption. Due to this generalized nature, these theories may not adequately represent all the factors that influence adoption and use in a mobile context [21]. Van Biljon and Kotzé [22] discuss the physical, social, mental and technological factors which uniquely differentiate the mobile context from the traditional computing environment. In a desktop computing setup, the user and devices are in the same location. Furthermore, the infrastructural environment is specifically designed to guarantee the completion of tasks with minimal interference. By contrast, mobile devices are used on the move and therefore the user environment may keep changing constantly. The quality of mobile technology infrastructure is highly susceptible to the capacity of network coverage, communication bandwidth, and geographical location [23]. Furthermore, traditional computer use is usually preceded by some form of formal training in operating devices and software applications [24]. The use of mobile devices, however, is highly personalized and often is based on the user's understanding of the technology rather than on any formal training.

In acknowledgment of these shortcomings of the traditional IT adoption models, several researchers [25–28] recommend integrative approaches to the development of concepts, theories, and models that explicitly establish relationships between various drivers of m-government and user adoption of e/m-government systems. This research proposes amalgamation of constructs from the Diffusion of Innovation and Technology Acceptance theoretical paradigms.

The proposed model in this research (Fig. 1) conceptualizes diffusion of m-government as a precursor to the adoption of e/m-government services by emphasizing the preceding innovation decision-making process [29]. Mobile government is a subset of, as well as a platform, for enhancing the uptake of electronic government services. The viability of the e/m-government synergy relies on the effectiveness of the government in identifying and leveraging key drivers of mobile technology diffusion to increase the uptake of e-government services. Figure 1 shows the proposed conceptual model for evaluating the adoption of electronic and mobile government services.

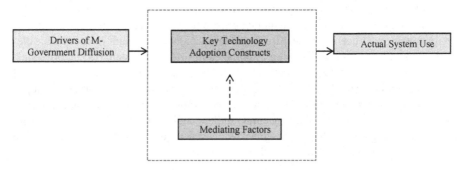

Fig. 1. Conceptual model for the adoption of electronic and mobile government services

DOI theory pinpoints specific characteristics of m-government innovations that users assess while evaluating available alternatives before deciding to adopt [30]. Thereafter, these variables may be employed as extensions of major acceptance theories to carry out empirical research on the adoption and actual use of e/m-government systems [31]. Incorporating m-government diffusion attributes enhances the specificity and extends the explanatory power of the technology adoption models within the mobile context [21]. It is anticipated that formal empirical testing and validation of the conceptual model will reveal its appropriateness in capturing and enhancing the e/m-government synergy in Kenya and other SSA countries.

2.2   Mobile Technology Innovation Attributes

Rogers [18] defines five stages that potential adopters of e/m-government services experience during the innovation-decision process: 1) *knowledge* (awareness about the innovation); 2) *persuasion* (conviction based on the characteristics of the innovation); 3) *decision* (choice to accept or reject); 4) *implementation* (actual use), and 5) *confirmation* (feedback).

At the knowledge stage, various information sources (media, public service announcements, face-to-face meetings, community meetings, email, and community leaders and public administrators) are used to communicate information about the m-government innovation to potential adopters in the social system [17]. However, it is the characteristics of the innovation itself that will persuade the adopter to form perceptions about the innovation [30] and the decision to accept or reject the m-government innovation is based on five attributes: relative advantage, complexity, compatibility, trialability, and observability. These attributes (Fig. 1) are synonymous with the drivers of m-government diffusion as presented in the conceptual model.

Relative Advantage. This is the degree to which m-government is perceived as being more beneficial than the preceding e-government desktop alternatives - personal computers at government offices, call centers, one-stop-shop service centers, and internet cafes. Mobile devices can access internet, voice, Unstructured Supplementary Service Data (USSD) codes, multimedia messaging service (MMS), social media applications and short message services (SMS) [32]. In this study, citizens were asked to identify relative advantages of m-government by considering the functional aspects of the mobile technology compared to previous methods of accessing e-government services.

Complexity. This is the extent to which citizens consider m-government innovations as challenging to comprehend and use. In this study, complexity was captured through the citizens' perceptions of ease-of-use of the m-government innovation. This innovation attribute was proposed by Moore and Benbaasat [33] in their Perceived Characteristics of Innovating (PCI) theory. As a measure, 'ease-of-use' is equivalent to complexity but is interpreted in reverse [34] and has a moderating impact on the user's opinion rather than the term 'complexity' which can be construed negatively.

Compatibility. This is the degree to which an innovation fits into users' existing values, habits, needs and experiences. Mobile devices offer connectivity anytime anywhere and services can be paid for instantly, making them very flexible and convenient [35]. In this study, citizens were asked to identify specific components of compatibility that increase their intentions to use mobile devices to access e-government systems. Previous studies [21] confirmed a significant positive effect between compatibility and perceived usefulness of, as well as intention-to-use, an e-learning system. The findings [36] demonstrated that compatibility had the most significant influence on citizens' intention to use e-government websites. A similar observation was made in the investigation of the adoption of online banking services [37].

Trialability. This is the extent to which an innovation may be tested before committing to usage. Participants in this exploratory study were asked to confirm whether they had an opportunity to test m-government innovations before they were deployed as e-government systems. In an online banking context [38], trialing reduced reluctance among users once they realized that errors or difficulties encountered could be corrected prior to actual system use. In SSA countries, citizens' experience with e-government has been inadequate due to, among others, insurmountable infrastructural challenges [15]. If successfully leveraged through trials and pilot studies, the high mobile technology penetration rates offer a unique opportunity to overcome citizens' fears, negative attitudes, and hesitancy towards adopting e-government services.

Observability. This is the extent to which the benefits of the innovation can easily be seen and demonstrated to others. As a strategy, m-government extends the benefits of e-government to citizens because a high mobile penetration implies wider outreach, increased citizen participation, and inclusion of the most marginalized people in society. In SSA there is evidence of m-government implementations in healthcare, agriculture, SMS alerts/notifications, mobile finance applications, and interconnectivity between government agencies [39]. In this study, participants identified tangible visible characteristics of m-government innovations. In liberalized telecom markets such as Kenya, South Africa, and Tanzania, the use of mobile devices to access e-government services is likely to accrue where these benefits are manifested.

3 Research Methodology

A qualitative approach based on grounded theory [40–42] was adopted in this exploratory study. To collect data, a questionnaire was administered in face-to-face interviews. The first part of the questionnaire (Fig. 2) enlisted three demographic questions to compile the profile of the participants (Table 2), plus two questions to identify mobile service providers used and whether the participants had used their mobile devices to access e-government services (Table 3). The second section of the questionnaire covered the five m-government innovation attributes (Table 1) and comprised of five structured open-ended questions [43] to collect rich qualitative data in the form of in-depth accounts of participants' experiences and expectations with m-government. This also allowed for consistency in the specific manner and type of questions posed to interviewees [44]. Each participant was asked the same questions with discussions focusing only on the main themes of the study.

The sampling strategy was non-random [36, 45] with participants identified through two sampling methods. Purposive sampling was used to identify participants who own mobile phones and have access to the internet, which increased the potential of collecting responses relevant to the study. Theoretical sampling prioritized participants who use their mobile phones to access e-government systems in line with the study's main theoretical aims.

To ensure data saturation the recommended sample size for grounded theory studies is 20–30 interviews [46]. With respect to the research question in this exploratory study, the participant profiles were not specific to a single characteristic, for example - age, gender, location, or education level. From the literature review, the theoretical foundation for investigating mobile government innovation attributes is also not well established.

Table 1. Survey questions

Attribute	Survey item	Reference
Relative advantage	What are the advantages of using mobile phones to access e-government services compared to previous methods?	[18, 30]
Complexity	In your opinion, is the use of mobile phones for e-government services simple?	[30, 33]
Compatibility	Are mobile phones well-suited for accessing e-government services? Explain	[21, 46]
Trialability	Have you tested e-government functions on a mobile phone?	[30, 38]
Observability	What direct benefits have you observed when accessing e-government services using a mobile phone?	[18, 30]

Besides, the interview setting did not allow for an in-depth exploration of the study aims. Therefore, the information power model [47] was applied to guide the sample size selection. A larger sample size was required to capture a wide enough range of participant experiences and achieve saturation [48]. 91 interviews were conducted in all the 17 sub-counties in Nairobi city.

Data collection in the field was performed by six expert researchers using Open Data Kit (ODK) Collect Apps on android mobile phones. The raw data consisted of text and audio recordings and was uploaded to an online server. To avoid bias, a separate researcher was employed to transcribe, edit, examine the transcripts and code the qualitative data. The qualitative data was coded using ODK Aggregate and analyzed for theme frequency distribution using SPSS software [41, 49].

4   Presentation and Discussion of Results

4.1   Profile of the Participants

The participants were fairly uniformly derived from each of the 17 sub-counties of Nairobi, with the mean number being 5 from each sub-county. Of the 91 participants interviewed, 40% were female and the majority where aged between 20–30 years-old. There was a broad distribution of education levels, with 33% having only completed high school and 40% having obtained a Bachelor's degree. Only 5% of participants had a post-graduate degree. 2% of participants had received no formal education (Table 2).

4.2   Participants' Mobile Service Providers and E-government Systems Used

Safaricom was the most popular mobile service provider in Kenya (57%). 30% of the participants answered that they use *Safaricom* and *Airtel*. *Orange Telkom* was the least used provider at 5%. *I-Tax* and *E-Citizen* were the most frequently used e-government systems at 42% and 44% respectively. The e-government systems were accessed for a variety of reasons including business registration (10%) and license renewal (26%), applying for driving school (12%), and filing tax returns (20%).

Table 2. Demographic profile of the participants

Characteristic	%	Characteristic	%
Gender		**Education Level**	
Female	40	Post-graduate/Master's degree	5
Male	60	Bachelor's degree	40
Age		Diploma/Certificate	13
Below 20	7	O level/A level	33
20–30	57	Primary level	7
31–40	21	No formal education	2
41–50	8		
51–60	5		
Over 60	2		

4.3 Driving Factors of M-government Diffusion

In line with previous qualitative studies, the codes identified from the *in vivo* phrases of the participants were analyzed for theme frequency distribution. Table 4 provides a summary of the thematic driving factors concerning each innovation attribute.

An important revelation in this study was the tendency of driving factors of m-government diffusion to cut across the various attributes rather than being specific to individual innovation attributes. For example, accessibility was rated as an important driver of m-government diffusion across all factors, excluding trialability. This was also apparent in the participants' descriptions of the various driving factors. Extracts of the participants' exact phrases when referencing each driving factor are paraphrased in Table 5, 6, 7 and 8.

Accessibility, efficiency, connectivity and time-saving appear to be the most dominant driving factors. Cost and security were cited under multiple attributes but the number of citations was low. Convenience, user-friendly, features, and service-provider had a relatively higher number of citations but specific to individual attributes.

Relative Advantage. Participants were asked to explain the relative advantages of using mobile phones to access e-government systems compared to previous methods. The most frequently cited advantage was time-saving with 34% of the participants feeling that it was faster to use a mobile phone rather than a personal computer or physically lining up for services at the designated centers. Accessibility (24%) also featured highly and is due to the widespread mobile services coverage and ease of owning a phone and purchasing data bundles in Kenya. 22% of the users felt that mobile phones were convenient to use. They are light and easy to carry around. The proximity of a phone to the owner minimizes the need for contact with government officials or any other third party. Furthermore, infrastructural requirements are low and phones can be used even when there is no electricity as long as they are charged in advance. Efficiency 10% was a

Table 3. Mobile service providers and use of e-government services

Characteristic	%
Mobile service providers	
Airtel	8
Safaricom	57
Orange Telkom	5
Airtel + Safaricom	30
E-government systems used	
E-jiji Pay	6
I-Tax	42
E-Citizen	44
NTSA	8
Use	
Booking vehicle inspection	4
Account transaction	2
Apply for driving school	12
Certificate of good conduct	2
Business registration	10
Business license renewal	26
Apply for a passport	8
File tax returns	20
Apply for a PIN	16

factor that elicited diverging comments from participants. Finally, cost 8% and security 2% were the least cited factors as shown in Table 5.

Compatibility. Participants were asked to explain whether they considered mobile phones well suited for accessing e-government services. Accessibility (45%) was the most frequently cited feature of compatibility. Services are available anywhere and any-time in Kenya as long as one owns a mobile phone, can purchase data bundles and there is network coverage. 24% of the respondents considered connectivity an important factor of compatibility with regards to mobile phones, citing fast internet connection through the 4G network. Of these, 5% highlighted fluctuations in connectivity which results in slow speeds and poor service. Some users (17%) also emphasized the limitations of mobile phones (Table 6) where the whole range of e-government services is not available. Some websites are not compatible with mobile phones and hence not suitable. Phones are efficient (7%) because they offer quick service with minimal effort. Finally, the service provider (7%) was a factor because to be compatible, respondents believe

Table 4. Drivers of m-government diffusion in relation to the five attributes of innovation

Drivers of m-government diffusion	Theme frequency distribution (%)				
	Relative advantage	Compatibility	Complexity	Trialability	Observability
Accessibility	24	45	30	*	44
Efficiency	10	7	16	*	7
Connectivity	*	24	16	*	10
Time-saving	34	*	*	*	37
Cost	8	*	15	*	*
Convenience	22	*	*	*	*
User-friendly	*	*	21	*	*
Features	*	17	*	*	*
Service-provider	*	7	*	*	*
Security	2	*	*	*	2

they should be able to access e-government services effectively through any mobile service provider.

Complexity. Respondents were asked to consider whether the use of mobile phones for e-government services is simple. From the responses obtained (Table 7), mobile phones were perceived to be user-friendly (21%). They are not complicated; they don't require any special skills and are easy to navigate. They are efficient (16%) without additional requirements for setup and operation. Another factor that enhances the simplicity of mobile phones is accessibility (30%). All that is needed is an internet connection to get services anywhere – no queuing or need for physical contact with public officers. The low cost of mobile usage (15%) because data bundles are cheap and there is no need for installation or monthly subscription charges also moderates complexity. Divergent views about simplicity centered on challenges with connectivity (16%), for example, slow speeds and system delays make usage difficult.

Trialability. None of the participants reported testing an e-government service on a mobile phone before it was officially deployed for use by the general public. 36 participants discussed errors or challenges encountered while using e-government systems on a mobile phone. 33% of those participants believed that despite these challenges accessing e-government systems on a mobile phone was not a problem and had no complaint. 47% of them believed that this was a problem because it took a long time to respond to their complaints and in some cases, there was no feedback at all. 20% believed there was a problem, but their complaints were responded to promptly. Therefore the effectiveness in responding to and resolving user complaints is a driving factor that needs to be taken into consideration.

Observability. Respondents identified four main direct benefits that they observed when accessing e-government services using a mobile phone (Table 8). The majority of those interviewed identified accessibility (44%), followed by time-saving (37%), then connectivity (10%) and efficiency (7%) as the most observable attributes. 2% of the interviewees believed that mobile phones offer better security of passwords and personal information than shared terminals and laptops.

5 Conclusion

Kenya, like many Sub-Saharan countries, is characterized by a large and relatively poor population, many of whom live in remote rural areas. Widespread mobile network coverage and the fact that ownership of mobile phones greatly exceeds that of traditional fixed terminals, indicate that the country is primed to integrate mobile-government with the country's electronic-government for the provision of public services. However, the adoption of e/m-government has not kept pace with the growth of the mobile telecommunications industry. This study attempted to understand why this e/m-government synergy is not optimal by investigating the driving factors for m-government diffusion from the Kenyan citizens' perspectives.

To commence, a conceptual model was proposed to explain the process of m-government diffusion of innovations. Focusing on the first component of the model, namely, the drivers of m-government diffusion, five innovation attributes that influence the decision to adopt m-government were investigated. Using a questionnaire as an interview guide, themes related to those attributes were proposed. In the study context, trialability was found not to influence the adoption of innovations since none of the participants interviewed had the opportunity to test m-government services before they were implemented. Themes cut across the other four attributes, indicating that the decision to adopt m-government is multi-faceted, with accessibility, efficiency, connectivity and the ability to save time being the most often cited reasons.

Future research should consider how the key driving factors for m-government diffusion can be leveraged to facilitate greater adoption of and synergy between e- and m-government. Empirical validation of the conceptual model to confirm its appropriateness in enhancing the adoption of electronic and mobile government services in Sub-Saharan Africa is recommended. E-government services that are already in use, for example, I-Tax and E-Citizen should be investigated to identify best practices that could be adopted in other areas of m-government service provision. An investigation of the civil servants' perspectives of the challenges to implementing e/m-government services would also be insightful.

Owing to the study being based on interviews, the sample population was relatively small. For future research, the sample size could be increased to provide more insight into the themes identified in this study. Additionally, the study context should be extended to other SSA countries to establish whether there may be any significant differences in the driving factors to mobile diffusion and adoption of e/m-government services as a whole.

In developing nations characterized by large populations of relatively poor people dispersed across vast areas, mobile-government service provision has the potential to greatly improve efficiencies in service delivery. This paper has identified the most important driving factors for m-government diffusion via the adoption of mobile innovations by local citizens. Discussions with the government need to be facilitated to encourage enhanced provision and adoption of e/m-government.

Appendix

See Fig. 2, Table 5, 6, 7 and 8

KEY INFORMANT INTERVIEW GUIDE

The objective of this survey is to evaluate the role of mobile government within the overall e-government ecosystem from the perspective of general citizens. The study is strictly confidential and will not be used for any other purpose except for academic research and the respondents' personal details will not be disclosed in the results. The questionnaire has two sections: **participant profile** (with characteristics of the interviewee) and **m-government innovation attributes** (relative advantage, compatibility, complexity, triability, and observability).

SECTION 1:   PARTICIPANT PROFILE

1.1   Age Group (Years):
     a. 20-30   b. 31-40 c. 41-50 d. 51-60   e. Over

1.2   Gender:
     a. Female b. Male

1.3   Highest level of education:
     a.   Post-graduate/Master's degree
     b.   Bachelor's degree
     c.   Diploma / Certificate
     d.   'O' level / 'A' level
     e.   Other

1.4   Mobile subscriber:
     a.   Safaricom
     b.   Airtel
     c.   Orange (Telkom Kenya)
     d.   Yu (Essar)

1.5   Have you accessed any e-government systems using your phone? Please list

SECTION 2:   MOBILE TECHNOLOGY INNOVATION ATTRIBUTES

2.1   Relative advantage
     ▪   What are the advantages of using mobile phones to access e-government services compared to previous methods?

2.2   Compatibility
     ▪   Are mobile phones well suited for accessing e-government services? Explain

2.3   Complexity
     ▪   In your opinion is the use of mobile phones for e-government services simple?

2.4   Triability
     ▪   Have you tested e-government functions on a mobile phone?

2.5   'Observability
     ▪   What direct benefits have you observed when accessing e-government services using a mobile phone?

Fig. 2. Interview questionnaire

Table 5. Driving factors - relative advantage

Driving factors	Freq (%)	Sample responses
Time-saving	34	"No more queues"; "Saves time, Saves money, Saves energy"; "Using a mobile phone is faster compared to pc"
Accessibility	24	"They require less bundles which can be bought easily"; "Mobile phone is more accessible and anybody can own a mobile phone compared to a computer"; "Mobile phones allow access from anywhere in Kenya"; "It allows one to access them from any location"; "Fast, you can access the services anywhere anytime"; "Mobile phones allow fast access to these services wherever you are"; "Mobile phone is more accessible and anybody can own a mobile phone compared to a computer"; "I can easily access these services from my phone without any trouble"
Convenience	22	"No need to meet with officials in order to get services"; "Faster and very convenient"; "Mobile phones come in handy when there is no electricity and I have to access these services" "They are more reliable than pc"; "Mobile phones are more reliable as they do not use electricity constantly"
Efficiency	10	"The mobile phone is more efficient compared to the Pc platform"; "I believe they can do more improvements to make the system efficient";
Cost	8	"They are cheaper compared to PC platforms"; "They are easier to access, cheaper in terms of money and time"; "The mobile phone is much more efficient this is because it's cheaper" "Phones rely on data bundles which are cheap"
Security	2	"Phones have more security"; "Personal details are not open to many parties"

Table 6. Driving factors – compatibility

Driving factors	Freq (%)	Sample responses
Accessibility	45	"Anytime I have data bundle I can access it"; "Everybody can access"; "I have seen services offered through the internet translate well to mobile"; "My phone has what it takes to access these services"
Connectivity	24	"My phone easily connects to the various platforms"; "Phones connect to the internet easily"; "The services require smartphones hence delivery will be slow"; "Low networks connection reduces the compatibility"
Efficiency	7	"The services once connected to the server they are efficient"; "Much has to be done to maximize consistency of offering services"; "The services are well compatible with the mobile phones hence this leads to efficiency of the services"
Service-provider	7	"The use of service providers is useful most of the time"; "They can be used with any service provider"; "Use of the most widespread service provider serves a lot of people but locks out a few"
Features	17	"They are compatible but more features need to be added"; "The websites are not mobile friendly"; "Inability to access the entire services compared to when using a computer"; "Only useful on a smartphone"; "They function for selected services and not others"

Table 7. Driving factors – complexity

Driving factors	Freq (%)	Sample Responses
User-friendly	21	'It's very simple'; 'Phones are less complicated'; 'They don't call for experts in order to use them'; 'Phones are simple to operate'; 'No special skills needed'; 'Easy to navigate'; 'I love the simple language used to ensure everyone understands how it operates'
Accessibility	30	'All I need is an internet connection and I can access the services'; 'I can access services from anywhere'; 'No long queues'; 'Some services are conveniently accessible through the phone'; 'It removes the agony of going to public offices for services'; 'I only need data bundles to access the internet'; 'Yes, you are near it can be in everyone's pocket'
Cost	15	'All I need is a data bundle which is cheap'; 'You don't incur much charges'; 'Yes, I don't need to pay for installation or monthly subscription'
Efficiency	16	'It's more suitable because there aren't many extra requirements when using a mobile phone'. 'For efficiency I would use a computer rather than mobile phones'
Connectivity	16	'Network problem'; 'No, my phone can't access network'; 'Delay in provision of services due to congestion of systems'; 'System will load slower on a mobile phone'

Table 8. Driving factors - observability

Driving factors	Freq (%)	Sample responses
Security	2	'More secure operations as no one will get an opportunity to see your password and other personal information'; 'I use a password to keep my confidential information safe'
Efficiency	7	'Phones do not go off easily with electricity surges'; 'Do not require electricity to run fully'; 'They are faster and efficient'
Connectivity	10	'More rapidly and speed of access'; 'Wider reach even in remote areas'
Time-saving	37	'They are less time consuming';' I get to save on time I would have gone to a cyber'; 'Saves time used in going to queue in government offices'; 'Does not require one to be physically present to acquire services'; 'Avoidance of long queues'
Accessibility	44	'Services are easily accessible anytime'; 'Mobile phones enable access of these services from anywhere'; 'They are easily accessible'; 'Versatility and flexibility of phones'; 'Services are accessible on the go'

References

1. Gichoya, D.: Factors affecting the successful implementation of ICT projects in government. Electron. J. E-gov. **3**(4), 175–184 (2005)
2. Mpinganjira, M.: Delivering citizen-centric m-government services in Africa: critical success factor. Afr. Insight **44**(3), 129–144 (2014)
3. Ngulube, P.: The nature and accessibility of e-government in Sub-Saharan Africa. Int. Rev. Inf. Ethics **7**(9), 1–13 (2007)
4. International Telecommunication Union: The State of Broadband 2016: Broadband Catalyzing Sustainable Development. ITU, UNESCO (2016). https://www.broadbandcommission.org/Documents/reports/bb-annualreport2016.pdf. Accessed 26 Jan 2020
5. Mengistu, D., Zo, H., Rho, J.J.: M-government: opportunities and challenges to deliver mobile government services in developing countries. In: Proceedings of Fourth International Conference on Computer Sciences and Convergence Information Technology, pp. 1445–1450. IEEE, Seoul (2009)
6. Mwirigi, G.B., et al.: An empirical investigation of m-government acceptance in developing countries: a case of Kenya. Securing Government Information and Data in Developing Countries, pp. 62–89. IGI Global, Pennsylvania (2017)
7. Oteri, O.M., Kibet, L.P., Ndung'u, E.N.: Mobile subscription, penetration and coverage trends in Kenya's telecommunication sector. Int. J. Adv. Res. Artif. Intell. **4**(1), 1–7 (2015)
8. Communications Authority of Kenya First Quarter Sector Statistics Report for the Financial Year 2018/2019. https://ca.go.ke/document/sector-statistics-report-q2–2018-19/. Accessed 26 Jan 2020
9. UNDESA: United Nations E-Government Survey 2018: Gearing E-Government to Support Transformation towards Sustainable and Resilient Societies. United Nations, New York (2018)
10. Nkosi, M., Mekuria, F.: Mobile government for improved public service provision in South Africa. In: Proceedings of 2010 IST-Africa, pp. 1–8. IEEE (2010)

11. Ishengoma, F., Mselle, L., Mongi, H.: Critical success factors for m-government adoption in Tanzania: a conceptual framework. Electron. J. Inf. Syst. Dev. Countries **85**(1), e12064 (2019)
12. Munyoka, W., Manzira, M.F.: From e-government to m-government-challenges faced by Sub-Saharan Africa. In: Proceedings of The International Conference on Computing Technology and Information Management (ICCTIM), p. 86. Society of Digital Information and Wireless Communication (2014)
13. Amanquah, N., Mzyece, M.: Mobile application research and development: the African context. In: Proceedings of the 2nd ACM Symposium on Computing for Development, p. 20. ACM (2012)
14. Kyem, P.A.K.: Mobile phone expansion and opportunities for e-governance in Sub-Saharan Africa. Electron. J. Inf. Syst. Dev Countries **75**(1), 1–15 (2016)
15. Sekyere, E., Tshitiza, O., Hart, T.: Levering m-governance innovations for active citizenship engagement. HSRC, South Africa (2016)
16. Mpekoa, N., Dlamini, D.R: M-government maturity model: a qualitative investigation. In: Proceedings of International Conference on Information Society (i-Society), pp. 87–91. Infonomics Society, Dublin (2017)
17. Crandall, A., Mutuku, L.: M-governance: exploratory survey on Kenyan service delivery and government interaction. In: Proceedings of the IST-Africa 2012 Conference Proceedings. IST-Africa, Tanzania (2011). http://www.ist-africa.org/home/outbox/ISTAfrica_Paper_ref_84_4750.pdf
18. Rogers, E.M.: Diffusion of Innovations. Free Press, New York (2003)
19. Davis, F.D., Bagozzi, R.P., Warshaw, P.R.: User acceptance of computer technology: a comparison of two theoretical models. Manag. Sci. **35**(8), 982–1003 (1989)
20. Venkatesh, V., Morris, M.G., Davis, G.B., Davis, F.D.: User acceptance of information technology: toward a unified view. MIS Q. **27**(3), 425–478 (2003)
21. Lee, Y.H., Hsieh, Y.C., Hsu, C.N.: Adding innovation diffusion theory to the technology acceptance model: supporting employees' intentions to use e-learning systems. J. Edu. Technol. Soc. **14**(4), 124–137 (2011)
22. Van Biljon, J., Kotzé, P.: Modelling the factors that influence mobile phone adoption. In: Proceedings of the 2007 Annual Research Conference Of The South African Institute Of Computer Scientists And Information Technologists On It Research In Developing Countries, pp. 152–161. ACM Press, Port Elizabeth, South Africa (2007)
23. Kushchu, I., Kuscu, H.: From e-government to m-government: facing the inevitable. In: Proceedings of The 3rd European Conference on E-government, pp. 253–260. MCIL Trinity College Dublin, Ireland (2003)
24. Kwon, H.S., Chidambaram, L.: A test of the technology acceptance model: the case of cellular telephone adoption. In: Proceedings of the 33rd Annual Hawaii International Conference on System Sciences, p. 7. IEEE, Maui, Hawaii (2000)
25. Bwalya, K.J., Healy, M.: Harnessing e-government adoption in the SADC region: a conceptual underpinning. Electron. J. E-gov. **8**(1), 23 (2010)
26. Kanaan, R.K., et al.: Implementation of m-government: leveraging mobile technology to streamline the e-governance framework. J. Soc. Sci. (COES&RJ-JSS) **8**(3), 495–508 (2019)
27. Shareef, M.A., Archer, N., Dwivedi, Y.K.: Examining adoption behavior of mobile government. J. Comput. Inf. Syst. **53**(2), 39–49 (2012)
28. Shareef, M.A., Kumar, V., Dwivedi, Y.K., Kumar, U.: Service delivery through mobile-government (mGov): driving factors and cultural impacts. Inf. Syst. Front. **18**(2), 315–332 (2014). https://doi.org/10.1007/s10796-014-9533-2
29. Min, S., So, K.K.F., Jeong, M.: Consumer adoption of the Uber mobile application: insights from diffusion of innovation theory and technology acceptance model. J. Travel Tourism Mark. **36**(7), 770–783 (2019)

30. Rogers, E.M.: Diffusion of Innovations. Free Press, New York (1995)
31. Sanni, S.A., Ngah, Z.A., Karim, N.H.A., Abdullah, N., Waheed, M.: Using the diffusion of innovation concept to explain the factors that contribute to the adoption rate of e-journal publishing. Serials Rev. **39**(4), 250–257 (2013)
32. Oghuma, A.P., Libaque-Saenz, C.F., Wong, S.F., Chang, Y.: An expectation-confirmation model of continuance intention to use mobile instant messaging. Telematics Inform. **33**(1), 34–47 (2016)
33. Moore, G.C., Benbasat, I.: Development of an instrument to measure the perceptions of adopting an information technology innovation. Inf. Syst. Res. **2**(3), 192–222 (1991)
34. Kapoor, K.K., Dwivedi, Y.K., Williams, M.D.: Empirical examination of the role of three sets of innovation attributes for determining adoption of IRCTC mobile ticketing service. Inf. Syst. Manag. **32**(2), 153–173 (2015)
35. Aker, J.C., Mbiti, I.M.: Mobile phones and economic development in Africa. J. Econ. Perspect. **24**(3), 207–232 (2010)
36. Carter, L., Bélanger, F.: The utilization of e-government services: citizen trust, innovation and acceptance factors. Inf. Syst. J. **15**(1), 5–25 (2005)
37. Giovanis, A.N., Binioris, S., Polychronopoulos, G.: An extension of TAM model with IDT and security/privacy risk in the adoption of internet banking services in Greece. EuroMed J. Bus. **7**(1), 24–53 (2012)
38. Tan, M., Teo, T.S.: Factors influencing the adoption of internet banking. J. Assoc. Inf. Syst. **1**(1), 5 (2000)
39. Hasbi, M., Dubus, A.: Determinants of mobile broadband use in developing economies: evidence from Sub-Saharan Africa. Telecommun. Policy **44**(5), 101944 (2020)
40. Creswell, J.W., Hanson, W.E., Clark Plano, V.L., Morales, A.: Qualitative research designs: selection and implementation. Couns. Psychol. **35**(2), 236–264 (2007)
41. Harrison, H., Birks, M., Franklin, R., Mills, J.: Case study research: foundations and methodological orientations. In: Proceedings of Forum Qualitative Sozialforschung/Forum: Qualitative Social Research, vol. 18(1) (2017)
42. Korstjens, I., Moser, A.: Series: practical guidance to qualitative research. Part 2: context, research questions and designs. Eur. J. Gen. Pract. **23**(1), 274–279 (2017)
43. Turner III, D.W.: Qualitative interview design: a practical guide for novice investigators. Qual. Rep. **15**(3), 754–760 (2010)
44. Kallio, H., Pietilä, A.M., Johnson, M., Kangasniemi, M.: Systematic methodological review: developing a framework for a qualitative semi-structured interview guide. J. Adv. Nurs. **72**(12), 2954–2965 (2016)
45. Ritchie, J., Lewis, J., Nicholls, C.M., Ormston, R. (eds.): Qualitative Research Practice: A Guide for Social Science Students and Researchers. Sage, Thousand Oaks (2013)
46. Moser, A., Korstjens, I.: Series: practical guidance to qualitative research. Part 3: sampling, data collection and analysis. Eur. J. Gen. Pract. **24**(1), 9–18 (2018)
47. Malterud, K., Siersma, V.D., Guassora, A.D.: Sample size in qualitative interview studies: guided by information power. Qual. Health Res. **26**(13), 1753–1760 (2016)
48. O'Reilly, M., Parker, N.: 'Unsatisfactory Saturation': a critical exploration of the notion of saturated sample sizes in qualitative research. Qual. Res. **13**(2), 190–197 (2013)
49. Saunders, B., et al.: Saturation in qualitative research: exploring its conceptualization and operationalization. Qual. Quant. **52**(4), 1–15 (2017). https://doi.org/10.1007/s11135-017-0574-8

Research on the Tax Base of Income Tax of Smart Mobile Commerce

Qi Wei[✉] and Peiyan Zhou

School of Management of Jilin University, Changchun, China
rzweiqi@163.com, zh-peiyan@163.com

Abstract. With the rapid development of mobile communication technology and Internet intelligent terminal technology, mobile commerce with mobility and convenience has become a new direction of e-commerce development. Mobile commerce is a new e-commerce mode that carries out data transmission through mobile communication network and participates in various business activities by using mobile information terminals. Mobile commerce is the extension of e-commerce, which has greatly developed e-commerce, and its influence on economic development has been gradually enhanced. It is very different from traditional e-commerce. Mobile e-commerce is not limited by time and space, which is also one of the biggest advantages of mobile e-commerce compared with traditional e-commerce.

However, the rapid development of mobile commerce, driving economic growth, but also brought a series of tax management problems. In the new environment of digital economy, e-commerce and mobile commerce, the existing tax management system has exposed many loopholes. The incomplete tax system of digital economy and e-commerce has led to serious tax loss, and the tax rate of digital economy is less than half that of traditional business model. At the same time, the absence of relevant laws also increases the difficulty of collection and administration, which is not conducive to maintaining the fairness of taxation. Therefore, the research on the tax management of mobile commerce is the protection of the tax rights of the country and also the general trend to adapt to the development. Among them, the tax base as the basis of calculating the tax payable, mobile commerce income tax base is the most important issue. Therefore, on the basis of the original e-commerce tax system and digital economy, combined with the actual situation in China, this paper further explored and improved the tax base of income tax under mobile commerce.

International research on digital economy, e-commerce tax management is in full swing. In this context, this paper is divided into six parts from the perspective of improving the tax base. Firstly, the research background, current tax management status and existing problems of the emerging field of mobile commerce income tax are expounded. The second part expounds the relevant concepts of the income tax base of mobile commerce, the theoretical analysis of the composition scope and the determination principle at home and abroad, and studies the influencing factors of the tax system from the political, economic and social aspects. The third part discusses the determination of the income tax base of mobile commerce. Starting from the macro tax data, this paper specifically studies the taxable income, deduction items and tax preferences of mobile commerce income tax. The fourth part will focus on research the existing problems of tax management system in the

© Springer Nature Switzerland AG 2020
G. Salvendy and J. Wei (Eds.): HCII 2020, LNCS 12216, pp. 138–151, 2020.
https://doi.org/10.1007/978-3-030-50350-5_12

tax base, as well as the problems of expense deduction, tax preferential policies, the fifth part, comparing the selected OECD countries based on the same taxable income, deductions, tax breaks for the analysis of the specific Settings and change trend of enterprise income tax base, the last part in view of the above analysis, combined with the actual situation of our country, put forward suitable for China's national conditions of further optimization measures of mobile business income tax base and legislative Suggestions.

Keywords: Mobile commerce · The tax base · The digital economy · The income tax · The electronic commerce

1 Introduction

With the gradual maturity and rapid development of communication technology in recent years, China's mobile Internet has entered a period of rapid development. With 5G network optimization, wireless network development, the popularity of smart phones and application software innovation, mobile phones have become the main form of Internet access for netizens. Smart terminal Internet has become a new driving force for the development of the Internet, which has promoted the new growth of the Internet economy. The innovation boom based on mobile Internet has provided a new business model and development space for traditional Internet businesses. With the development of mobile Internet and the popularization of intelligent terminals, mobile e-commerce will become an important driving force for future economic growth. In particular, the issuance of 5G licenses and the immediate commercial deployment provide more new development momentum for mobile e-commerce, marking the advent of a new round of changes in mobile e-commerce.

2 Relevant Theories of Mobile Commerce

2.1 The Concept and Connotation of E-Commerce

E-commerce refers to all over the world in the commercial trade activity widely, in the Internet open network environment, based on client/server applications, buyers and sellers are not met in various business activities, realize consumer online shopping, online transactions between merchants and online electronic payment and various business activities, trading activities, financial activities and related comprehensive service activities of a new type of commercial operation mode. Generally speaking, e-commerce is based on traditional commerce, relying on modern information technology and computer network, the whole trade activities digitization and electronic business activities.

The key to e-commerce activities lies in two aspects, one is how to verify the identity of online transactions, and the other is how to carry out payment activities. Ma xiuling proposed that the difference between e-commerce and traditional business activities lies in the change of the transaction mode that originally must be conducted by contact or physical exchange, so that it can also be realized by electronic means. CAI chang holds the same view with previous scholars. In addition, he believes that the core of e-commerce lies in transforming capital flow and logistics into information flow by relying on modern information technology.

2.2   The Concept and Characteristics of Mobile Commerce

Mobile commerce (m-business or MobileBusiness) is a branch of e-commerce. Mobile commerce refers to a new e-commerce mode that carries out data transmission through mobile communication network and participates in various business activities by using mobile information terminals. It is a new e-commerce form under new technological conditions and new market environment. Many scholars believe that mobile commerce is the combination of "mobile" and "commerce". They use mobile phones and other terminal devices to conduct business activities through wireless network.

The components of mobile commerce should include buyers and sellers, information integrators, financial payment platforms, mobile operators and mobile terminal providers.

Compared with traditional e-commerce, mobile commerce has more advantages.

1. It is ubiquitous, anytime and anywhere.

The biggest characteristic of mobile commerce is "freedom" and "individuation". Traditional commerce has made people feel the convenience and happiness brought by the network, but its limitation lies in that it must be connected by wire. However, mobile e-commerce can make up for this deficiency of traditional e-commerce, allowing people to check out, order tickets or go shopping anytime and anywhere, and feel the unique business experience.

2. Be more open and inclusive.

Because of the wireless access mode, mobile commerce makes it easier for anyone to enter the network world, thus extending the network scope wider and more open. At the same time, make the network virtual function more with reality, so more inclusive.

3. Mobile e-commerce is easy to promote and use.

The flexible and convenient characteristics of mobile communication determine that mobile e-commerce is more suitable for popular personal consumption.

4. It is not controlled by time and space

Mobile commerce is the extension of e-commerce from wired communication to wireless communication, from fixed location business form to business form anytime and anywhere. Its biggest advantage is that mobile users can get needed services, applications, information and entertainment anytime and anywhere. Users can use a smartphone or tablet to find, select and purchase goods or other services at their own convenience.

5. Large scale of potential users

China has nearly 400 million mobile phone users, the most in the world. Obviously, in terms of the popularity of computers and mobile phones, mobile phones far surpass computers. From the perspective of consumer groups, mobile phone users basically include middle and high-end users with strong consumption ability, while traditional Internet users are mainly young people who lack the ability to pay. From this, it is not difficult to see that the mobile e-commerce with mobile phone as the carrier is superior to the traditional e-commerce in terms of both user scale and consumer power.Second, the current situation of mobile commerce income tax collection.

In the digital economy and e-commerce environment, the tax situation is not satisfactory. At present, China's digital economy and e-commerce tax have serious problems such as tax loss, lack of laws and difficulties in collection and administration. At the same time, the Chinese government is also actively exploring relevant tax practices.

1. Tax is not levied on digital economy and e-commerce, resulting in serious tax loss. In terms of tax loss measurement, zhujun (2013) used the "average tax burden method" to estimate the scale of tax loss caused by e-commerce. Guopeiting and li haoyuan (2017) believe that due to the particularity of online transactions, the "average tax burden method" and "tax loss rate method" can be used in the selection of tax loss measurement methods. Based on the tax loss estimation, wanghuochen (2018) calculated that the tax rate of digital economy is less than half that of traditional business model. CAI chang (2017) estimated the loss of value-added tax and income tax in China from 2012 to 2015 by using the average tax rate method, and estimated the loss of tax in 2016 to be 53.1 billion yuan based on this.

2. Relevant tax laws are relatively absent in China at present. Sun yuhong and liujintao (2012) found that it is generally believed that C2C e-commerce is not taxed, mainly because there are no explicit regulations on C2C taxation in China. Yao gongping and wangxiaojie (2016) found that due to the lack of relevant tax laws and difficulties in tax collection and management, enterprises that operate completely online have lower tax burdens than those with physical existence.

3. Due to their differences from traditional business, they have difficulties in tax collection and management. Zhu haitao (2016) believes that e-commerce tax has the characteristics of virtualization, vagueness and concealment compared with traditional business model tax. As a result, it is difficult to collect and manage the tax. Shen yali, Beixin Lin, liaoweimin (2015) believe that in the digital economy environment, ma wei, yujing, cheng ping (2016) believe that in the e-commerce environment, multinational enterprises can achieve direct and indirect tax avoidance through a variety of ways. At the same time, when both the buyer and the seller are individuals, renguozhe (2018) believes that C2C tax collection and management is the most difficult.

4. At the same time, China has been actively implementing relevant tax practices. Dai hsinzhu and huangxun (2016) believe that although China has made some achievements in electronic invoices, it still needs to learn from foreign successful experience and actively promote reform. Di changya (2016) believes that the Chinese government constantly guides the e-commerce industry into a standardized path to make the tax more fair. It can be seen from this that scholars' research on the current situation of relevant taxation in China mainly focuses on the estimation of tax loss, tax legislation, tax collection and management, and the positive practice in China has made good progress.

From China's current tax system, mobile commerce in the income tax is not blank. According to China's income tax law, enterprises and individuals engaged in mobile commerce are also required to pay corporate and individual income taxes.

Among them, the nature of mobile commerce enterprises are divided into complete mobile commerce and incomplete mobile commerce.

3   Provisions on Resident Income Tax for Mobile Commerce

Under the condition of complete mobile commerce, the enterprise income tax shall be paid at the place where the enterprise is registered and in accordance with the provisions of the income tax law. However, in a completely mobile commerce environment, due to online business activities, relevant information is "hidden", leading to the situation of hidden income of enterprises more likely to occur. In accordance with the provisions of the individual income tax law, individual income tax shall be paid on income derived by individuals at home and abroad. Similarly, in a fully mobile commerce environment, situations such as individuals hiding their income are more likely to occur.

Under the condition of incomplete mobile commerce, enterprise income tax, logistics and other activities are part of normal business activities, which are not different from the traditional business model. Therefore, the tax regulations of income tax are relatively less challenged. For individual income tax, similar to incomplete mobile commerce corporate income tax, the tax regulations on income tax are relatively less challenging. In a mobile commerce environment, it is common for the seller to be an individual, but the compliance of individual taxpayers is low. So additional measures are needed.

It can be seen that incomplete mobile commerce poses relatively little challenge to income tax for resident enterprises and individuals. Since in the context of mobile commerce, the number of sellers increases for individuals, the government needs to take relevant measures to improve individual tax compliance. Due to the online operation of complete mobile commerce, relevant transaction information is "hidden", which may lead to hidden income and bring challenges to income tax management. Therefore, it is necessary for the government to strengthen information exchange with relevant third-party platforms in the process of income tax collection.

4   Provisions on Non-resident Income Tax for Mobile Commerce

Under the condition of complete mobile commerce, if a non-resident enterprise has an institution or place in China, it shall pay enterprise income tax on the income of the institution or place in China and the income related to the institution or place obtained abroad. If there is no institution or place, income tax will be paid on the income from China. However, in the context of mobile commerce, enterprises often do not need to have an entity in a certain place to carry out business activities, which brings challenges to the identification of income tax authorities and places. In addition, non-resident enterprises only need to pay income tax on their income from China, so how to judge the nature of income and the division of domestic and foreign profits is particularly important. Individual income tax is paid on income derived from China.

Under the condition of incomplete mobile commerce, the enterprise income tax is consistent with the enterprise income tax of complete mobile commerce. Incomplete mobile commerce will go through the customs in the process of commodity import, and relevant tax-related information will be collected more comprehensively. However, it is difficult to identify institutions and places. Individual income tax is paid on income derived from China. Incomplete mobile commerce will go through the customs in the process of commodity import, and relevant tax-related information will be collected more comprehensively.

It can be seen from this, when collecting enterprise income tax for non-resident enterprises, the determination of institution, place or permanent establishment is very important. In a mobile commerce environment, companies can trade with China without a "physical presence". Therefore, without a clear definition of "permanent establishment" in the context of mobile commerce, China may lose tax revenue in non-resident enterprises. In addition, it is also necessary to pay attention to the income characterization and profit distribution in corporate income tax, so as to cope with the challenges brought by mobile commerce.

To sum up, China is not a blank in the field of income tax management of mobile commerce. For resident enterprises and individuals, the tax challenges brought by mobile commerce are mainly reflected in the two aspects of information acquisition by tax authorities and tax compliance degree of individual taxpayers, which requires the government to strengthen information exchange with third-party intermediary platforms and so on during tax collection and management. For non-resident businesses and individuals, the tax challenges posed by mobile commerce are reflected in the judgment, income characterization and profit distribution of the "permanent establishment". But whether China's current regulations can cope with the mobile commerce environment requires a more detailed analysis.

5   Existing Problems

Scholars' research on the three related tax management problems is mainly carried out from the two aspects of tax legislation and tax collection and administration. In the aspect of tax legislation, it is divided into direct tax legislation and indirect tax legislation. (1) the direct tax legislation mainly focuses on how to define the permanent institution in the digital environment and how to determine the tax jurisdiction; How to characterize the income generated by the transaction, different income characteristics may lead to different tax methods; How to determine the profit should belong to which organization and so on. (2) the discussion of indirect tax legislation mainly focuses on how to determine the place of tax payment. In terms of tax collection and management, the following aspects are as follows: the low compliance of current online transaction taxpayers, the unapplicable current tax collection and management process, the low efficiency of tax collection and management, and the weak links in tax collection and management.

The legislative problems of direct taxation are mainly embodied in: (1) the definition of permanent institutions. Wang fengfei (2013) believes that failure to clearly divide tax jurisdiction will lead to competition for international tax interests. Therefore, the concept of permanent establishment needs to be clarified and adapted to economic development. Chen yongsheng, pan guozhong and wangwenlai (2016) believe that in the digital economy environment, many enterprises lack physical existence, which may lead to the situation that countries of origin cannot exercise tax power. Cui xiaojing and sun qimin (2017) found that in the challenge of information technology to traditional tax system, the problem of "permanent institution" judgment is the primary problem. Jones, Basu (2002); Meharia and Priyanka (2012) found that when American online retailers transact across states, they can only be taxed if there is "physical presence". Therefore, Choudhary (2011) believes that whether servers or Internet service providers constitute permanent institutions is an important issue that puzzles decision makers. (2) income qualitative aspect. Deng ziji (2001) believes that in the current environment, it is difficult to judge the nature of intangible transactions, which may lead to tax loss. Zhang yan (2013) also believes that in the digital economy environment, it is difficult to accurately judge the nature of digital products for online transactions. Buchan and Jenny (2014) believe that the current law is really difficult to adapt to all aspects of franchise operation practice. Zhang li (2018) believed that the reason why it was difficult to judge the income quality was that the defining standard of commodities was vague. (3) profit distribution. Wang haochen (2018) believes that the characteristics of digital economy, such as data, liquidity and network, will pose challenges to tax legislation. At the same time, nihongri (2016) also proposed that the actual attribution of profits is difficult to determine. Pinson and Julian (2017) believe that it is very complicated to distribute profits to branches or permanent institutions.

The main problem with indirect tax legislation is that it is difficult to determine where to pay taxes. Liang ping and xu Chen (2000) believe that in the digital economy environment, it is difficult to determine the location of goods or services, which will pose challenges to VAT tax collection. Conley, John, Makowski and Roberte (2004) argue that new payment methods and new commodity categories will increase VAT.

Steven and Salbu (1998) believe that e-commerce is characterized by complexity and ambiguity, which will bring challenges to tax collection and management. In addition, Kathleen and Ramona (2010) believed that even if relevant taxes were legislated, the implementation of policies was not satisfactory. Current scholars' studies on the difficulties in tax challenges are mainly reflected in: (1) low compliance of taxpayers in online transactions. Alm and Meinik (2010) investigated the sales tax situation of e Bay and found that the compliance degree of the seller was very low. (2) in terms of tax collection and management process and tax registration, Chen qiang (2009) proposed that in the context of e-commerce, it is difficult for tax authorities to determine the basic information and transaction information of taxpayers. Wang fengfei (2013) found that e-commerce enterprise registration was poor. Zhao qinghua, Lou wanhai and xiongyifeng (2016) also found difficulties in the implementation of e-commerce tax registration system. In terms of tax inspection, wangfengfei (2013) found that the current tax authorities lack reliable technical support for the management of paperless vouchers. In paperless trading environment, Liang Jun jiao (2013), Meng Shu Tian (2019) argue that this brings to the tax authorities to obtain evidence of legitimacy and authenticity of the challenge. Zhu haitao (2016) believed that tax authorities did not make full use of third-party payment platforms when collecting taxes on e-commerce. (3) in terms of tax collection and administration evaluation, li jianye qi-xin et al. (2016) and most scholars quantitatively evaluated tax collection and administration in terms of the results of tax collection and administration. Cao haisheng and tang bingyong (2012, 2014) started from the process of tax collection and management, built evaluation indexes and models for the process of tax collection and management, and looked for the weak links of tax collection and management. This paper analyzes the causes of weak links in e-commerce tax collection and management by using fishbone diagram. Combined with the reading of relevant literature, scholars pay more attention to the digital economy tax, e-commerce tax, and pay more attention to the three aspects of tax source control, tax rate determination and tax collection and management. The control of tax source mainly involves the determination of tax jurisdiction, while the determination of tax amount mainly involves the recognition of the amount of relevant business activities and the distribution of profits. In other words, for direct tax, mainly income tax, scholars focus on the determination of tax linkage, income characterization and related profit distribution. As for indirect tax, scholars' discussions mainly focus on tax payment location and tax collection and management process.

6 Determination of Tax Base and Influencing Factors

The Connotation of the Tax Base. The tax base refers to the objective basis for the government to collect tax. It describes the extent of the government to collect tax, that is, to solve the problem of who's "what" to tax. From the perspective of tax practice, the objective basis of tax system can be divided into national income type, national consumption type and national wealth type. From the perspective of the middle meaning, tax base refers to the objective basis for taxation of a certain tax, that is, the object of taxation. It describes the scope of taxation of a certain tax in terms of its qualitative stipulation. In a narrow sense, the tax base refers to the basis for calculating tax, which defines the scope of taxation of a certain tax category from the stipulation of quantity, and is the legal basis and basis for calculating tax payable.

As the basis for calculating the tax payable, the tax base includes two meanings:

The quality of the tax base. That is, the specific object of the tax. Different taxes, tax base is also different, if the tax base of commodity turnover tax is commodity sales or value-added, the tax base of income tax is all sorts of income, the tax base of property tax is all sorts of property.

The amount of the tax base. That is, how much of the tax object can be used as the base for calculating the tax payable.

For a tax object, the tax base can be wide or narrow. If there are more non-taxable items deducted from the income amount, the tax base is relatively small. Tax base is the unity of quality and quantity of tax basis.

A country to formulate a tax system, to properly choose the tax base. The alternative tax base varies with socio-economic development. Under the condition of commodity economy, the range of tax base that can choose is wider. Merchandise turnover, corporate profits, personal income, investment and consumption expenditures, as well as property and property transfers, can all serve as tax bases. The tax base should be selected according to certain principles and needs. If we want to ensure the steady growth of fiscal revenue, we must choose the tax base that is common and often exists in the national economy. If the government wants to use tax to adjust the national economy, the scope of choosing tax base should be relatively broad, and it should be beneficial to realize the optimal combination of tax fairness and efficiency principle, which is feasible in practice.

The Scope of the Tax Base. The basis of enterprise income tax is the basis for enterprises to calculate the amount of income. But in general, corporate income tax is a tax on corporate profits. Enterprise. Total income, the balance after deducting all costs and expenses and allowing for the recovery of losses.

Specific to the following circumstances, the enterprise income tax according to different types of business income respectively, mainly three categories: the treatment of investment income, the taxation method of capital gains, and the treatment of overseas income. At the same time, various tax-free and non-taxable income, such as interest income from national debt, Income from dividends and dividends among resident enterprises. The enterprise income tax is levied on the basis of the profits of the enterprise. The following items are also deducted from the income: costs, expenses, losses and loss recovery. But countries are deducting items. There are different ways of measuring inventory, depreciation of fixed assets, and carryover of losses. And other deductions. In addition, there are a variety of tax incentives, in general. Reflected in the following aspects: industrial policy, enterprise investment, scientific research and development, regional development, employment. And the development of small and medium-sized enterprises, these preferential tax policies, so that the government's industrial policy and social policy objectives. In order to realize. Each country according to the needs of their own, to the enterprise income tax base for different forms of tax payment method, in addition to the corporate income tax, and other special tariffs, however, is also enterprise operating profits tax, has the nature of the enterprise income tax in the previous section mentioned some surcharge: crisis tax, education tax, surcharge, AIDS or separately apart from the enterprise income tax base to impose a tax, such as capital gains tax. We will take these taxes of the same nature as a unified study of the tax base of corporate income tax.

Determination of the Tax Base. From China's current tax system, mobile commerce in the income tax is not blank. According to China's income tax law, enterprises and individuals engaged in mobile commerce are also required to pay corporate and individual income taxes.

First, the scope of the transaction. Transaction scope refers to taking into account the revenue generated by which transactions. It is generally defined as the income generated by signing contracts between two or more parties through digital platforms.

When collecting enterprise income tax for non-resident enterprises, it is very important to determine the institution, place or permanent establishment. In a mobile commerce environment, companies can trade with China without a "physical presence". Therefore, without a clear definition of "permanent establishment" in the context of mobile commerce, China may lose tax revenue in non-resident enterprises. In addition, it is also necessary to pay attention to the income characterization and profit distribution in corporate income tax, so as to cope with the challenges brought by mobile commerce.

In accordance with the relevant provisions of the income tax law: (1) if a non-resident enterprise constitutes a "permanent establishment" in China, that non-resident enterprise is the taxpayer and shall pay the enterprise income tax on income derived from within the People's Republic of China and income derived from outside the People's Republic of China but actually connected with the "permanent establishment". (2) if the non-resident enterprise does not constitute a "permanent establishment" in China; Or constitute a "permanent establishment", but the income obtained has nothing to do with it, and only the income from China is subject to income tax. Withholding tax shall be withheld by withholding tax on payers within the territory of China who are withholding agents. The effective tax rate in subparagraph (2) is lower than that in subparagraph (1).

Secondly, the qualitative analysis of income. For the non-resident income type of judgment, here mainly on the royalty. When a non-resident enterprise obtains royalties, it needs to withhold income tax. Therefore, in many cases, non-resident companies prefer to classify their revenues as operating profits rather than royalties. In accordance with the relevant provisions of the income tax on royalties, royalty income includes income from patent rights, non-patented technology, trademark rights, Copyrights and other use rights. At the same time, as can be seen from the rules, royalties focus on "use" and "transfer". It does not constitute a royalty if the right to "use" is exercised only with respect to the contents of the royalty and no "transfer" of the right is made. The distinction between service contracts and royalties also requires attention to whether rights are "transferred"; When the recipient of the service has no right to use the contents of the royalty, it is not a royalty and belongs to the service contract. In a mobile commerce environment, a user who downloads music to a mobile phone for the sole purpose of listening to it for himself does not constitute a royalty. If the recipient of the service has the right to transfer the contents of the royalty, it shall constitute a royalty.

In addition, for the mobile commerce enterprise profit distribution problem. According to document no. 18 [2010] of the state council of taxation, there are two types of profit accounting for the permanent establishment of non-resident enterprises. When the permanent establishment has a sound account book, the permanent establishment can be regarded as an independent enterprise according to the account book, and the tax payable by the permanent establishment can be calculated. When the books of the permanent establishment are not sound, the profit of the permanent establishment shall be calculated in accordance with the approved profit margin method. Determine which side of the expenditure or income can be accurately calculated and then the tax payable on the permanent establishment can be calculated based on this and the approved rate of profit.

The current profit distribution system treats the permanent establishment as an independent enterprise and distributes profits according to functions, assets and risks. This applies to the "physical presence" of the state in the market; However, "significant economic presence" enterprises have little or no "physical presence". Therefore, the traditional profit distribution method will not be applicable to the case of "significant economic existence". On this basis, OECD puts forward two proposed methods of profit distribution, namely the approved profit distribution method and the sporadic distribution method. (1) approved profit method. For "significant economic existence", the profit of the enterprise in the market country is calculated based on the prescribed profit margin of the market country and the income of the non-resident enterprise, and then the tax payable is calculated. In this case, the establishment of profit margin is particularly important, need to consider the industry, commodity type and other factors. (2) sporadic distribution method. Distribution of profits to the portion of "significant economic existence" calculated according to a certain formula can be adjusted according to the actual situation. Specific steps are: first, determine the income range for distribution, that is, the determination of the tax base; Secondly, the factors of tax base distribution should be clarified. Finally, the tax base is divided according to these distribution factors and relevant weights.

Factors affecting the tax base. The following factors should be considered when choosing a reasonable tax base:

1. Changes in tax source distribution

The structure of the selected tax base should be adapted to the distribution of tax sources, and those tax sources that are relatively extensive and abundant should be selected as the leading tax base as far as possible. At the same time, according to the changes in tax sources, timely adjust the structure of the tax base.

2. Tax revenue

Tax base and tax rate are two main factors that affect tax revenue. Narrow the tax base and reduce revenue.

3. National policies

If the tax rate remains unchanged and the tax base width and narrowness directly affect the burden level of taxpayers, the state can guide taxpayers' behaviors and reflect the national policy by stipulating allowances, pre-tax deduction and pre-tax loan repayment.

6.1 International Practice on Income Tax Administration

The OECD. In the second half of 2015, the OECD released 15 action plans on tax base erosion and profit shifting, in which it made recommendations on income tax in the digital economy. On the one hand, the definition of permanent institutions has been partially modified to pay more attention to the substantive judgment of preparatory and auxiliary activities, mainly because such activities may play a major role in commercial activities in the context of the digital economy; Some cases of agent-type permanent establishment are specified in greater detail. On the other hand, the concept of "significant economic presence" is introduced, which is mainly applicable to the situation where digital enterprises can still carry out core business with little or no physical presence in the country of source.

The European Union. The eu introduced a "significant number presence" in direct taxes, while innovating the principle of profit distribution. The eu defines "significant economic presence" from the perspectives of income factor and user factor. At the same time, the profit distribution principle of the permanent organization under the environment of innovative digital economy in the eu has two schemes: (1) the reason for profit distribution is based on the proportion of intangible assets expense or cost used in the "significant economic existence" to the total expense or cost of the headquarters. (2) the European commission wishes to take into account the important fact that user data and information create enterprise value in the distribution of profits. This is conducive to following the trend of globalization and avoiding the occurrence of profit transfer and tax base erosion.

India. The original definition of permanent establishment in India is consistent with international tax treaties, which can be divided into two types: place permanent establishment and agency permanent establishment. The approved profit margin method is adopted for the profit distribution of the permanent establishment. The reason for the Indian government's introduction of "significant economic presence": mainly due to the greater challenges posed by the digital economy, India's active participation in global economic activities will lead to massive tax losses if the concept of permanent institutions is not broadened. Therefore, the Indian government has accepted the OECD's recommendation to introduce a "significant economic presence" to broaden the concept of a permanent institution.

6.2 Mobile Commerce Income Tax Improvement Suggestions

Determination of the "Permanent Establishment" of a Non-resident Enterprise.
It is suggested to introduce the concept of "significant economic presence" into China mobile commerce tax, and the judging factors include:

1. income;
2. digitalization factor, local domain name or APP downloadable by local users, local digital platform (including APP), local payment method selection (also considering the combination with mobile payment software such as alipay and WeChat);
3. user factors, monthly active users, amount of online contracts concluded through digital platforms and apps, and relevant data collection;
4. other factors.

Profit Distribution of Permanent Establishment of Non-resident Enterprises.
At present, China adopts the approved profit distribution method. China has a huge mobile commerce market. Big data analysis of user data and information can improve marketing accuracy, reduce enterprise costs, and thus improve enterprise profits. Therefore, if China does not consider the value of user data and information in the profit distribution process of the permanent organization, it may lead to the loss of tax revenue in China to some extent. Therefore, it is recommended that China consider the market value of user data or information in the distribution of profits of the permanent organization.

1. adopt the sporadic distribution method, first determine the income range to be divided; Second, consider income distribution

To determine the formula for profit distribution by taking into account the market value of user data and information; Finally, the tax base is divided according to the formula. Advantages: convenient operation; Disadvantages: formula determination needs careful consideration and promotion in the international community needs some time.

2. verify the profit margin method, and consider the market value of user data and mobile commerce services when determining the profit margin. Advantages: more countries in the international community adopt this method, which is convenient for international tax coordination; Disadvantages: because the market value of user data and information varies in different industries or other factors, it is difficult to set the profit margin.

Therefore, in the short term, it is suggested that China should adopt the approved profit margin method when it comes to profit distribution division of mobile commerce. With the international community's recognition of the sporadic distribution method gradually improved, China can gradually prefer to choose the sporadic distribution method.

7   Conclusion

With the popularization of Internet and mobile communication, the rapid development of mobile commerce has brought opportunities and challenges to China. In this context, this paper illustrates the connotation and characteristics of mobile commerce; The status quo and existing problems of income tax for smart mobile commerce are analyzed. Clarify the connotation of the tax base and how to determine; Comparative analysis of reforms with OECD countries; On the basis of China's current income tax legislation, combined with China's national conditions and interests, this paper puts forward appropriate Suggestions for China's mobile commerce income tax legislation.

Therefore, the Suggestions of the study on China mobile commerce income tax legislation and countermeasures are as follows: (1) for foreign enterprises that do not have "physical existence" in China but have sales behaviors, the concept of "significant economic existence" is introduced to determine whether it constitutes "economic existence"; (2) in terms of income definition, China's current legislation and implementation process is relatively complete; (3) China has a large number of mobile commerce users. It is suggested that China take into account the data and information value of users in the process of profit margin setting in the current profit distribution method – the method of determining profit rate. Big data analysis of user data and information can improve marketing accuracy, reduce enterprise costs, and thus improve enterprise profits. Therefore, if China does not consider the value of user data and information in the profit distribution process of the permanent organization, it may lead to the loss of tax revenue in China to some extent. Therefore, it is recommended that China consider the market value of user data or information in the distribution of profits of the permanent organization.

References

Ballard, C.L., Lee, J.: Internet purchases, cross-border shopping, and sales taxes. Natl. Tax J. **60**(4), 711–725 (2007)

Einav, L., Knoepfle, D.T., Levin, J., et al.: Sales taxes and internet commerce. Soc. Sci. Electron. Publishing **104**(1), 1–26 (2014)

Li, Y.: Research on tax base erosion and profit shifting under digital economy

Duo, Z., Pei, X.: On the control of tax base. Explor. Think.

Li, L.: Analysis of tax planning of enterprise income tax base. Work Res.

OECD: Addressing the Tax Challenges of the Digital Economy, Action 1–2015 Final Report, OECD/G20 Base Erosion and Profit Shifting Project. OECD Publishing, Paris (2015). https://doi.org/10.1787/9789264241046-en

Redpath Esq, I.J., Redpath, E.M., Ryan, K.: Sales and use taxation in e-commerce: where we are and what needs to be done. J. Inf. Syst. Manag. **24**(3), 239–245 (2007)

Problems and Suggestions in the Initial Construction of Running Campuses in Different Places

Xiang Xie, Qianru Zhang[✉], and Haihong Su

School of Economics and Management, Beijing Jiaotong University, Beijing, China
{xxie,19120626,15113141}@bjtu.edu.cn

Abstract. As the country attaches more importance to education and the number of students increases, universities have taken measures to recruit and cultivate high-quality talents. In the process of running universities, some universities have adopted the strategy of running campuses in different places, which helps universities to expand their development space and promote the development of education in the places where university branch campuses are located. However, in the process of implementing the strategy of running campuses in different places, many problems have arisen in the management of university branch campuses, especially in newly-built university branch campuses. These problems make newly-built university branch campuses unable to meet the needs of students, resulting in lower students' satisfaction with the campus. This article first investigates the factors that affect students' satisfaction with the campus through questionnaire surveys, testes the data using regression analysis, and selects significant influencing factors, which includes students' satisfaction with curriculum arrangements, teacher resources, and scientific research atmosphere. Then take these three factors as the research direction, and use questionnaire surveys again, from the perspective of students to discuss the current problems in the construction and development of newly-built university branch campuses. The survey results show that from the perspective of students, there are many problems in newly-built university branch campuses in terms of curriculum arrangements and scientific research resources. Finally, this article puts forward suggestions for problems that arise in development of newly-built university branch campuses: 1) Don't rush to recruit students; 2) Don't rely on main campuses' resources; 3) Establish a strict teacher supervision system.

Keywords: Student satisfaction · The development of university · University branch campus · New campus

1 Introduction

Running campuses in different places is a phenomenon that universities establish campuses in regions other than the original region due to the expansion of the education scale and government policies. The policy of running campuses in different places is

© Springer Nature Switzerland AG 2020
G. Salvendy and J. Wei (Eds.): HCII 2020, LNCS 12216, pp. 152–165, 2020.
https://doi.org/10.1007/978-3-030-50350-5_13

to provide development conditions for universities by using its own brand in conjunction with regional government support, the region's socio-economic and the region's educational resources [1]. Meanwhile, the development of the campus education can cultivate more talents for the region. In response to the concept of "rejuvenating the country through science and education", the Ministry of Education issued the *Education for the 21st Century Revitalization Action Plan* in 1999. In this plan, the concept of "increased enrollment" was introduced [2]. Due to the enrollment expansion policy, universities have gradually expanded their enrollment scale, which has resulted in the shortage of resources such as teaching and dormitory. Therefore, various universities have taken measures to solve these problems. The most common solution is to establish a branch campus in a new region, that is, to run a university branch campus. In addition, China faces the problem of imbalanced development of education resources. Education resources are more developed in first-tier cities such as Beijing, while education resources are relatively poor in third-tier cities. The lack of education resources has prevented these cities from developing rapidly, so local governments have adopted certain measures to attract universities to establish new campus in their city. Due to the promotion of various policies, running campuses in different places has gradually emerged and become a regular means for universities to expand enrollment [3]. Running campuses in different places can not only improve the competitiveness of universities in the education market, but also promote the educational development of the region that university branch campuses located [4].

For students, the construction of university branch campuses provides students with more education opportunities, and enables more students to receive undergraduate education. A lot of project 211's university branch campuses' admission line are lower than main campuses, so some students who cannot apply for the project 211's main campuses can choose to apply for the university branch campuses, so that some students can receive the same education as main campuses, which improves the level of education students received. What's more, the graduation certificates issued by some university branch campuses are consistent with main campuses, which makes more students choose to study in university branch campuses. Most courses in university branch campuses are taught in small classes, which is easier for students to accept than large classes in main campuses. Therefore, the development of the strategy of running campuses in different places not only helps universities respond to the policy of expanding enrollment, helps universities recruit more students, but also helps students improve their chances of choosing a university.

The strategy of running campuses in different places has solved the problems of the enrollment scale of various universities, but has also brought many problems to the development of university branch campuses. For instance, the management system of the campus is inadequate, the management of students and teachers lacks standards, and university branch campuses lack excellent resident teaching staff. Because university branch campuses are relatively far from main campuses, the two campuses cannot communicate timely. Teachers in main campuses need to spend a lot of time in transportation to teach in university branch campuses, so only a few teachers volunteer to teach at university branch campuses. Newly-built university branch campuses often lack scientific research facilities which results in fewer resources available to students, so it is not conducive to students' independent and innovative development [5]. In view of the current situation of running campuses in different places, this article mainly analyzes the problems existing in running newly-built university branch campuses from the perspective of students, and proposes solutions to these problems.

2 Literature Review

According to the survey, more than half of the project 211 have adopted a policy of running campuses in different places, and some universities have not only established university branch campuses in one region. For example, Harbin Institute of Technology has established campuses in Weihai and Shenzhen, and Shandong University has established campuses in Weihai and Qingdao. In addition to the campuses that have already recruited students, many universities have signed contracts or are building their university branch campuses. When investigating the selection of regions to build university branch campuses, it is found that the regions are mostly concentrated in coastal regions such as Shenzhen, Zhuhai, Weihai and Qingdao. The number of universities in coastal regions is relatively small compared to developed regions, but coastal regions need high-quality talents to drive economic development. Therefore, building campuses in coastal regions not only meets the needs of universities but also meets the needs of talents in coastal areas [6].

Qiuheng Shi and Min Kang [7] introduce the multi-campus university system in the United States and Japan, and compared it with university branch campuses in China. The authors propose that the current definition of university branch campuses is not clear. Generally, most people position university branch campuses as a platform for expanding the discipline space. In addition, university branch campuses lack the actual investigation and rational judgment on the needs of local higher education. Zhigan Qian [8] points out that newly-built university branch campuses have problems in the students' ideological education, including the contradiction between functional positioning and student development needs, obstacles to communication between teachers and students, an unformed mature life community. Weak strength of ideological and political is not conducive to the education and management of students' ideological and political affairs, and it is not conducive to the condensing of campus atmosphere. Zhenming Lyu and Guoping Zhou [9] think that there exist problems in university branch campuses in terms of resource allocation, multiple governance, and campus culture construction. Due to the distance, it is not convenient for university branch campuses to exchange information with main campuses, and it cannot guarantee that all the teachers in university branch campuses will be teachers from main campuses, so the quality of teaching cannot be guaranteed to be consistent with main campuses. And because university branch campuses are more oriented towards serving local needs in terms of school running philosophy, the university branch campuses and main campuses have formed two inconsistent campus cultures. Meilin Gong and Jie Yang [10] argue that there is a large gap between university branch campuses and main campuses in terms of discipline construction, teaching staff, and scientific research hardware facilities and resources. The authors conclude that main campuses can apply and obtain more projects supported by *The National Natural Science Funds* than university branch campuses by counting and comparing the projects in two campuses. Due to the lack of discipline construction and other aspects, the scientific research development of university branch campuses and main campuses is unbalanced, resulting in the scientific research construction of university branch campuses is far behind main campuses. Philip G. Altbach [11] indicates that the lack of appropriate laboratory equipment and personnel may make scientific research projects on university branch campuses impossible. Therefore, for university branch campuses, the campus is teaching-oriented rather than research-oriented. However, some part-time teachers in university branch campuses may not be able to reach the teaching level of teachers in main campuses, which brings challenges to the teaching quality of university branch campuses. Philip G. Altbach [12] also indicates that university branch campuses have many problems in teachers, students and replicating the main campus. First of all, it is difficult for university branch campuses to attract teachers from main campuses to teach in university branch campuses for a long time. Therefore, the curriculum arrangement is relatively intensive. Secondly, the intensive curriculum arrangement will cause students to study under pressure. Finally, university branch campuses cannot be consistent with the main campus in terms of the breadth and depth of research facilities and courses. Hence, when establishing university branch campuses, sustainability should be a core issue. So, whether university branch campuses can last for a long time remains to be verified. Jeff Hoyt and Scott Howell [13] use Brigham Young University as an example to analyze the reasons why students choose university branch campuses, including less class size, less group lessons, strong interaction with teachers, and being able to get higher scores, so there are more students choose to study at university branch campuses.

In summary, running campuses in different places can alleviate the lack of educational space brought by the increase in the number of professional disciplines in universities, and promote the development of education in the places where university branch campuses are located. However, there have also been many problems that affect the quality of university branch campuses. Only by solving these problems can play the role of university branch campuses to cultivate talents in universities.

3 Research Methods

According to the literature, there are certain problems in the construction of university branch campuses in many aspects. This article studies the problems of the development of university branch campuses from the perspective of students. Before investigating problems in the construction of university branch campuses, this article uses questionnaire survey to investigate the factors that affect students' satisfaction with the university. First, we process the obtained data, then use regression analysis to test, and finally select the more significant influencing factors. Only by understanding which factors have an impact on student satisfaction, can study the problems of university branch campuses from a more detailed perspective. According to the influencing factors selected, this article analyzes the problems of newly-built university branch campuses from these aspects.

3.1 Analysis of Students' Satisfaction

Jianfang Zhu [14] proposes to build a "student-centered" teaching quality guarantee system in universities, and strengthen the construction of laboratories to ensure that scientific research facilities are complete. The result of Yuanlin Hu's [15] research on influencing factors of undergraduate college students' learning satisfaction shows that teaching level, teaching relationship and learning atmosphere are the main factors affecting the undergraduate college students' learning satisfaction. Therefore, students' satisfaction with the university will be affected by many factors, and the influence degree of each factor on university satisfaction is not the same. This article takes students' satisfaction with curriculum arrangements, teacher resources, scientific research atmosphere, teaching facilities, university environment, and student activities as the characteristic variables that affect students' satisfaction, and proposes hypotheses: students' satisfaction with curriculum arrangements, teacher resources, research atmosphere, teaching facilities, university environment, and student activities positively affect students' satisfaction with the university, and students' satisfaction with curriculum arrangements, teacher resources, and research atmosphere have a significant impact on students' satisfaction. Curriculum arrangements mainly refer to cultivating scheme and teaching arrangements. Teacher resources mainly refer to teachers' professional knowledge and ethics. Scientific research atmosphere mainly refers to academic information communication, innovative activities and academic atmosphere. Teaching facilities mainly refer to laboratories and other equipment. University environment mainly refers to the humanities and natural landscapes. Student activities mainly refer to activities' type, activities' content and support of the university.

According to various influencing factors, establish a model to analyze the relationship between students' satisfaction with the university and various characteristic variables. The model was constructed as follows:

$$Y = \alpha_1 + \beta_1 X_1 + \beta_2 X_2 + \ldots + \beta_6 X_6 + \varepsilon \tag{1}$$

Keep the students' satisfaction with the university unchanged, analyze the impact of various variables on satisfaction, and gradually eliminate the characteristic variables that have little or no impact. In the model expression (1), it is assumed that Y is students' satisfaction with the university, and X_i ($i = 1, 2, 3, 4, 5, 6$) is each characteristic variable that affects the students' satisfaction with the university, that is, X_1 is the degree of students' satisfaction with curriculum arrangements. X_2 is the degree of students' satisfaction with teacher resources. X_3 is the degree of students' satisfaction with the scientific research atmosphere. X_4 is the degree of students' satisfaction with teaching facilities. X_5 is the degree of students' satisfaction with the university environment, and X_6 is the degree of students' satisfaction with the student activities.

The data of this survey are obtained by publishing an online questionnaire. The questionnaire uses "Likert five-level scale" to assign values to all variables from low to high, which 1 is very dissatisfied, 2 is relatively dissatisfied, 3 is average, 4 is more satisfied, and 5 is very satisfied. The magnitude of the value indicates the students' evaluation of the various influencing factors.

We use SPSS to test the data collected in the questionnaire, and obtain the following results:

According to the multiple regression model, use SPSS to comprehensively analyze the six factors of students' satisfaction with the curriculum arrangement, teacher resources, scientific research atmosphere, teaching facilities, university environment and student activities. Table 1 shows the fitting degree according to the six characteristic variables of curriculum arrangement, teacher resources, scientific research atmosphere, teaching facilities, school environment, and student activities. From the table, the correlation coefficient R is 0.991, and the coefficient of determination R square is 0.981, the adjusted R square is 0.980, so the six variables have a strong explanatory power for university satisfaction, so the judge index selected in this article have a certain feasibility. According to Table 2, the VIF values of the six characteristic variables are all less than 10, which indicates there is no multicollinearity problem among the independent variables. The coefficient of each variable is greater than 0, and the *sig* of curriculum arrangement, teacher resources, and scientific research atmosphere are less than 0.05, that is, the significance is strong. The hypothesis in this article is verified. Therefore, this article starts from these three aspects, and sets up a new questionnaire to analyze the problems of university branch campuses in these three aspects.

Table 1. Model summary

Model	R	R square	Adjusted R square	Std. error of the estimate	Change statistics				
					R square change	F change	df1	df2	Sig. F change
1	.991ᵃ	.981	.980	.092	.981	806.446	6	92	.000

ᵃPredictors: (Constant), Student Activities, University Environment, Curriculum Arrangement, Teaching Facilities, Scientific Research Atmosphere, Teacher Resources

3.2 Analysis of the Problems in University Branch Campuses

Due to the different forms and times of running campuses in different places, there are different problems in different universities branch campuses. In response to the problems of running campuses in different places raised in the proposal of *The First Meeting of The Thirteenth National Committee of The Chinese people's Political Consultative Conference*, the Ministry of Education replied that "China's higher education should not be scaled up blindly. It supports university branch campuses for universities that have improved school conditions and the teaching quality, but it will strictly monitor universities that are eager to compete and develop blindly". In addition, according to the Ministry of Education, building university branch campuses is always disagreed. As the method of running campuses in different places is being adopted by more and more universities, the Ministry of Education has issued that running campuses in different places should be managed strictly. There are many problems in the management of university branch campuses, so the management of university branch campuses will become a major problem for the development of universities.

This article uses a case study method to deeply study the current problems of newly-built university branch campuses. The data was collected using online questionnaires. The same questionnaires were issued to a newly-built university branch campus and the main campus. The questionnaires were for students in the newly-built university branch campus and the main campus. The questionnaire includes 17 questions. The

Table 2. Coefficients

Model		Unstandardized coefficients		Standardized coefficients	t	Sig.	Collinearity statistics	
		B	Std. Error	Beta			Tolerance	VIF
1	(Constant)	−.328	.146		−2.240	.028		
	Curriculum arrangement	.118	.032	.114	3.625	.000	.206	4.851
	Teacher resources	.250	.038	.249	6.668	.000	.146	6.866
	Scientific research atmosphere	.622	.033	.631	18.913	.000	.182	5.485
	Teaching facilities	.031	.027	.035	1.143	.256	.215	4.649
	University environment	.029	.027	.021	1.067	.289	.529	1.891
	Student activities	.041	.022	.044	1.837	.069	.346	2.892

[a]Dependent Variable: Student Satisfaction

main question is to investigate students' satisfaction of curriculum arrangement, the resources they enjoy and the overall impression of the campus. Some of the questions are: whether students can digest the knowledge learned during the course arrangement. If not, whether the reason is related to the time or method of the course arrangement; whether the student has access to take part in more scientific research projects in school period and obtain teachers' guidance during the completion of the projects. Compare the survey result of these two campuses to obtain the difference of students' learning situation and scientific research between the newly-built university branch campus and the main campus.

4   Research Results

According to the results of the questionnaire, on the whole, students from the main campus mainly scored 80–90 points on the main campus, with 11% above 90 and below 70. The result is shown in Fig. 1. The score of students from the newly-built university branch campus is concentrated on 70–80 points, 90–100 points account for 0, and less than 70 points account for 30%. The result is shown in Fig. 2.

Judging from the results, students in the newly-built university branch campus are less satisfied with the campus, so there are still some problems in the construction of newly-built university branch campuses in meeting the requirements of students.

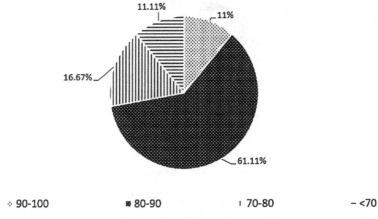

Fig. 1. The main campus's score

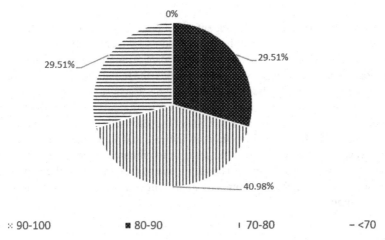

Fig. 2. The newly-built university branch campus's score

4.1 Curriculum Arrangement

Regarding the curriculum arrangement, the results of the questionnaire survey show that compared with the students in the main campus, it is more difficult for students in the university campus to digest their knowledge within a specified period of time. The main reason is that the course is too tightly scheduled and before taking this course students have taken a long time for other courses. The result is shown in Fig. 3. As a result, students' energy cannot be focused.

In order to maintain the same teaching quality as the main campus, the newly-built university campus had to rely on the teachers of the main campus in the early stages of running the campus. Because the teachers teach the courses in the two campuses, the same courses will be arranged centrally, and most of courses are arranged in the

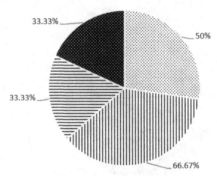

33.33%

50%

33.33%

66.67%

∴ The curriculum is too tight (More lessons a day)   ꟾ Have taken more courses before taking this course

– Teaching speed is too fast   ▪ Irrational study schedule

Fig. 3. Reasons why students in the newly-built university branch campus cannot digest what they have learned

same time period. During this time, students must not only digest the knowledge taught by the teachers, but also complete the exams and assignments, which leads to greater learning pressure for the students. In addition, when arranging courses, the university first considers the schedule time of the main campus, the remaining time of the teacher is arranged to teach in the newly-built university campus. Because some courses are related, if the two courses are taught separately, it may cause students to forget the knowledge of previous subjects and not be able to contact the knowledge of other courses. Some students in the newly-built university campus indicate that there are still more courses in the senior year, which results in insufficient time to prepare for the IELTS, TOFEL and postgraduate entrance examination. Therefore, due to the reliance of the main campus, there are many unreasonable phenomena in curriculum arrangement of the newly-built university campus.

4.2 Scientific Research Resources

Due to the incomplete facilities of the newly-built university campus, students cannot enjoy the same resources as the main campus. By investigating the participation of scientific research competitions of students in the main campus and the newly-built university campus, it is found that students in the main campus participate in scientific research competitions more times, the survey results are shown in Fig. 4 and Fig. 5.

Secondly, we investigate the reasons why fewer students participate in scientific research competitions in the newly-built university campus. The number of students who choose "no contact with instructors" in the newly-built university campus accounts for 47.5%. The result is shown in Fig. 6.

Finally, we investigate the reasons why students in different campuses think they can win a prize after participating in scientific research competitions. In the main campus, 50% of the students choose "teacher's guidance". The result is shown in Fig. 7. In the newly-built university campus, only 9% of the students choose "teacher's guidance". The result is shown in Fig. 8.

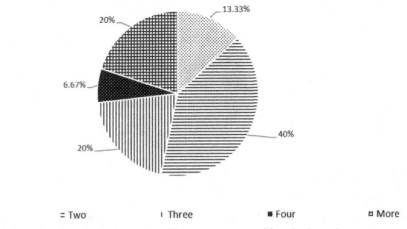

·∴ One   ≡ Two   ı Three   ■ Four   ▫ More

Fig. 4. Number of participating in scientific research competitions in the main campus

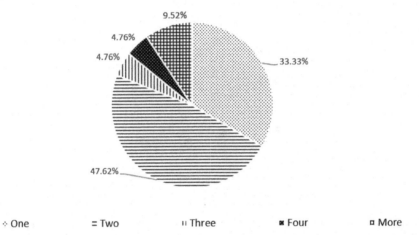

·∴ One   ≡ Two   ıı Three   ■ Four   ▫ More

Fig. 5. Number of participating in scientific research competitions in the newly-built university campus

Students in the newly-built university campus have less access to obtain scientific research resources and receive long-term and stable guidance from teachers, so they often do not participate in scientific research competitions. Generally, teachers have more scientific research projects in the main campus. Because the newly-built university campus lacks research facilities, if teachers transfer research projects to the newly-built university campus, the lack of scientific research facilities may lead to the inability to complete projects and affect the projects' progress. So, teachers generally do not transfer research projects to the newly-built university campus. Because teachers' work on the main campus, there are hardly any teachers are resident in the newly-built university campus. As a result, when students need teachers' guidance in scientific research or study, they cannot communicate with the teachers in time and get timely help. Therefore, in terms of enjoying scientific research resources and teacher resources, students in the newly-built university campus cannot able to ask teachers about academic and scientific

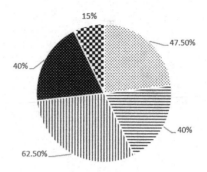

Fig. 6. Reasons why fewer students participate in scientific research competitions in the newly-built university campus

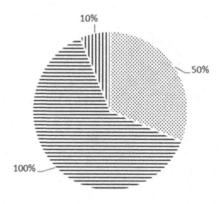

Fig. 7. Reasons students think for winning a prize after participating in scientific research competitions in the main campus

research issues in teachers' free time. So, the newly-built university campus unable to get the same resource support as the main campus.

In the last question of the questionnaire, students can put forward suggestions for the development of their own campus. Some suggestions made by students in the newly-built university campus are shown in Fig. 9. From the student's suggestions, more suggestions from students in the newly-built university campus are directed to management to campus, curriculum arrangements and teacher resources.

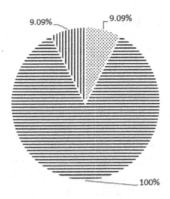

Teacher's guidance   – Team effort   Stable project facility

Fig. 8. Reasons students think for winning a prize after participating in scientific research competitions in the newly-built university campus

	A	B
1	Answer	
2	Hope to have a stadium	
3	Facilities need to be perfect and system management is chaotic	
4	Everyone cannot learn useful knowledge, which increases the cost of education for classmates and schools	
5	Teachers need to be better	
6	Contact with the main campus	
7	Don't arrange so many lessons in junior and senior years, and there are about ten coursework at the same time, it is difficult to have time to prepare for GRE and language	
8	The campus is too small. I hope to expand it.	
9	I hoped that major hardware facilities such as supermarkets will be out of monopoly operation as soon as possible	
10	Hurry to recruit students and teachers!	
11	The infrastructure is perfect, but I cannot get more and satisfactory help in many aspects related to teaching such as competition teaching	
12	Improve the management of educational administration	
13	Too many classes!	
14	Hope that the campus's administrative teacher do not always put students on the opposite side of the campus	
15	Improve the faculty, lecture activities and scientific research base	
16	Hope to provide more opportunities for large-scale volunteer activities	
17	Many places are unreasonable	

Fig. 9. Student's suggestions to their campus (the newly-built university campus)

5 Discussion and Conclusion

Based on the results of the questionnaire, in view of the problems existing in the newly-built university campus proposed, this article puts forward suggestions for the development of newly-built university campuses.

5.1 Don't Rush to Recruit Students

Some newly-built university campuses begin to recruit students after completing the construction of infrastructure, and improve campus facilities while training students. Although students can successfully complete the required courses, the lack of teaching and scientific research facilities may result in students not being able to use campuses' facilities resources to meet their needs for scientific research, and then complete their scientific research goals. At the same time, if campuses build some facilities later than planned, it will increase students' dissatisfaction with the campus. Based on this, newly-built university campuses should recruit students after the various facilities of the campus have been perfected, so that not only there will be complete promotional materials, but also students can use the resources available in the campus to plan their study and scientific research. Students' evaluation of the campus will affect the enrollment of the campus to a certain extent in the next few years. If the campus meets the needs of students, then the increase of students' satisfaction with campus will increase the publicity of the campus, and the enrollment quality of the campus will be improved. The government can also play a supervisory role in the recruitment of newly-built university campuses, and work with the campus to plan a reasonable recruitment time, which avoid the campus's rush to recruit students to ignore the construction and management of the campus.

5.2 Don't Rely on Main Campuses' Resources

In order to lay the foundation of the educational resources of the campus, newly-built university campuses need teachers from main campuses to complete the teaching tasks of the campus. Teachers traveling between the two places will not only consume teachers' time, but also reduce the teachers' energy during the class, so the quality of teaching will be affected. Therefore, using external teachers will reduce the teaching pressure of teachers in main campuses. However, using external teachers do not mean that newly-built university campuses recruited teachers independently. Teacher recruitment in newly-built university campuses should have the same requirements as main campuses, and the teacher must pass the same assessments as teachers recruited in main campuses. Only qualified teachers who have been recruited and selected by main campuses can work in newly-built university campuses. When main campuses recruit teachers, newly-built university campuses can mark the lack of subject teachers. Teachers who pass the assessment can choose whether to teach in the newly-built university campus or in the main campus. Teachers in newly-built university campuses should carry out the research projects in newly-built university campuses. In this way, not only can teachers be spared from running around and have sufficient time to complete their own scientific research projects, but also enable students to complete their courses and participate in certain scientific research projects to improve their scientific research knowledge and level.

5.3 Establish a Strict Teacher Supervision System

If external teachers are used in newly-built university campuses, in order to avoid the inattention of external teachers to the teaching tasks of newly-built university campuses, it is necessary to strengthen the supervision of teachers. Teacher morality is the top priority of teacher supervision. Campuses can regularly allow students to evaluate teachers in terms of teaching attitude and teaching quality in the assessment system. Campuses should give warning to teachers that students think the teaching attitude is poor and the teaching quality is low. If teachers who are warned do not change their teaching attitude, campuses can choose to fire the teacher. Teachers should be assessed regularly, and campuses should warn or fire teachers who do not meet the requirements. In addition, establish a suitable teacher incentive system, and give certain rewards to teachers of good teaching quality, which have a certain stimulating effect on teacher's teaching and make the teacher teach more seriously. Teachers in newly-built university campuses need to report the teaching results and the next stage of teaching tasks to the main campus on a regular basis to ensure that the teaching tasks are recognized by the main campus, so that the newly-built university campus have the same teaching arrangements and quality as the main campus.

References

1. Nan, W.: The rational examination of long-distance education in colleges and Universities-Zhangjiagang in Jiangsu university of science and technology campus as reference. Forum Contemp. Educ. (04), 10–19 (2015)
2. Zhang, W.: Reflections on the path of multi-sectional and multi-campus management. Guide Sci. Educ. (04), 4–6 (2015)
3. Jia, X.: Research on the development model of higher education in central cities—taking Shenzhen as an example. Educ. Rev. (05), 14–17 (2019)
4. Liu, B., Zhong, Y.: Research on the development and problems of the model of running campuses in different universities. New Curric. Res. (04), 134–136 (2017)
5. Cheng, Y.: Analysis of some problems needing attention in the process of running campuses in China. Mod. Bus. Trade Ind. **39**(20), 160–162 (2018)
6. Ma, R., Li, W., Xu, F.: On the development of higher education in coastal areas—taking Jiangsu province as an example. Heilongjiang Res. High. Educ. **30**(02), 74–76 (2012)
7. Shi, Q., Kang, M.: Research and comments on universities with multi-campuses in different cities. J. Natl. Acad. Educ. Adm. (07), 21–27 (2017)
8. Qian, Z., Ye, F., Liu, Y.: Study on ideological education and management of college students in campuses of different regions. Sci. Educ. Artic. Collects (02), 6–8 (2017)
9. Lyu, Z., Zhou, G.: Evolution, dilemma and countermeasures of running branch campuses of Chinese Universities. J. Ningbo University (Educ. Sci. Edition) **40**(04), 64–68 (2018)
10. Gong, M., Yang, J.: The difficulties and their corresponding measures on the different area campus scientific research in the multi-campus university mode. Sci. Technol. Manag. Res. **37**(12), 91–96 (2017)
11. Altbach, P.G.: Twinning and branch campuses. In: Altbach, P.G. (ed.) The International Imperative in Higher Education. GPHE, pp. 107–109. SensePublishers, Rotterdam (2013). https://doi.org/10.1007/978-94-6209-338-6_23
12. Altbach, P.: Why branch campuses may be unsustainable. Int. High. Educ. (58) (2015)
13. Hoyt, J., Howell, S.: Why students choose the branch campus of a large university. J. Continuing High. Educ. **60**, 110–116 (2012)
14. Zhu, J.: Research and practice of student-centered internal teaching quality assurance system in colleges and university. Heilongjiang Res. High. Educ. **37**(05), 138–141 (2019)
15. Hu, Y.: The study of the influencing factors on learning satisfaction in local universities. High. Educ. Explor. (03), 43–50 (2018)

An Empirical Research on Factors Influencing Virtual Community Members Shift Toward E-Commerce Buyers

Guangming Yang[1], Zhongwei Gu[2(⊠)], and June Wei[3]

[1] Zhejiang University of Science and Technology, Hangzhou, China
holycloud@sohu.com
[2] Shanghai Dianji University, Pudong, Shanghai, China
zwgu@qq.com
[3] University of West Florida, Pensacola, FL, USA
jwei@uwf.edu

Abstract. With the growing number of virtual community providers entering the e-commerce transactions market, the mechanism affecting the community users shift to e-commerce buyers has gradually aroused the concern of industry and academia. Based on trust mechanism, the value of information and risk cost theory, this paper constructs the transformation model of the virtual community of users. To select members of the community survey, we collected a total of 269 valid questionnaires. After data processing and analysis, the results indicate that perceived purposeful value of virtual community members significantly positively affects community trading platform trust. Perceived purposeful value of virtual community members has a significant positive impact on their purchase intention of virtual community trading platform, and thus significantly affect the purchase intention. Community trading platform trust significantly positively affects users' purchase intention.

Keywords: Virtual community users transformation · Trust · Information value

1 Introduction

According to the 2019 research report of Chinese community users and webmasters published by IRESEARCH Consulting Group, by Q1 2019, the monthly coverage of Chinese online communities was 370 million people, the monthly browsing time was 300 million hours, and the monthly visiting page number was 15.85 billion pages. The rapidly developing network virtual community has a large scale of users, and at the same time has a good user stickiness and user access depth, which is very conducive to the development of other forms of new applications or network marketing, in order to create better market value. Traditional community enterprises almost all rely on selling advertising to survive, lack of an effective way to convert community popularity into commercial value. With the continuous development of internet applications, a new "community + e-commerce" model has become a new way for many community enterprises

G. Salvendy and J. Wei (Eds.): HCII 2020, LNCS 12216, pp. 166–173, 2020.
https://doi.org/10.1007/978-3-030-50350-5_14

to survive. TIEXUE has established an e-commerce platform for TIEXUE's conduct. 80% of the company's turnover comes from e-commerce, while traditional advertising accounts for less than one-fifth of the business. Table 1 shows more examples of community enterprises establishing e-commerce transaction platforms. Another situation is that e-commerce enterprises establish communities to promote the communication and purchase of members, such as TAOBAO community, PDD community.

Table 1. Examples of virtual communities establishing community trading platforms

Virtual community	Community trading platform	Trades
TIEXUE	www.junph.com	Military articles, clothing, bags, boots, etc.
TIANYA	mall.tianya.cn	A wide variety of goods
HAICI	store.dict.cn	Learning materials, software, electronic equipment
19LOU	www.19lou.com/haodian	Various goods and services

Community users communicate with each other, release information and obtain information, which is a long-term process to establish a certain circle of discussion. Circle members trust each other based on common topics. This sense of trust is key to sustaining community development. But when it comes to community trading platforms, will the trust of community users be transferred correspondingly? This is trust transfer. Although a large number of literatures at home and abroad have studied online purchasing behaviors from the perspective of consumer trust, these studies have all considered consumers' trust in online and mobile stores under online and mobile environments, and less considered the problem of users' trust in virtual communities turning to the trust of community shopping platforms. Community users sharing knowledge and information together for a long time will have a certain impact on their purchasing decisions. Research shows that about 61.7% of community users make purchase decisions based on other people's opinions. A virtual community is an information exchange platform where users can obtain the consumption experience of other members. For example, when many people buy a certain product or service, they will look at other consumers' comments on the product or service. Through this sharing of information to reduce their own concerns. However, the influence of information sharing is based on the judgment of users on the perceived value of information. Users only need to pay a certain amount of time, physical strength and energy to participate in the virtual community, but they need to pay the monetary cost for shopping and bear the possible risks in the transaction process. That is, community users often consider perceived risks and costs when they turn to community trading platforms. Therefore, based on trust transfer theory, information theory and risk cost, this paper builds a virtual community users into the community trade influence model, the research community trust whether impact on community trust trading platform, how the user's trust and perceived risk value and cost effect on purchase intentions together, in the hope of promoting the transformation of community of users to the community trade.

2 Study Models and Hypothesis

For information value, from the perspective of consumers, it is not defined by commercial enterprises, but by the value of information perceived by consumers, that is, perceived value. Zeithaml proposed the concept of perceived value as early as 1988. He described perceived value as the evaluation of the overall utility of a product or service made by consumers after weighing and comparing the benefits they feel with the costs they pay in the process of acquiring the product or service [1]. Spreng also believes that customer perceived value is the customer's expectation of the outcome of the purchase from the perspective of future gains and losses [2]. Blackwell et al. investigated customer loyalty of service products and proposed a value loyalty model. They believed that customer perceived value was a balance between customer perceived gain and perceived loss, and believed that this balance was formed gradually [3]. The definition of perceived value studied by these scholars later became a widely accepted concept among researchers. Herrmann et al. believe that the main factors influencing perceived value are information acquisition ability, experience, learning ability, time and economic factors, such as money [4]. Extending these studies, this paper proposes the following hypotheses:

H1: Perceived purposeful value of virtual community members significantly positively affects community trading platform trust.
H2: Perceived purposeful value of virtual community members has a significant positive impact on their purchase intention of virtual community trading platform.

McKenna et al. believe that virtual community members have strong social drivers, namely social connection and social reinforcement [5]. In a virtual community, certain social benefits can be obtained through connection and communication with others, such as intimacy among members, elimination of loneliness, meeting people with similar views, establishment of benefits among people and acquisition of certain social support. In addition, community members can gain recognition and attention from others due to their contributions, so that the status of individuals in the virtual community can be improved, so as to receive respect from others and have a certain sense of achievement. Fan Xiaoping believes that the network, anonymity, online interaction and borderless nature of virtual communities make communities have special cultural and social characteristics. Virtual community with strong gathering power is essentially because it can bring benefits to community members and meet their different needs. Virtual community is the extension of the real society on the Internet, and in some aspects, it is the supplement and reinforcement of the real society. Virtual community is a place where members and organizers create value together and share value together [6]. Extending these studies, this paper believes that the higher the social value perceived by community members, the more likely it is to influence their trust in and purchase intention of community trading platform. Therefore, it proposes the following hypothesis:

H3: Perceived social value of virtual community members significantly positively affects community trading platform trust.
H4: Perceived social value of virtual community members significantly affects the purchase intention of community members.

Bauer introduced the psychological concept of perceived risk into the research of marketing earlier. He believed that perceived risk was caused by consumer behavior, which consumers could not predict for sure and was inconsistent with their own wishes [7]. Engel believes that perceived risk is a consumer's cognition of whether there is a risk before buying a certain commodity or service. Hsin believes that perceived risk is a consumer's perception of the uncertainty of purchasing goods and services and the opposite result of activity, which is generally used to explain consumers' purchasing decision behavior [8]. Dowling believes that perceived risk is the uncertainty that consumers perceive when they buy a product or service about the adverse structure that might occur. At the same time, consumers are accustomed to avoid risks, so consumer behavior is closely related to perceived risks [9]. Compared with traditional face-to-face transactions, online transactions have more uncertainties. Therefore, in recent years, more scholars have conducted researches on consumers' perceived risks in the network environment. Therefore this paper proposes the following hypothesis:

H5: Perceived risk of virtual community members significantly negatively affects community trading platform trust.
H6: Perceived risk of virtual community members significantly negatively affects the purchase intention of community members.

Lee et al. studied the transfer of offline trust to online trust, pointing out that trust transfer is a cognitive process in which people's trust in one field affects their trust and attitude towards other fields. He also studied different trust transfer processes, that is, trust transfer within channels and trust transfer between channels. The transfer of trust in a channel means that the trust of a user in a product will affect his trust in another product in the same channel. Trust between channels refers to the transfer process of trust between different channels [10].

H7: Community trading platform trust significantly positively affects users' purchase intention.

To sum up, the research model proposed in this paper is shown in Fig. 1.

3   Research Method

On the basis of a large number of related literature studies, the research scale of this paper is developed by referring to the previous research results and combining with the background of this paper. After the initial scale was designed, three scholars in this field and five users of the virtual community trading platform were invited to put forward their views and opinions, and some adjustments were made based on their Suggestions. Then, the modified scale was pre-tested in a small range, and the scale description was modified according to the results of the pre-test and the questions of the tested objects. All measure terms adopt 7 points Likert method, 1 means strongly disagree, 7 means strongly agree.

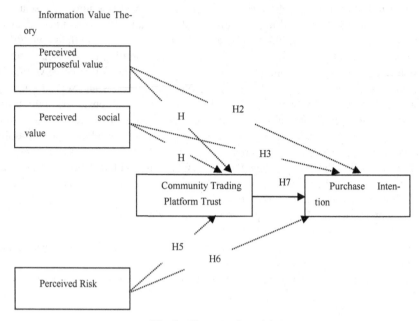

Fig. 1. Conceptual model

This study selected TIEXUE, TIANYA, HAICI and 19LOU as data sources. Since the respondents are users with shopping experience on the community exchange platform, the questionnaire is mainly published in the community forum in the form of rewards, but the questionnaire recovery rate is relatively low. After that, questionnaires were sent out by mutual recommendation of friends in the community, with a high recovery rate. After sorting out the recovered questionnaires, a total of 269 valid questionnaires were obtained. The men surveyed are slightly more than the women, with the age distribution concentrated between 18 and 30, the most active group of Internet users.

4   Data Analysis and Hypothesis Testing

Principal component factor analysis and confirmatory factor analysis were used to test the measurement model. Bartlett's Test of Sphericity showed that the KMO (Kaiser - Meyer-Olkin) value of the sample data was 0.821 and significant at the level of 0.01, indicating that the scale was suitable for principal component analysis. According to the standard that the characteristic value is greater than 1, 7 factors are extracted, the variance interpretation rate is 78.564%, and the load value of each indicator's corresponding factor is greater than 0.5, while the factor load value of the cross variable is less than 0.5, indicating that each indicator can effectively reflect its corresponding factor and the scale validity can be guaranteed.

This paper uses confirmatory factor analysis to test the reliability and validity of variables. AVE of each variable was greater than 0.6, indicating that the scale had good validity. Cronbach's alpha of each factor is greater than 0.7, indicating that the scale has good reliability. Composite Reliability (CR) was used to evaluate the internal consistency of the model, and the results showed that the CR value of each variable was higher than 0.7, indicating that the scale had good reliability. Since the standard load of some measures is too low, these indicators, such as PSV3 and PR3, are deleted. The results of confirmatory factor analysis are shown in Table 2.

Table 2. Load measurement standards and average variance extracted

Factor	Item	Standard loading	AVE	CR	Cronbach's Alpha
Purchase intention	INT1	0.73	0.72	0.83	0.901
	INT2	0.81			
Trading platform trust	TOP1	0.67	0.79	0.86	0.827
	TOP2	0.82			
	TOP3	0.79			
	TVC2	0.85			
	TVC3	0.64			
Perceived purposeful value	PPV1	0.72	0.64	0.84	0.754
	PPV2	0.71			
	PPV3	0.69			
Perceived social value	PSV1	0.78	0.63	0.71	0.821
	PSV2	0.76			
Perceived risk	PR1	0.65	0.62	0.75	0.801
	PR2	0.70			
	PC2	0.68			

LISREL is used to test the hypothesis of the model. It shows the results after the hypothesis test. Perceived purposive value and perceived social value significantly affect purchase intention, verifying H2 and H3, but not H1 and H4. Perceived risk significantly negatively affects the trading platform's trust and purchase intention, while perceived cost significantly negatively affects purchase intention, which verifies H5, H6 and H7.

5 Conclusion

Based on trust transfer theory, information value, this paper constructs a research model to influence the transformation of virtual community users to community transaction users. Based on the data collection and analysis of the users who have successfully transferred from virtual community services to e-commerce, it is found that the trust of virtual community plays an important role in influencing the trust of community members to the community trading platform and the purchase decision process. The results are as follows.

Perceived purposive value and perceived social value significantly positively affect users' purchase intention, but have no significant impact on the trust of the trading platform. This is consistent with the findings of Dodds et al. The perceived value of users to the virtual community includes purposive value, self-discovery, social reinforcement, maintenance of interpersonal relationship and entertainment value, all of which strengthen users' perception of the usefulness and quality of the virtual community and thus influence users' behaviors. Virtual community service providers should, through various channels, such as in-depth rational discussion of people's life concerns, enhance users' perceived value of virtual community through rational analysis, so as to potentially guide users' purchase behavior.

Perceived risk significantly negatively affects purchase intention. In the context of the transformation of virtual community users into community trading platform customers, the traditional risk and cost perception still has a significant negative impact on the purchase intention of customers, but the degree of such impact is relatively small compared with the trust and value perception of virtual community. Virtual community service providers to build e-commerce trading platform, still need to take some traditional marketing methods to promote the success of the trading platform.

References

1. Zeithaml, V.A.: Consumer perceptions of price quality, and value: a means-end model and synthesis of evidence. J. Mark. **52**(3), 2–22 (1988)
2. Spreng, R.A.: A desires congruency model of consumer satisfaction. J. Acad. Mark. Sci. **21**(3), 169–177 (1993)
3. Blackwell, S.A., Szeinbach, S.L., Barnes, J.H.: The antecedents of customer loyalty. J. Serv. Res. **1**(4), 362–375 (1999)
4. Huber, F., Herrmann, A., Morgan, R.E.: Gaining competitive advantage through customer value oriented management. J. Consum. Mark. **18**(1), 41–53 (2001)
5. McKenna, K.Y.A., Bargh, J.A.: Causes and consequences of social interaction on the internet: a conceptual framework. Media Psychol. **1**, 249–269 (1999)
6. Fan, X.: Participation motivation of non-trading community members: empirical research and management implications. J. Manag. Eng. (1), 1–6 (2009)
7. Bauer, R.A.: Consumer behavior as risk taking: dynamic marketing for a changing world. In: Proceedings of the 43rd Conference of the American Marking Chicago: American Marketing Association, pp. 389–399 (1964)

8. Chang, H., Chen, S.W.: The impact of online store environment cues on purchase intention trust and perceived risk as a mediator. Online Inf. Rev. **32**(6), 818–841 (2008)
9. Dowling, G.R., Staelin, R.A.: Model of perceived risk and intended risk handling activity. J. Consum. Res. **21**(June), 119–134 (1994)
10. Lee, K.C., Kang, I., McKnight, D.H.: Transfer from offline trust to key online perceptions: an empirical study. IEEE Trans. Eng. Manag. **54**(4), 729–741 (2007)

Characteristics of Online Transaction Dispute Mediation Cases in Mobile Electronic Commerce

Lifan Yang[1(✉)] and Jingjing Xing[2]

[1] East China University of Political, Science and Law, Shanghai, China
cnyanglifan@163.com
[2] School of Management, Shanghai University of Science and Technology, Shanghai, China
305202591@qq.com

Abstract. Online dispute resolution (ODR) mode is an effective mechanism to resolve mobile e-commerce disputes. However, there are some obstacles in the development of ODR, such as low public acceptance, difficult technology realization and lack of uniform management standards. At present, the problem that needs to be studied urgently in the field of ODR is to analyze the characteristics of the case according to the ODR mediation case, to study which characteristics have an impact on the mediation results, and then to improve the efficiency of mediation. Based on the collection of mobile e-commerce transaction dispute mediation applications, this paper carries on the text mining, observes and summarizes the original text, extract variables from the text that can describe the case attribute information. The variables found to be able to distinguish the type of case are: X4 (whether the platform was involved), X9 (type of dispute), Y (case status), X8 (number of claims), X10 (type of product), X5 (number of respondent), X3 (number of applicant), X6 (amount of claim), X7 (difference ratio). The difference variables feature distribution can better describe the characteristics of the cases. According to the characteristics of case attributes, the second-order clustering method is used to cross-classification. In this paper, the ODR cases are divided into four categories. The paper find that the cases of mediation failure are mostly type I and type II, while the cases of mediation success are mostly type III and type IV. This kind of classification is advantageous to the mediator to the dispute case classification processing, enhances the mediation success rate.

Keywords: Online dispute resolution · Case mediation · Text mining · Second-order clustering

1 Introduction

Mobile e-commerce has become the most important way of e-commerce transactions. According to iResearch statistics, by November 2019, the number of independent devices in the APP industry used for online shopping reached 1.38 billion pieces, and the number of APP industry use for online shopping reached 60.26 billion times; in the APP hot use ranking, online shopping ranked first[1].

---

[1] iResearch. Mobile APP index [EB/OL] (2019-11-15)[2020-01-20]. https://index.iresearch.com. cn/new/#/app.

© Springer Nature Switzerland AG 2020
G. Salvendy and J. Wei (Eds.): HCII 2020, LNCS 12216, pp. 174–189, 2020.
https://doi.org/10.1007/978-3-030-50350-5_15

Because mobile e-commerce buyers and sellers are usually in a long space distance, information exchange mostly depends on online third-party trading platform, and generally need to use logistics as an intermediate link to complete the transaction. Therefore, compared with the traditional offline transactions, online transactions have the characteristics of asymmetric information between buyers and sellers, and there are risks in the intermediate links, which are more likely to cause disputes.

Taking China as an example, the China Consumer Association published on Jan 17,2020, "An Analysis of the Complaints Received by the National Consumer Association in 2019" [2] shows that 821,377 complaints were received by the National Consumer Association in 2019, of which 33,436 complains were remote shopping complaints, ranking third in the top 10 service complaints[2]. In 2019, the number of online shopping complaints reached 28,741, accounting for 85.9% of the number of remote shopping complaints. The frequent infringement of online shopping is needed to further strengthen the protection of consumer rights and interests. Figure 1 reflects the growth of complaint cases in the field of e-commerce in China in recent years[3] .

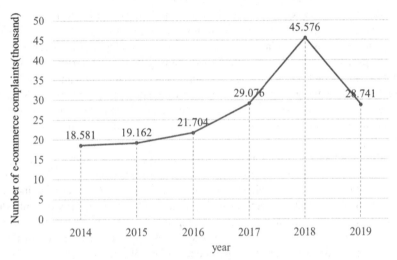

Fig. 1. The number of complaints in the field of e-commerce in China in recent years (thousand) Data source: China Consumer Association, website: http://www.cca.org.cn.

A large number of mobile e-commerce disputes cannot be resolved only by the courts. Litigation should not be the first choice for dispute resolution, and judicial justice should be the last line of defense for right relief. The disputes of mobile e-commerce should be solved efficiently and quickly in a proper way, and online dispute resolution (ODR)

---

[2] The top 10 service complaints are: operating Internet services, network access services, remote shopping, training, catering, beauty salon, mobile phone, accommodation, fitness, education services.

[3] China Consumer Association. Analysis of complaints received by the National Consumer Association in 2018[EB/OL]. (2019-01-23)[2019-12-21]. http://www.cca.org.cn/tsdh/list/19. html.

is a kind of solution that can meet the requirements of e-commerce. In the Internet age, ODR capacity has become an important part of the modernization of national governance system and governance capacity.

2 Literature Review

2.1 Research on ODR

Due to the appearance time of ODR is not long, the relevant research is relatively few, and the existing relevant literature mainly has the following categories.

The first category is a more systematic discussion of the ODR system itself. Stephanie (2003) [1] discussed the feasibility of ODR mechanism based on ADR (Alternative Dispute Resolution) dispute resolution mechanism. Ethan (2007) [2] studied the rules and standards of ODR. Pablo (2011) [3] analyzed the development of ODR in Europe based on the European consumer environment. Zheng Shibao (2012) [4] systematically studied the type and operation mechanism of ODR.

The second category is the discussion specific operation of the ODR. Karolina (2015) [5] takes the consumer regulation as an example to explore the specific methods of law formulation and unified regulation to resolve online disputes in e-commerce. Li Tao (2017) [6] proposed that China's online mediation system can be improved by incorporating online mediation into the legal system, standardizing relevant rules, building supporting systems and giving executive power to mediation agreements. Ju Ye (2013) [7] discussed the problem of consumer protection from three aspects: the formation of online transaction contract, the assumption of legal responsibility and the settlement of network dispute.

The third category is research on the solution effectiveness evaluation of the ODR platform. Zhao lei, Guo wenli (2019) [8] introduced the main recommendations for the ODR platform operation evaluation of the 19th world ODR conference, including: ① Evaluation of the ODR service provider, if the ODR service provider introduces advanced technology to expand the carrying capacity of the platform; ② Evaluation of the program rules, if the ODR program rules are rationality; ③ Evaluation of the user experience, if the user's reflection are good and the use of platform is ease. At the same time, it is suggested that the evaluation of users' feeling of using ODR should be carried out in terms of time cost, monetary cost, access mode, information access and use, and system guidance about resolution results; the justice of the evaluation procedure should take into account the differences with other procedures, the user's right to speak, respect, fairness and transparency; and the justice of the evaluation results, mainly in terms of whether the solution reflects the demands of the parties, whether there is an effective agreement, whether the solution plays a role and how it is implemented.

From the current world research situation, most of the existing research on ODR revolves around the legal significance and practical significance of the improvement or extension of the system itself, the vast majority of which are qualitative analysis, almost no use of practical application data as research materials, let alone the use of text analysis method to do quantitative analysis of the characteristics of ODR cases, there are gaps in this research.

2.2 Study on Text Classification

The origin of text classification technology can be traced back to the late 1950s, and after the 1990s, the text classification technology based on machine learning began to develop rapidly. Especially in the last two decades, with the continuous development of Internet technology and computer science, text classification technology has achieved many major breakthroughs.

Feature Selection. Text feature selection is to evaluate all the features in the original feature set according to some rule or some method after the text is preprocessed, and then to select the set of feature subsets that contribute the most to the text classification according to the evaluation results. Tabakhi (2014) [9] proposed an unsupervised feature selection algorithm based on ant colony optimization algorithm to find the optimal feature subset by several iterations without using any learning algorithm. Xie Juanying (2014) [10] combined order forward, order backward, order forward floating and order backward floating, and used support vector machine to guide feature selection process, and proposes four feature selection algorithms based on feature subset differentiation measurement criterion. Maruf. S (2016) [11] introduced feature selection algorithm based on random forest into the text classification domain. Liu Y N (2016) [12] proposed a hybrid feature selection method combining document frequency information and word frequency information, and presented a new feature subset evaluation parameter optimization method.

Method of Text Classification

1. Text classification based on machine learning. Wu Q Y (2014) [13] proposed an integration approach based on stochastic forest to address unbalanced text classification. Pang G S (2015) [14] proposed an extensible classifier, CenKNN, combining the K-nearest neighbor algorithm and the text classification method based on efficient centroid for solving unbalanced class distribution and redundancy and noise feature problems. Salles T (2017) [15] proposed a fully automatic time weighting function FA-TWF to reduce the time effect in text automatic classification and incorporated it into Rocchio, KNN and naive Bayes.
2. Classification of texts based on statistical methods. Li Ronglu (2005) [16] first used the maximum entropy model to study the Chinese text classification problem, and compared the classification performance with Bayes, KNN and SVM by experiments. Wang P (2009) [17] established a concept dictionary of synonyms and related relationships based on Wikipedia, and using the dictionary to expand the semantic relationship of the word bag which helps to improve the coverage of the word bag.
3. Classification of texts based on neural networks. Rossi (2014) [18] proposed a classification algorithm for text documents using the dichotomous network structure to derive the classification model, and assigned weight to the terms of each category association in the document using the derivation model based on bilateral heterogeneous networks. Du C (2018) [19] proposed a combination of the advantages of the text classification method based on the classification of keywords and classification of neural network semantic synthesis.

Although the research of text mining technology itself has been quite mature, the application of text mining technology in the field of ODR to analyze the characteristics of online transaction dispute cases is still in a blank state, which belongs to a very research potential direction.

3 Cluster Analysis Based on Property Characteristics of Online Transaction Disputes Cases

3.1 Basic Status of Cases

Table 1. Examples of case applications

Case ID	36305	
Type of case	Electronic commerce	
Place of occurrence	No. **, Streets **, Hangzhou City, Zhejiang Province, China	
Information of Plaintiff	Name: ***	
	Sex: Male	
	Age: 60	
	Contact: ******	
Information of defendant	Defendant I	Name:***
		Sex: Male
		Age: 51
		Contact:******
	Defendant II	Name: *** (Legal representative of defendant's enterprise)
Cause of the case	On April 15, 2018, plaintiff bought 4 boxes of goods named "Thailand original authentic *** active oil" through Taobao (taobao.com) online shopping platform. The brand of oil is ***, 50 ml, special treatment for analgesia injury, bone pain, package mail. The plaintiff paid 312.00 RMB Yuan for transaction, order number is 135***". After the plaintiff paid, the defendant I used express delivery the goods, the waybill number is: 7701*** (Shentong express). After receiving the package, the plaintiff opened the package and found that the package box of the product was marked with "Taiquan active oil", the main treatment: falling injury, mosquito bite, soothing muscles and activating collaterals, abdominal pain and wind. It's a definite drug. China's "Drug Administration Law" clearly stipulates that drugs for import and sale without authorization approval shall be treated as counterfeit	

(continued)

Table 1. (*continued*)

	After inquiry, the criminal judgment of the Guangxi Zhuang Autonomous Region *** People's Court (2017) Gui No. *** Xingchu No. *** shows in the No."** case "*** active oil"is a fake medicine, the sale of the product is a sale of fake medicine. So the product plaintiff received is fake medicine clearly To sum up, the drugs involved in the case are clearly counterfeit drugs according to article 48, paragraph 2(ii) of the "Drug Administration Law". In the absence of a "Drug Trading License", the defendant registered an online shop to sell counterfeit drugs and open an online pharmacy is not only a clear criminal violation of article 23 of the "Amendment to the Criminal Law of the People's Republic of China", but also an infringement of the plaintiff's rights and interests and caused economic losses to the plaintiff. In accordance with Article 15 of the "Provisions on Certain Questions Concerning the Application of the Law in the Trial of Cases Concerning Food and Drug Disputes", the court shall be requested to make a just judgment in accordance with the law in support of the plaintiff's claim According to Article 26 of the "Measures on the Administration of Network Transactions", the defendant II should close the network store opened by defendant I on its platform, and report the illegal acts of the defendant I to the administration department for market regulation and the public security department. The plaintiff requested a just judgment from the court in support of the plaintiff's claim
Plaintiff's claim	(1) The defendant I should refund the original purchase, and compensate at 10 times the price (2) Defendant I should make an apology; (3) Defendant II should bear joint and several liability, and in accordance with the law, close the network shop opened by defendant I on its platform illegally, disclose the defendant I's illegal acts and report the illegal acts of the defendant I to the administration department for market regulation and the public security department
Type of appointment mediation	Offline mediation
Mediation outcomes	The mediation was successful, and both sides confirmed the mediation agreement and reached a settlement

3.2 Data Preprocessing

From Table 1, we can see that the case data contain some privacy information such as name, contact information, order number and so on, so we first desensitize the data and delete the relevant privacy information. In addition, the case description of the specific commodity brand name, efficacy description, as well as the relevant laws and regulations are not related to the issues studied in this paper, so it is also deleted treatment.

Most of the data used in this paper are stored in text form, and there are a small number of classified variables and quantitative variables. For this kind of composite data, this paper adopts the method of separate extraction and separate analysis for data processing.

For example, each case is classified as "type of dispute" and "type of product". The "dispute type" and "product type" here mentioned refer to "China e-commerce user experience and complaint monitoring report 2018"[4] and Tmall mall's classification of product types[5] respectively.

Considering that too detailed classification will cause the problem of data too sparse, so combining the characteristics of the cases studied, it is stipulated that the classification of "dispute type" and "product type" of the cases studied in this paper and the corresponding codes are shown in Table 2, in which the corresponding variables of the cases that cannot be classified are all coded as "0" and are not listed separately.

Table 2. Classification numbers and names of "types of disputes" and "types of products"

Variable name	No.	Category name	No.	Category name	No.	Category name
Disputes type	1	Product liability disputes	4	After-sales service	7	False shipments
	2	Product quality	5	Logistics issues	8	False propaganda
	3	Fake	6	Information security	9	Intellectual property rights
Products types	1	Electronic products	5	Air Ticket Hotel	9	Food
	2	Dress shoes and hats	6	Beauty care	10	图书音像Books, audio and video
	3	Household goods	7	Maternal and child supplies	11	Information technology services
	4	Household appliances	8	Automotive supplies	12	Drugs

The variable information finally extracted and deformed from the case text is shown in Table 3.

3.3 Cluster Analysis Based on Case Attributes

In order to understand the attribute characteristics of online transaction dispute cases, we can classify the cases according to the variable information related to the attributes

---

[4] Economic Society—E-Commerce Research Center, China Electronic Commerce User Experience and Complaint Monitoring Report 2018[EB/OL]. (2019-03-12)[2019-12-20]. http://www.100ec.cn/zt/2018yhts/.

[5] Tmall Select Website.Home page [2020-01-20]. https://www.tmall.com.

Table 3. Description and properties of extracted variables

	Variable name (symbol)	Variable description	Type of variable
案件属性	(ID) Case No. (ID)		Label data
	Sex of applicant (X1)		Classification data
	(X2) Age of applicant		Quantitative data
	Number of respondent (X3)	Count the number of respondents	Quantitative data
	(X4) Whether the platform is involved (X4)	Does the respondent include the merchant's platform	categorical data
	(X5) Amount of matter involved (X5)	Commodity prices involved in the dispute	Quantitative data
	Amount of claim (X6)	Amount of merchant compensation claimed by the applicant	Quantitative data
	Difference ratio (X7)	The ratio of the amount claimed to the amount involved	Quantitative data
	Number of claims (X8)	Number of claims included in the appeal information	Quantitative data
	Type of dispute (X9)	Different types of cases by cause of dispute	categorical data
	Type of Products (X10)	Different categories by type of commodity involved	categorical data
	Type of appointment mediation (X11)	Online/Offline	categorical data
	Status of cases (Y)	Successful/unsuccessful mediation	categorical data

of the cases, and analyze the characteristics of the cases. Since there are 6 classification variables and 6 quantitative variables at the same time, the number of variables of the two types is the same, so it is difficult to use the traditional clustering method to deal with them. Because most of the traditional clustering methods are only suitable for continuous quantitative variables, it is difficult to apply them directly to classification variables. Moreover, quantifying the classification variables into quantitative variables will bring about a certain degree of information loss. The second order clustering can be used based on the classification variables and the continuous type variables simultaneously, and the final classification number can be determined automatically, which is suitable for the mixed type data in this paper. Therefore, this paper keeps the attribute of the original variable unchanged, and uses the second order clustering method to cross classify the attribute characteristics of the case.

Second order clustering requires that there is no collinearity between variables, so the correlation between variables is first tested. The results are shown in Table 4, where the correlation coefficient is selected as Pearson correlation coefficient. It can be seen that the correlation coefficient between variables is mostly below 0.5, which basically accords with the condition of mutual independence.

Table 4. Correlation test between variables in Case Properties "(Part)"

		X4	X2	X1	X5	X6	X7	X9	X10	X11
X2	Correlation coefficient	0.04	1							
	P value	0.45								
X1	Correlation coefficient	0.00	0.15	1						
	P value	0.99	0.01							
X5	Correlation coefficient	0.02	0.03	0.10	1					
	P value	0.71	0.61	0.06						
X6	Correlation coefficient	0.06	0.01	0.14^*	0.51**	1				
	P value	0.27	0.82	0.01	0.00					
X7	correlation coefficient	0.06	0.08	0	0.19**	0.11*	1			
	P value	0.29	0.14	0.94	0.00	0.04				
X9	Correlation coefficient	0.10	0.11^*	0	0.09	0.11*	0.11^*	1		
	P value	0.08	0.04	1.0	0.10	0.04	0.04			
X10	Correlation coefficient	0.14^{**}	0.05	0.04	0.11	0.05	0.06	0.06	1	
	P value	0.00	0.39	0.51	0.05	0.40	0.25	0.27		
X11	Correlation coefficient	0.06	0.01	0.01	0.2**	0.13*	0.03	0.09	0.07	1
	P value	0.25	0.92	0.91	0.00	0.02	0.53	0.09	0.21	
Y	Correlation coefficient	0.02	0.04	0.06	0.13*	0.11*	0.04	0.09	0.09	0.16^{**}
	P value	0.70	0.48	0.30	0.02	0.04	0.41	0.08	0.10	0.00

** at 0.01 level (bilateral) significantly.
* at 0.05 level (bilateral) significantly.

Using SPSS for second-order clustering, the above 12 variables were used as data input to get the result of clustering, as shown in Fig. 2. It can be seen that cases are divided into four categories according to the case attribute, the number of cases is more evenly distributed. Specific classification basis for each type can be referred to Table 5.

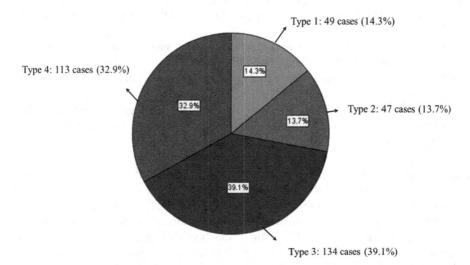

Type 1: 49 cases (14.3%)

Type 4: 113 cases (32.9%)

14.3%

32.9%

13.7%

Type 2: 47 cases (13.7%)

39.1%

Type 3: 134 cases (39.1%)

Fig. 2. Number and proportion of cases in the result of second-order clustering

Table 5. Importance of input variables in cluster types

Type	X4 (Whether the platform is involved)	X9 (Type of dispute)	Y (Case status)	X8 (Number of claims)	X10 Type of product)	X5 (Amount of matter involved)
1	0(否) (No)	2 (Product quality)	0 (Failure)	0.59	9 (Food)	1510.7
2	0(否) (No)	0 (Other)	0 (Failure)	0.64	0 (Other)	9266.8
3	1(是) (Yes)	3 (Fake)	1 (Success)	1.23	12 (Medicine)	1052.7
4	0(否) (No)	3 (Fake)	1 (Success)	0.35	12 (Medicine)	794.2
类型 Type	X3 (Number of respondents)	X6 (Amount of claim)	X7 (Difference ratio)	X1 (Sex)	X2 (Age)	X11 (Type of mediation appointment)
1	1.14	10161.4	15.4	1 (Male)	36.4	2 (Offline)
2	1.23	20581.4	5.7	1 (Male)	36	2 (Offline)
3	1.34	7471.6	8.3	1 (Male)	36.8	2 (Offline)
4	1	6079.2	11.8	1 (Male)	38.5	2 (Offline)

On the one hand, Table 5 reflects the most frequent categories of input variables of classifying variables in four different attributes cases. For example, the most frequent category of ×4 variables in type I is 0 (i.e., no platform participation), indicating that most cases in type I are without platform participation, that is, "no platform participation" is a feature of type I.

On the other hand, Table 5 also reflects the input variable mean of quantitative variables in four different attribute cases. For example, the average value of ×5 in type I is $1510.7, that is the average amount of matter involved in all cases that are classified as type I is $1510.7.

The input variables in Table 5 are arranged according to the degree of importance, that is, the most important variables for the classification of types are "whether the platform participates", followed by "dispute type", "case status" and so on. It can be seen from the table that the last several variables located in the table, such as "applicant sex", "applicant age", "type of mediation appointment", have similar characteristics in different types, and there is not enough distinction, so these variables have little contribution to the classification of case types and are omitted in the analysis of case types.

In order to see more intuitively the proportion of different types of variables, we can refer to Fig. 3, Fig. 4 and Fig. 5. The light color section in the figure is the frequency distribution of all cases in the variable, where the dark color part is the case frequency distribution of this type in the variable. The frequency ratio of the type can be seen from the area size of the deep and shallow part.

结合图表可以概括四种网上争议解决类型案件的基本特征：

Combine the figure and table, the basic features of the four types of ODR cases can be summarized as follows:

1. Type I: The product type is mostly "food", and the dispute type is mostly "product quality". There is usually no platform for participation in such cases. The average amount involved is about 1500 RMB yuan, and the average amount of appeal is about 10,000 RMB yuan, which is more evenly distributed, but the difference between the amount of claim and the amount involved is very large, and the result of mediation is mostly failure.

2. Type II: The types of products are mostly "other" and the types of disputes are mostly "other". Such cases usually have no platform to participate, the average amount involved is close to 10,000 RMB yuan, the average amount of claims is about 20,000 RMB yuan. Compared with the overall distribution, large disputes cases are more. Although the difference between the amount of claims and the amount involved is small than the average, but the result of mediation is also mostly failure.

3. Type III: The types of products are mostly "medicine" and the types of disputes are mostly "fakes". This kind of case usually has the platform to participate in it, the applicant's appeal is many and specific, the average amount involved in the matter is about 1000 RMB yuan, the average amount of the appeal is about 7500 RMB yuan,

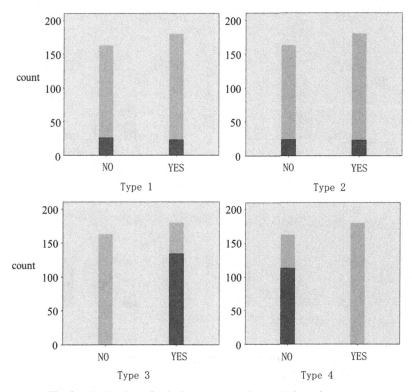

Fig. 3. Distribution of "platform participation" (x4) in various types

concentrated in the small dispute, the difference ratio is also small, the mediation result is mostly successful.

4. Type IV: The type of product and the type of dispute have the same characteristics as type III. Similar to type III, mostly small disputes. The difference is that the applicant's claim is generally only refundable compensation, the claim description is not specific, and the difference between the amount of the claim and the amount of the matter involved is relatively large, there is generally no platform to participate, and the result of mediation is mostly successful.

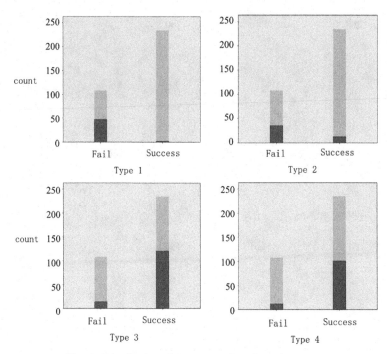

Fig. 4. Distribution of "case status" (y) in various types

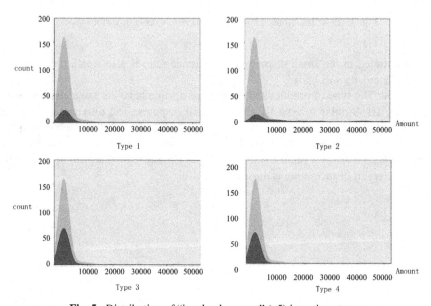

Fig. 5. Distribution of "involved amount" (x5) in various types

4   Conclusion: The Characteristics of Different Types of Online Transaction Dispute Mediation Cases

From the classification results of the third part of the cluster analysis, the variables of all variables that can distinguish the type of case are: X4 (whether the platform participates), X9 (type of dispute), Y (case status), X8 (number of claims), X10 (type of product), X5 (amount of matter involved), X3 (number of applicants), X6 (amount of claim), X7 (difference ratio). These variables have different value distribution in different cases, which can better describe the characteristics of different cases, which is beneficial to the mediator's classification of dispute cases and improve the success rate of mediation.

4.1   Type I

This kind of case mainly involves the large amount of food products trade dispute, its main dispute contradiction is the product quality, and the amount of compensation claimed by the applicant is very different from the amount of matter involved, most of the claims do not propose additional joint and several liability to the online shopping platform.

In terms of product types and types of disputes, there are more subjective descriptions of the reasons for the product quality disputes, such as "bad food", "bad taste" and "unfresh", in which the buyers and sellers are prone to some degree of dispute in the definition of this subjective feeling, which is an important reason for the high rate of mediation failure. In terms of the amount of money involved, when the difference is larger than the value, the amount of the applicant's claim for compensation is also greatly increased, and it is easy to cause mediation failure for the merchant to accept it.

4.2   Type II

This kind of case is mainly other types of product transaction disputes, the amount involved in the matter is large, the difference ratio is small, and there is no joint liability for the online shopping platform in the appeal.

The proportion of this type cases is minimal, the main issue of which is the unspecified type of product and the inability to define the type of dispute. This kind of case has the characteristic that the amount of the matter is large, but the amount of the applicant's claim is very low, the general claim is original price compensation or the "Refund of original products and three times compensation", also does not require the platform to assume the responsibility. The reasons for the failure of mediation in this type of case are more complicated, which may be due to the difficult mediation of disputes, or the special types of products, such as information technology service products, which is difficult divided the scope of responsibility of the buyer and seller, and difficult negotiated compensation.

4.3   Type III

Such cases are mainly disputes over counterfeit goods in the pharmaceutical category. The amount of matter involved is small, the margin ratio is small, and the appeal is clear and requires the platform to assume joint and several liability.

This type of case has the highest success rate of mediation. First of all, from the product type and dispute reasons, the sales drugs generally is needed to record through the State Food and Drug Administration, and usually the government has strict laws and regulations, the determination of the truth and false of drugs is also relatively clear, there are few subjective judgment, buyers and sellers can easily reach a consensus. Secondly, from the amount of money, the characteristics of small transactions and low proportion of the amount of claims make it easier for merchants to accept. In addition, from the appeal point of view, applicants for such cases require the platform to assume joint liability, as an online shopping platform, whether the dispute can be resolved related to the credibility of its own platform, so this kind of dispute mediation can arouse the platform's attention, and urge the platform to promote the settlement of disputes between buyers and sellers.

4.4 Type IV

This kind of case is similar to type III case, it is also a small dispute of drug type fake goods. The different is that this kind of case lacks platform participation, the number of claims is small, and the difference between the amount of claim and the amount involved is larger than the value of type III.

Although the success rate of mediation in such cases is lower than that of type III, the majority is mediated successful on the whole. It can be seen that the platform participation, the number of claims, the difference ratio and other variables affect the mediation results, but they are also not decisive factors in the success of mediation of the cases, the main reason is that the amount of matter involved is small and the sale of counterfeit drugs is regulated by law. In such cases, even if there is no platform to participate in the supervision, businesses in the face of a higher proportion of compensation will also choose to settle compensation. But there may also be cases where some businesses sell counterfeit medicines at the risk of breaking the law and are found by buyers to choose to pay compensation. Online shopping platforms have the responsibility to review and supervise such businesses. This phenomenon should be taken seriously.

Acknowledgments. We thank "301-12" "E-commerce Innovation and Entrepreneurship Management" as the model course for the international students." Supported by Shanghai Municipal Education Commission. (2018-2020) "CLS(2018)D164" Study on the implementation rules of the United Nations technical notes on online dispute resolution, China Law Society. Construction of virtual simulation experiment platform for intelligent justice based on cloud computing, First-class undergraduate construction leading plan Cultivation of major teaching reform results, East China of Political Science and Law support.

References

1. Bol, S.H.: An analysis of the role of different players in E-mediation: the (legal) implications. In: Second International ODR Workshop (2003)
2. Katsh, E.: Online dispute resolution: some implications for the emergence of law in cyberspace. Int. Rev. Law Comput. Technol. **21**(2), 97–107 (2007)

3. Cortés, P.: Online Dispute Resolution for Consumers in the European Union, p. 55. Taylor & Francis Group, Abingdon (2011)
4. Zheng, S.: Online Dispute Resolution Mechanism (ODR) Study. Law Press, Beijing (2012)
5. Mania, K.: Online dispute resolution: the future of justice. Int. Comp. Jurisprud. **1**, 76–86 (2015)
6. Li, T.: On the development of online mediation mechanism in China. Law Expo (13) (2017)
7. Ju, Y.: Legal Protection of Consumer Rights and Interests in B2C Electronic Commerce. Law Press, Beijing (2013)
8. Zhao, L., Guo, W.: Technology and Future ODR Intelligent Development and Establishment of Digital Ecosystems - Review of the 19th World ODR Congress [EB/OL] (2019-12-08) [2019-12-20]
9. Tabakhi, S., Moradi, P., Akhlaghian, F.: An unsupervised feature selection algorithm based on ant colony optimization. Eng. Appl. Artif. Intell. **32**, 112–123 (2014)
10. Xie, J., Xie, W.: Several feature selection algorithms based on the discernibility of a feature subset and support vector machines. Chin. J. Comput. **37**(8), 1704–1718 (2014)
11. Maruf, S., Javed, K., Babri, H.A.: Improving text classification performance with random forests-based feature selection. Arab. J. Sci. Eng. **41**(3), 951–964 (2016)
12. Liu, Y.N., Wang, Y.W., Feng, L.Z., et al.: Term frequency combined hybrid feature selection method for spam filtering. Pattern Anal. Appl. **19**(2), 369–383 (2016)
13. Wu, Q.Y., Ye, Y.M., Zhang, H.J., et al.: FORESTEXTER: an efficient random forest algorithm for imbalanced text categorization. Knowl.-Based Syst. **67**, 105–116 (2014)
14. Pang, G.S., Jin, H.D., Jiang, S.Y.: CenKNN: a scalable and effective text classifier [J]. Data Min. Knowl. Disc. **29**(3), 593–625 (2015). https://doi.org/10.1007/s10618-014-0358-x
15. Salles, T., Rocha, L., Motirao, F., et al.: Inf. Syst. **69**, 40–58 (2017)
16. Li, R., Wang, J., Chen, X., et al.: Chinese text classification using the maximum entropy model. Comput. Res. Dev. **42**(1), 94–101 (2005)
17. Wang, P., Hu, J., Zeng, H.J., et al.: Using Wikipedia knowledge to improve text classification. Knowl. Inf. Syst. **19**(3), 265–281 (2009). https://doi.org/10.1007/s10115-008-0152-4
18. Rossi, R.G., Lopes, A.D., Faleiros, T.D., et al.: Inductive model generation for text classification using a bipartite heterogeneous network. J. Comput. Sci. Technol. **29**(3), 361–375 (2014). https://doi.org/10.1007/s11390-014-1436-7
19. Du, C., Huang, L.: Text classification research with attention-based recurrent neural networks[J]. Int. J. Comput. Commun. Control **13**(1), 50–61 (2018)
20. Fleury, M.-J., Grenier, G., Bamvita, J.-M.: Predictive typology of subjective quality of life among participants with severe mental disorders after a five-year follow-up: a longitudinal two-step cluster analysis. Health Qual. Life Outcomes **13**(1), 150 (2015)
21. Okosun, I.S., Okosun, B., Lyn, R., Henry, T.L.: Chronic medical conditions based obesity phenotypes: a two-step cluster analysis of a representative sample of obese American adults. Diabetes Metab. Syndr.: Clin. Res. Rev. **13**(5), 2897–2905 (2019)
22. Calogero, A.M., Giuseppe, P., Vittoria, T., Felicia, P., Carla, G.: Phenotyping of type 2 diabetes mellitus at onset on the basis of fasting incretin tone: results of a two-step cluster analysis. J. Diabetes Invest. **7**(2), 219–225 (2016)
23. Sun, L., Yang, W.: Research on customer classification management based on two step clustering analysis. J. Harbin Univ. Commer. (Nat. Sci. Ed.) **35**(05), 630–633 (2019)
24. Anna, C.E., et al.: Adverse childhood experiences and clinical severity in bipolar disorder and schizophrenia: a transdiagnostic two-step cluster analysis. J. Affect. Disord. **259**, 104–111 (2019)

Optimization of Online Dispute Resolution Process in Mobile Electronic Commerce—A Case of the ODR Platform's Process Optimization in China Zhejiang Province

Lifan Yang[1][✉] and Tianjiao Niu[2]

[1] Business School, East China University of Political Science and Law, Shanghai 201620, China
cnyanglifan@163.com
[2] School of Management, Shanghai University of Science and Technology, Shanghai 200093, China

Abstract. On the basis of the overall operation process of the ODR platform, this paper comprehensively evaluates the quality problems such as the process efficiency and the operation cycle, and describes the dispute resolution process of the platform by using the IDEF0 model, and establishes a process activity analysis table through the FMEA, in combination with the problems that may exist in the actual operation data analysis process of the ODR platform of Zhejiang Province, including the lack of the detailed time standard of each link, the long feedback time of the consultation link, the too strict information restriction in the submission of the mediation application, the excessive communication links, the lack of feedback evaluation links, and etc. On this basis, by using the methods of expert empowerment and scoring and Pareto rule classification, the paper puts forward some suggestions for improving the problems existing in the process, including setting the process link, defining the running time standard, removing the redundant communication link, strengthening the management of consultation link and adding evaluation link, in order to promote the ODR platform to perfect its own operation flow and promote the promotion and application of ODR service through the above improvement measures.

Keywords: Mobile e-commerce · Online Dispute Resolution · Process optimization

1 Introduction

With the rapid development of mobile e-commerce, the settlement of transaction disputes has become a problem that must be faced. The excessive strictness of arbitration requirements and the low efficiency of litigation make the parties forced to abandon arbitration or litigation, these difficulties hinder the popularity of mobile e-commerce, online dispute resolution (ODR) arises. Therefore, how to play the role of ODR, fair, efficient, low-cost settlement of transaction disputes, to promote the healthy development

© Springer Nature Switzerland AG 2020
G. Salvendy and J. Wei (Eds.): HCII 2020, LNCS 12216, pp. 190–210, 2020.
https://doi.org/10.1007/978-3-030-50350-5_16

of mobile e-commerce has become a common concern of today's consumers, enterprises and the government.

1.1 Mobile e-Commerce Develops Rapidly and Disputes Increase

Taking China as an example, by the end of June 2019, the number of mobile Internet users in China reached 847 million, and the proportion of Internet users using mobile phones was as high as 99.1%. Among of them, the mobile phone network shopping users reached 622 million, accounting for 73.4% of the mobile phone Internet users. Users use 7.2 GB of mobile traffic per month,1.2 times the global average.[1]

The rapid development of mobile e-commerce has also caused many consume disputes. In 2018, China's market regulators accepted a total of 1.682 million online shopping complaints, up 126.2% year-on-year. Complaints are mainly: false advertising, fake and shoddy, unqualified quality, business operators refuse to fulfill the contract, and so on.[2]

"2018 consumption status scoreboard" of the European Commission shows[3] that more EU consumers are favoring cross-border online shopping, and trust in e-commerce is rising. In the 10 years from 2007 to 2016, the share of online shopping among EU consumers rose from 29.7% to 55%. Consumer trust in online shopping by domestic retailers has risen 12% since the 2016 scoreboard was released, and trust in online shopping by other countries has risen 21%. In addition, consumer scoreboard showed that 30.8% of EU consumers faced consumer disputes did not take any steps to resolve the issue, with half choosing to negotiate with sellers and only about 3.7% taking the ODR solution. For the consume dispute resolution mechanism, 34.6% and 32.5% of the respondents thought that the amount of consume dispute was small, it took longer and no settlement measures were taken, while about 45% of the traders surveyed were not aware of the existence and application of the ODR mechanism. Therefore, it is very important to improve consumers' understanding of dispute resolution mechanism, improve the efficiency of transaction dispute resolution, and enhance the confidence of both parties to mobile e-commerce.

1.2 World ODR has Developed Rapidly and Relevant Policies and Regulations have been Introduced

The term ODR (Online Dispute Resolution) originated in the United State. ODR was originally proposed to resolve online dispute settlement of a mediation mechanism, faced with a large number of low-value e-commerce transactions dispute.

---

[1] China Internet Network Information Center. Statistical Report on Internet Development in China (August 2019). [R/OL] [2019-08-30] [2019-12-23]. http://www.cnnic.net.cn/hlwfzyj/hlwxzbg/hlwtjbg/201908/t20190830_70800.htm.

[2] China State Administration for Marketing Regulation. Consumer complaints and reports presents eight characteristics in 2018 [EB/OL] (2019-03-14) [2019-12-20]. http://www.samr.gov.cn/zt/315scjg/315fb/201903/t20190314_291987.html. European Commission.

[3] European Commission. Consumer Markets Scoreboard: making markets work for consumers - 2018 edition. Luxembourg: Publications Office of the European Union, 2018.

With the promotion of ODR, advanced information and communication technology has gradually merged into all aspects of legal mediation, giving new connotations to ODR, and its application of dispute resolution has expanded from business to civil fields, such as marriage disputes; the way of settlement has expanded from online mediation to online arbitration and trial; and the means of settlement have adopted kinds of ways of mobile communication and artificial intelligence.

The United States has developed a relatively complete ODR system. Small litigation disputes, traffic and parking disputes, tax assessment disputes, family disputes and other cases are mainly resolved through the ODR system. In addition to the court system, other representative ODR systems are SquareTrade, Cybersettle, Matterhorn, Modria, etc(see footnote 1).

Canada established the world's first government-sponsored ODR system, the Canadian Civil Disputes Tribunal (CRT), in 2015[4]. CRT disputes are primarily minor disputes of up to $25,000, involving types of cases such as borrowing, compensation for damages, specific property disputes, etc. In addition to government-led ODR systems, Canada also has private ODR platforms such as Smartsettle, Cyberjustice.

Japan has attached great importance to exploring ODR practices in the e-commerce trading environment in recent years. The Japanese Ministry of Justice's online case application system, the mediation platform EC network that provides ODR services, and the Dispute Supports platform for online mediation approved by the Ministry of Justice are typical of practical applications.

On December 13, 2016, the UN General Assembly adopted the Technical Notes on Online Dispute Resolution of the United Nations Commission on International Trade Law[5] (for short Technical Notes), which provide technical Notes for dispute resolution in electronic commerce.

On 21 May 2013, the European Parliament and the Council of the European Union promulgated the On Online Dispute Resolution for Consumer Disputes and Amending Regulation (EU)[6] which are applied to the settlement of disputes arising from online transactions (including cross-border transactions) between consumers and operators within the EU member States.

China's 12315 Internet platform (Phase II) has opened the channel of online settlement of consumer disputes (ODR), consumers can log in through mobile phone app and Wechat public number, mini programs and other functions, enterprises can directly negotiate and settle with consumers on the mobile platform. In October 2019, China's State Council issued the "Regulations on the Optimization of the Business Environment", in which Article 66 stipulates that the state should improve the diversified dispute

---

[4] Canadian Civil Disputes Tribunal ODR Web site: www.civilresolutionbc. Visit time: 2019-12-19.

[5] United Nations Commission on International Trade Law. Technical Notes on Online Dispute Resolution of the United Nations Commission on International Trade Law [EB/OL] (2016-12-13) [2019-12-20]. http://www.uncitral.org/pdf/chinese/texts/odr/17-00381_C_ebook_Technical_Notes_on_ODR.pdf.

[6] Regulation(EU) No 534/2013 of the European Parliament and of the Council of 21 May 2013 On Online Dispute Resolution for Consumer Disputes and Amending Regulation (EU) No 2006/2004 and Directive 2–9/22/EV (regulation on consumer ODR), Official Journal of the European Union L1 65, 18.6.2013, pp. 1–12.

resolution mechanism, through organic link-up and mutual coordination of mediation, arbitration, administrative adjudication, administrative reconsideration and litigation, so as to provide an efficient and convenient way for the main body of the market to resolve disputes.[7]

2 Literature Review

2.1 Research on Electronic Commerce Dispute Resolution

With the rapid development of e-commerce, after entering the 21st century, e-commerce dispute resolution has been attracting the attention of many disciplines professionals at home and abroad.

Stephanie (2003) [2], starting from ADR (Alternative Dispute Resolution) dispute resolution mechanism, discussed the feasibility of the ODR mechanism and the future development trend. Ethan (2007) [3] studied the importance of ODR in resolving ODR and advocated for a trading environment capable of producing agreed rules and standards. Pablo (2011) [4] based on the European consumer environment analyzed the development of ODR in European and assessed the challenges to its growth. Karolina (2015) [5] in its study, citing consumer regulations as an example, emphasized the importance of lawmaking and uniform regulation in using ODR to resolve online disputes in e-commerce.

Chinese scholars are also constantly looking for measures to solve the improvement of ODR mechanism. Ou dan (2017) [10] analyzed the problems still faced in the settlement of cross-border e-commerce disputes. Han Noxin (2018) [11] discussed the lack of industry standards, insufficient legal basis, low social recognition, immaturity of technology and small scope of cases in the operation of ODR. Zhou Xiang (2018) [12] started from the ODR mechanism of Taobao Net, analyzed the characteristics and process of the dispute resolution mechanism of Taobao Net, and explored the way to perfect the ODR platform.

2.2 Research on Evaluation of Solution Effectiveness of ODR Platform

At present, the research on the evaluation of the solution effect of the ODR platform mainly has the following two aspects.

(1) Operational evaluation of the ODR platform. Zhao lei, Guo wenli (2019) [13] introduced the main recommendations for the ODR platform operation evaluation of the 19th world ODR conference, including: ① Evaluation of the ODR service provider, if the ODR service provider introduces advanced technology to expand the carrying capacity of the platform; ② Evaluation of the program rules, if the ODR program rules are rationality; ③ Evaluation of the user experience, if the user's reflection are good and the use of platform is ease. At the same time, it is suggested that the evaluation of users' feeling of using ODR should be carried out in terms

---

[7] State Council of China. Optimal Business Environment Ordinance [EB/OL] (2019-10-22) [2019-12-20]. http://www.gov.cn/zhengce/content/2019-10/23/content_5443963.htm.

of time cost, monetary cost, access mode, information access and use, and system guidance about resolution results; the justice of the evaluation procedure should take into account the differences with other procedures, the user's right to speak, respect, fairness and transparency; and the justice of the evaluation results, mainly in terms of whether the solution reflects the demands of the parties, whether there is an effective agreement, whether the solution plays a role and how it is implemented.

(2) Research on policy effectiveness assessment. Sang Ye (2013) [14] from the perspective of public policy management, determined the evaluation criteria (value standards and target standards) for the implementation effect of China's e-commerce policy, constructed the evaluation system for the implementation effect of China's e-commerce policy in combination with the analytic hierarchy process, and made an empirical evaluation of the implementation effect of China's e-commerce policy. The method of this paper is worth learning from the evaluation of ODR solution effect.

3   The Basic Process and Optimization Method of Online Solution Mechanism

3.1   Basic Processes Set Out in the Technical Guidelines on Online Dispute Resolution of United Nations

The Technical Guidelines adopted by the United Nations Commission on International Trade Law set the basic process for ODR. The Technical Guidelines divide the basic process of ODR into three phases: negotiation phase (phase I), assisted mediation (phase II) and final phase (phase III), as shown in Fig. 1.

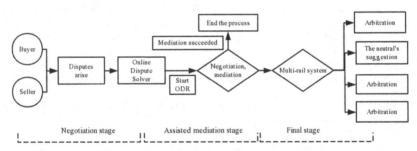

Fig. 1. Three phases of Online Dispute Resolution

The actual application of the ODR process is much more complex than Fig. 1 and needs to be continuously optimized under the guidance of the basic process. The main methods of process optimization are IDEF0 modeling, FMEA process activity analysis table, et. On this basis, we can use the methods of expert empowerment and scoring and Pareto rule classification to improve the possible problems in the process, so as to optimize the process.

3.2   Build Process Using IDEF0 Model

IDEF0 (ICAM definition method) known as functional modeling, is a method in the family of modeling methods, which forms an improved new model [15] by describing the functional activities and the interrelations that exist in the process. The basic unit of IDEF0 is shown in Fig. 2, where the box is the most basic original of IDEF0 and is commonly used to describe the characteristics of the activity; the input arrow indicates the resources and conditions required to complete the particular activity; the output arrow indicates the result or output after the activity has been processed; the control indicates the conditions required for the activity; and the mechanism represents the conditions required to complete the activity, including personnel, equipment and devices.

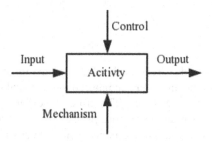

Fig. 2. The Basic structure of IDEF0

IDEF0 links the entire organizational process together through a basic structure diagram to refine the process activities, thereby achieving the purpose of process optimization [16]. From the perspective of process quality improvement, this paper uses IDEF0 model to explain the whole process of ODR, focusing on the results quality, limitation conditions and the results of each part of the process.

3.3   Determination of Process Problems and Evaluation Based on FMEA

FMEA (Failure mode and Effects analysis) is an important risk analysis tool in quality management [16]. FMEA is often used in the process design stage and the product design stage, analyzed the subsystem and the components of the product, the specific process and the intermediate link of the composition process, and analyzed to find out all the possible failure modes, so as to draw up the adjustment measures. This paper regards the process of ODR as a product process, using FMEA to establish a process activity analysis table (see Table 1), get the operation opinion through direct communication with the platform, combine the specific platform operation data to find the possible problems in the process, sort the existing failure mode, focus on improving the problems that have a great impact on the results.

3.3.1   Thought Train of Evaluating Process Issues

FMEA mainly evaluates possible problems in the product or process through the Risk Priority Number (RPN). RPN is the product of three indices (as shown in formula (1)).

Table 1. FMEA analysis form architecture

Serial number	Potential failure mode	Potential failure consequences	Potential failure causes

O is the degree of occurrence, that is, the probability or frequency of the occurrence of a problem; S is the degree of severity, that is, the degree of impact on the consequences when the problem occurs; and D is the degree of detection, that is, whether the problem is easy to be discovered.

$$RPN = R * S * D \tag{1}$$

Since there is no clear linear relationship between the three variables O, S and D, the relative importance of the three may be ignored in the calculation of the RPN value, which affects the judgment of the result. Therefore, the order of risk cannot be judged only according to the numerical size of the priority risk coefficient. To improve the problems existing in RPN evaluation, this paper invites experts to evaluate values to the three indicators (as shown in formula (2)).

$$RPN = aR * bS * cD \tag{2}$$

3.3.2 Evaluation of Process Issues Using Pareto Rule

Because there may be multiple failure modes for a given process, a large change in the process can be counterproductive. Therefore, based on the expert scoring results, this paper will use the Pareto rule to sort the failure modes of process activity according to the percentage of failure modes in all failure modes.

Pareto law, also known as the "Two and Eight Rule", is mainly used to identify the degree of influence of things, that is, based on the principle of "important minority and trivial majorit" to determine priorities according to the degree of importance of things [17]. This paper considers the failure mode as the first 60% of all failure modes as the most important problem in the process, and defines it as class I problem. If the two indicators of severity and occurrence in a process problem are evaluated as "L" or "VL" [1], this class of problems is defined as class II process problems, with precedence over class I. However, when the total number of class I and class II issues exceeds 60% of all issues, priority is given to optimizing class I process issues and class II as a secondary issue for improvement (see Table 2).

3.4 Process Quality Improvement Recommendations and Model Evaluation

(1) The flow optimization model structure of this paper is shown in Fig. 3, and the whole process optimization is divided into six basic steps.

Table 2. Optimal classification of failure models

Optimization category	Indicators	Optimization of order
Category I	Failure mode with a combined score of 60%	Take the lead in optimizing
Category II	Occurrence rating levels are L or VL	Take the lead in optimizing
	Severity rating levels are L or VL	
Special circumstances	If the total number of class I and class II issues is 60% of the total score	Take the lead in optimizing Class I Take the second in optimizing class II

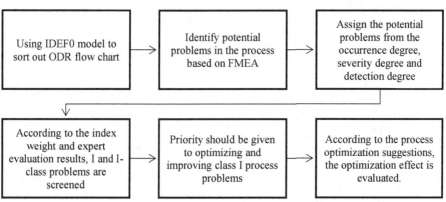

Fig. 3. ODR process optimization model

4 Empirical Analysis on Process Optimization of Zhejiang ODR Platform

In order to verify the rationality of the ODR platform process optimization proposed in this paper, this paper takes the Zhejiang Online Diversified dispute Resolution Platform (short for "Zhejiang ODR platform")[8] as an example to carry out the empirical study of ODR platform process optimization.

4.1 Introduction to Zhejiang ODR Platform

China Zhejiang ODR platform began trial operation in March 2017 and officially in October 2018. The Zhejiang ODR platform has many kinds of service ecology, such as pc, app and so on, using internet technology and intelligent means. Through using five service functions of online consultation, online evaluation, online mediation, online arbitration and online litigation, the contradictions and disputes are filtered step by

---

[8] Zhejiang ODR web site: https://yundr.gov.cn/, visit time: 2019-12-19.

step, and the simple and easy-to-solve disputes are filtered to non-litigation mediation methods, the cases that need arbitration and litigation to filter to the arbitration institution or court, thus the funnel-type mode of conflict and dispute resolution is formed.

Zhejiang ODR platform has achieved remarkable results, mainly in the following three aspects.

(1) The registration and access of platform are large. As of June 2019, more than 1 million parties had resolved the dispute through the platform. The total number of visitors to the platform is about 4.891 million, the number of users registered is 851,000, the total number of mediators registered is 42,000, and the total number of consultants registered is 1,445.

(2) The source of cases is wide. The source of cases of Zhejiang ODR platform is basically divided into five aspects: user individual application (3%), institutional registration case (47%), court registration case (1%), citation case (26%) and registration case of basic unit (23%). Of these, about half are from institutional registrations (see Fig. 4).

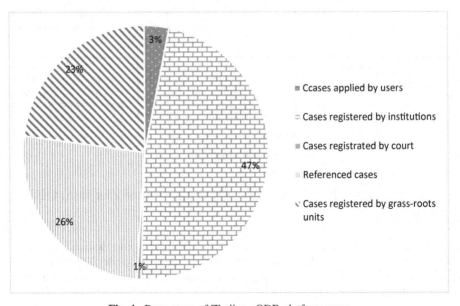

Fig. 4. Percentage of Zhejiang ODR platform cases

(3) The number of mediation cases is large and the success rate of mediation is high. From Fig. 5, it can be seen that since January 2018, the number of mediation cases in the platform has increased every month. In the first half of 2019, the average monthly growth rate of mediation cases on the platform remains at about 8%, and the volume of reconciliation cases exceeded 500,000. From June 2018 to June 2019, the success rate of case mediation basically remains at about 93%, the proportion of mediation failure was about 6%, and the remaining cases are mediation withdrawal,

mediation termination or inadmissibility of cases. The success rate of mediation in controversial cases has maintained a high level.

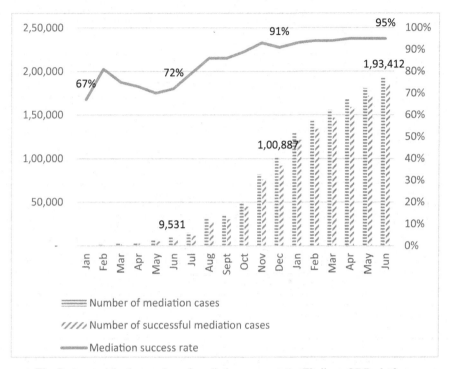

Fig. 5. Increase in the number of mediation cases on the Zhejiang ODR platform

4.2 Process Analysis of Zhejiang ODR Platform

4.2.1 Application of IDEF0 to Describe Zhejiang ODR Platform Service Flow

Before optimizing the Zhejiang ODR platform, the IDEF0 method is first used to adjust the ODR process of the enterprise and draw a detailed flow chart (see Fig. 6).

Zhejiang ODR platform is a comprehensive service platform, which provides a variety of dispute settlement models for both parties to the dispute. After users register on the platform with their personal mobile number or email address, they can choose to enter any mode in online consultation, online evaluation and online mediation.

4.2.2 FMEA Analysis of Failure Mode in Zhejiang ODR Platform Flow

1. Lack of time standards for each segment of the process

One of the principles of the ODR service is efficiency, but the entire dispute resolution process on the Zhejiang ODR platform lacks a time standard and is concentrated in the online mediation phase. Although the platform sets a maximum mediation time limit of

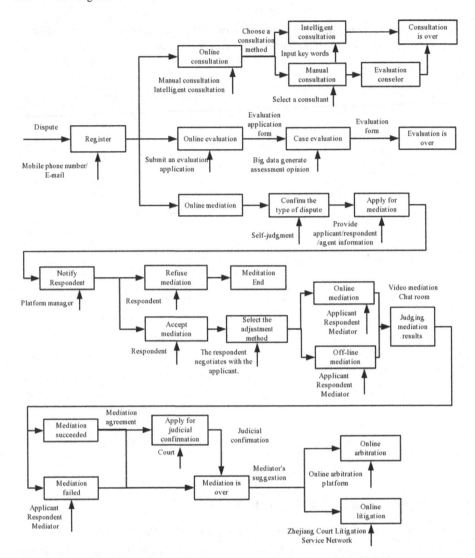

Fig. 6. Zhejiang ODR platform process adjustment using IDEF0

30 days for the entire submission process, the time limit for each link can only be known when the platform user actually enters the mediation link. In addition, mediation link time standard setting is not accurate enough, still need to be refined. Figure 7 reflects the detailed process of time consumption in the mediation process.

From Fig. 7, it can be found that the time of the whole process is difficult to control. First, the mediator needs to wait for feedback after informing the respondent. At this time, the platform does not set feedback time, if the respondent is unwilling to participate in mediation but also did not respond to the mediation notice, mediation is difficult into progress. Secondly, if the respondent agrees to participate mediation, both parties need

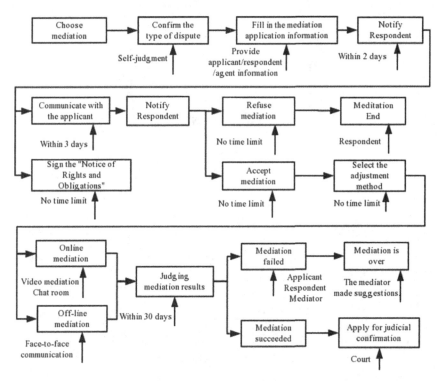

Fig. 7. Detailed flow of time consumption in mediation of Zhejiang ODR platform

to choose the method of mediation, and this link does not set the selection time standard. Thirdly, in the process of mediation, it is difficult for the two parties to know the whole process and time of mediation in advance, and it is difficult to control the progress of mediation, which ultimately affects the overall operational efficiency and the user's sense of experience.

When users enter the platform with controversial issues, they generally choose to consult first in order to have a preliminary understanding of the complaint case. The intelligent consultation provided by Zhejiang ODR platform plays a leading role, and manual consultation accounts for about 5% of the total cases of consultation. The biggest problem of intelligent consultation is that the questioner's key words and description of the case are not professional, resulting in the intelligent system cannot well analyze the main influencing factors of the case. The main problem of manual consultation is that the reply time is longer and it is difficult to meet the user's time requirement. The survey found that in January-May 2019, 1512 users of the Zhejiang ODR platform had used manual consultation, but 35.6% of the questions took more than 10 min to answer (see Fig. 8). This situation seriously affects the patience of users.

In order to further analyze the problems existing in the manual consultation link, this paper also collects 1000 user evaluation items of the platform manual consultation link, and obtains 260 text comment data. Using Python to segment these texts, the word clouds of praise and bad comments we*re obtained respectively (see Fig. 9, Fig. 10). It can be

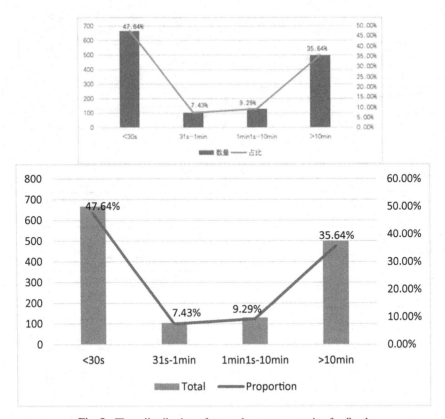

Fig. 8. Time distribution of manual customer service feedback

seen from the picture, the key words of praise are basically embodied as "very patient, timely solution, professional ", accounting for 3.88%, 3.36%, 2.84% respectively, and the key words of bad evaluation are" no reply, no response ", accounting for 11.38% and 4.88% respectively. It can be seen that the feedback speed of manual consultation and the timeliness of reply greatly affect the user's sense of experience, thus affecting the user's recognition of the platform service.

3. The application information filling is strictly restricted in the mediation application submission process

When applying for mediation, users are required to fill in some required information, as shown in Table 3, where the applicant needs to provide the name, contact information, address and other information of the respondent. However, if the respondent is a legal or non-legal person organization, the social credit code must be completed. In the absence of such accurate information, an application for conciliation cannot be submitted. However, in the environment of B2C e-commerce, the applicants are mostly individuals, and the respondents are mostly enterprises, so it is difficult for consumers to know the information of operators such as enterprise code, legal representative and so on. From this point of view, although the platform has strict restrictions on information from

Fig. 9. Favorable comment words cloud map of artificial consultation link user comments

Fig. 10. Bad comments words cloud map of artificial consultation link user comments

a security perspective, it does not consider the difficulty of obtaining information by individual applicants, and the setting of required items may affect the willingness of individual applicants to apply.

The new cases of Zhejiang ODR platform mainly come from institutional registration cases, and individual application cases account for only 3% of the number of cases (see Fig. 4). Therefore, how to improve the application amount of individual users from the process is also a key issue to be concerned in the process optimization.

4. Too many communication links in the process

After entering the mediation process, the platform first needs to confirm whether the respondent is involved in mediation, and after confirming the participation in mediation, the applicant and the respondent need to reach agreement on the way of mediation, that is, choose online mediation or offline mediation. At this time, it is necessary to communicate with the respondent twice, which can easily cause the disagreement between the two sides in the process of repeated communication in many times, thus reducing the participation of the respondent and affecting the subsequent mediation process. In the process, it is possible to inform the respondent whether to participate in the choice of mediation and

Table 3. Information required for mediation applications

Type	Applicant	Respondent
Natural person	Name Gender ID number Contact information Detailed address	Name Gender ID number Contact information Website address
Legal person	Name of enterprise Social Credit Code Legal Representative Contact information Detailed address	Name of enterprise Social Credit Code Legal Representative Contact information Detailed address
Non-legal organization	Name of institution Social Credit Code Agency representatives Contact information Detailed address	Name of institution Social Credit Code Agency representatives Contact information Detailed address

mediation mode at the same time, thus shortening the process cycle and entering the formal mediation link in time.

5. Lack of feedback evaluation in the process

Because the mediation service provided by Zhejiang ODR platform is assisted mediation, that is, the mediator participates in the whole process to assist the mediation agreement, the mediator's professionalism and ability have a certain influence on the result of mediation. How to better judge the mediator's ability and how to make the disputing parties choose the suitable mediator is also the key in the mediation process. And the platform currently has more than 39,000 mediators, and the management and evaluation of mediators is equally cumbersome. However, the current mediation process of the platform lacks the user's evaluation feedback link to the mediator, lacks the evaluation of the mediator, so it cannot better judge and improve the mediation results, and it is difficult to form an evaluation and competition mechanism.

6. Summary of analytical results

Based on the operation data analysis of Zhejiang ODR platform, combined with the investigation and interview with the platform operator, this paper believes that the following five potential failure modes exist in the process of Zhejiang ODR platform (see Table 4).

4.2.3   Identify the Sequence of Process Quality Improvements

Firstly, the weight ratio of occurrence O, severity S and detection D is given. Secondly, drawing on the research of Yu Jianxin et al. (Ref.17), it can be assigned to 0.4, 0.4, 0.2 respectively for O, S, D. Thirdly, five experts are selected to score the failure model.

Table 4. FMEA analysis of Zhejiang ODR platform service flow

Failure mode	Potential failure mode	Potential failure consequences	Potential failure causes
Failure mode 1	Lack of refinement of time standards for each link in the process	some links take too much time	Making the overall process less efficient
Failure mode 2	Long feedback time in consultation process	Poor user experience can affect the use of subsequent processes	Long response time for consultants
Failure mode 3	The process of submitting information of mediation application is too restrictive	The user cannot provide some information causes the process to stagnate	In the application process, the platform sets up to fill in the applicant's name, contact information, enterprise code and other information
Failure mode 4	Too many communication links in the process	Easily lead to ineffective communication	Low matching level for respondent
Failure mode 5	Lack of feedback evaluation in the process	Unable to assess mediation effect	Missing process

Finally, the evaluation results of the process quality problem are calculated according to the Fuzzy formula (see Table 5).

According to the evaluation index of the process quality problem in Table 5, the mean value of each index of each failure model is obtained separately according to the formula (1). Based on the average of each index, according to the weight distribution of the index (formula 3), the comprehensive evaluation is carried out. The comprehensive evaluation results and the percentage of each failure model in the population are shown in Table 6.

$$RPN = 0.4R * 0.4S * 0.2D \qquad (3)$$

According to the Pareto rule, the percentage of potential failure mode 1, failure mode 3, and failure mode 4 in the whole is 71.46%, which belongs to the classIproblem of process quality. They need to be improved first with limited time and energy. However, the severity of failure mode 2 and failure mode 5 are not up to the "high" standard, they do not belong to class I. They cannot be given priority to deal with. But after the class I problems are optimized, they can be followed up to improve the overall quality of the platform process.

4.2.4 The Recommendations of Process Optimization

According to the screening of the above steps, under the condition of limited energy and resources, priority should be given to improving failure mode 1, failure mode 3 and failure

Table 5. Experts evaluation form of process quality issues

Failure mode	Evaluation language	Expert 1	Expert 2	Expert 3	Expert 4	Expert 5	Mean value
Failure mode 1	O	H	VH	H	H	H	7.4
	S	VH	VH	H	VH	H	8.2
	D	M	L	M	M	M	4.6
Failure mode 2	O	M	M	L	L	M	4.2
	S	M	H	M	M	H	5.8
	D	VL	L	L	L	L	2.6
Failure mode 3	O	H	VH	H	M	H	7
	S	VH	VH	H	M	M	7
	D	M	M	L	L	L	3.8
Failure mode 4	O	H	H	H	H	H	7
	S	H	M	H	H	H	6.6
	D	H	VL	M	H	M	5
Failure mode 5	O	L	M	M	M	L	4.2
	S	L	L	VL	L	VL	1.8
	D	M	H	M	H	M	5.8

Table 6. Comprehensive scale form of process quality issues

Failure mode	Comprehensive results	Percentage share
Failure mode 1	7.16	25.29%
Failure mode 2	4.52	15.97%
Failure mode 3	6.63	23.42%
Failure mode 4	6.44	22.75%
Failure mode 5	3.56	12.57%

mode 4. For failure modes 2 and 5, follow-up improvements can be made. Therefore, the following optimization suggestions are put forward for the process optimization of Zhejiang ODR platform.

1. Setting time standards for each link

For the failure mode 1, that is, the process each link lacks the time standard, it should make the specific time standard for each link according to the platform operation data and experience, and make a clear explanation on the platform flow rules, so that the dispute parties and the mediator can complete the corresponding link within the specified time period to improve the efficiency of dispute resolution.

(1) The link of online assessment. Because the online evaluation of the platform adopts the "big data automatic analysis + manual audit" mode, the evaluation of the case is faster. According to the platform operation experience, the assessment application submitted by the applicant can respond within 30 min at the minimum, and the assessment report can be issued within 2 working days at the maximum. It is suggested that the online evaluation link can set a time limit of 2 working days to urge the platform to provide users with more rapid evaluation services.

(2) The link of notify the respondent. The success of the ODR platform gets in touch with the respondent is influenced by factors such as the completeness and correctness of the information provided by applicants and the timeliness of communications. It is recommended to set a time limit of 2 days, that is, after the platform sends a mediation notice to the respondent, if the respondent does not give an accurate reply within 2 days, it shall be deemed to have voluntarily waived its participation in the mediation.

(3) The link of mediation. According to the regulations of Zhejiang ODR platform, after entering the mediation stage, the mediation results need to be obtained within 30 days. According to the actual operation, case handling of the platform can be basically completed within 15 days. Therefore, it is proposed to set the duration of the dispute mediation to 15 days, and if the parties agree that the duration of the mediation should be extended, the maximum duration of the mediation period shall be 20 days.

After setting the time limit on the specific links of the process, only the actual mediation link can reduce the operating time of the platform by 10 days (the maximum time of the original mediation is 30 days). In addition, after the specific time limit is set, it is also necessary to mark on the flow guide diagram of each link of the platform, so that the user can have a general assurance on the overall operation time before entering the mediation link.

2. Adjustment of Mediation Application Information Form

For the failure mode 3, the original mediation application information form of the platform, such as enterprise social credit code, legal person representative and other information will cause some difficulties to the individual user applicant's mediation application, which is not conducive to the increase of users of the platform. Therefore, it is suggested to cancel some required information such as the enterprise social credit code and set it as a non-essential item, so as not to affect the normal submission of the mediation application by the users. After the platform formally accepts the mediation case, it can check and confirm the relevant enterprise information. In this way, on the one hand, it can solve the difficulty search of enterprise information, on the other hand, it can speed up the application volume of individual users and expand the influence of the platform.

3. Removing redundant communication links

In view of the failure mode 4, this paper proposes to remove the redundant communication link, that is, the parties to the dispute will choose the mode of mediation in the first stage, together with the notification of the respondent to participate in the mediation process. When applying for mediation, the applicant chooses his preferred form of mediation in order for the platform to confirm whether the respondent is involved in the mediation and to identify with the type of mediation chosen by the applicant. If the respondent and the applicant do not agree on the mode of mediation, the platform is responsible for communicating with both parties in this process. By adopting the method of process parallelization, the platform can first reduce the number of communication, improve the communication efficiency and save the process operation time; secondly, the platform can confirm multiple problems in one communication, avoid the problem of communication failure, and promote both sides to enter the formal mediation link more smoothly.

4. Strengthening management of advisory links

For failure mode 2, although the proportion of manual consultation in the overall number of consultation is relatively small, its service quality and feedback speed still need to be further improved. From the Fig. 6, 7, 8 and 9, we can see that the main reason for the poor evaluation of the manual consultation link is that the problem consultation of users is not timely feedback, and then affect the user's impression of the platform as a whole. In addition, 17% of users gave bad comments because they didn't get a timely response, or because their consultation time was not within the time set by the platform (Monday-Friday, 9:00–17:00). Therefore, Zhejiang ODR platform should strengthen the management of manual consultation customer service, analyze the centralized consultation period of users, and appropriately increase the number of consultants in this period, so as to respond to the needs of users more quickly and provide professional answers for users. In addition, for the user consultation generated outside the prescribed consultation time, the robot reply can be used to improve the overall service level and user satisfaction of the platform.

5. Adding the link of evaluation of mediators

For failure mode 5, it is necessary to adopt corresponding measures to improve the management of mediators. Therefore, this paper thinks that the platform can add the post-mediation evaluation link, and the parties to the dispute can evaluate the professional degree, attitude, mediation ability of the mediator, so as to establish a perfect evaluation mechanism within the platform, and promote the optimization of the mediator team, so as to enhance the service level provided by the Zhejiang ODR platform and promote the benign operation of the platform.

5   Conclusions

While the number of mobile e-commerce participants and the number of transactions are increasing, trading disputes are also increasing. How to resolve transaction disputes better in cyberspace has become a national concern. Online dispute resolution (ODR) plays an important role in promoting the sustainable development of e-commerce because of its high efficiency and convenience in dispute resolution.

The process and characteristics of the platform are analyzed by using process analysis, inductive contrast method and empirical model method, combined with the operation data of Zhejiang ODR platform. In view of the problems existing in the platform, this paper puts forward five suggestions for improvement: setting time standards for each link, adjustment of mediation application Information form, removing the redundant communication link, strengthening the management of the consultation link and adding the link of evaluation of mediators.

According to the above optimization proposal, the platform process transformation can improve the quality of the process to a certain extent, which is embodied in three aspects. First, from the point of view of the process cycle, setting the time standard of each link cannot only shorten the original adjustment period from 30 days to 20 days, but also shorten the original process by 10 days, and also allow the two parties to enter the formal mediation before entering the process of mediation clearly. Second, from the view of process quality point, adding evaluation links, deleting redundant links, make the whole process structure clearly, and form a complete closed loop, which is helpful for the platform to obtain user advice and increase the assessment of mediators. Third, from the view of the process specification point, the formulation of time standards, the removal of redundant links can set a certain standard for the process, and form a standardized process operation system with popularizing significance.

Online dispute resolution in the world is still a stage of exploration, how to make the mechanism more relevant to the development reality of countries needs continuous research and exploration. Starting from the existing development applications and exploring process optimization, the paper conclusion can play a guiding role. However, due to the lack of the massive detailed data of users' usage behavior, It is difficult to grasp the underlying problems in the process, and whether the existing process improvement suggestions apply to all the ODR platforms still need to be further studied.

Acknowledgments. . We thank "301-12" "E-commerce Innovation and Entrepreneurship Management" as the model course for the international students.", Supported by Shanghai Municipal Education Commission. (2018–2020) "CLS (2018) D164" Study on the implementation rules of the United Nations technical notes on online dispute resolution, China Law Society. Construction of virtual simulation experiment platform for intelligent justice based on cloud computing, First-class undergraduate construction leading plan Cultivation of major teaching reform results, East China of Political Science and Law support.

References

1. Zheng, S.: Improvement of China's online dispute resolution mechanism. J. Grad. Sch. Chin. Acad. Soc. Sci. (04), 126–136 (2017)
2. Bol, S.H.: An analysis of the role of different players in E-mediation: the (legal) implications. In: Second International ODR Workshop (2003)
3. Katsh, E.: Online dispute resolution: some implications for the emergence of law in cyberspace. Int. Rev. Law Comput. Technol. **21**(2), 97–107 (2007)
4. Cortés, P.: Online Dispute Resolution for Consumers in the European Union, vol. 55. Taylor & Francis Group, Abingdon (2011)

5. Mania, K.: Online dispute resolution: the future of justice. Int. Comp. Jurisprud. **1**, 76–86 (2015)
6. Dan, O.: Current situation and countermeasure of cross-border e-commerce dispute resolution: taking Zhejiang as an example. J. Heilongjiang Adm. Cadre Coll. Politics Law **01**, 69–72 (2017)
7. Han, N., Chen, L., Liu, Q., Xu, H.: Study of E-commerce online dispute resolution mechanism. Hebei Enterprises **06**, 147–148 (2018)
8. Xiang, Z.: Description and interpretation: description and explanation: Taobao dispute resolution mechanism—China experience of ODR. J. Shanghai Jiaotong Univ. (Philos. Soc. Sci.) [J/OL] [2018-06-05] [2019-12-23]. https://doi.org/10.13806/j.cnki.issn1008-7095.2018022
9. Lei, Z., Wenli, G.: Technology and future ODR intelligent development and the establishment of digital ecosystems. In: Review of the 19th World ODR Conference [EB/OL] (2019-12-08) [2019-12-20]. https://mp.weixin.qq.com/s/vq1qm92fopnefySci2wdVQ
10. Song, Y., Yang, J., Wang, Y.: Evaluation of China's e-commerce policy implementation. Financ. Econ. **9**, 148–150 (2013)
11. You, J., Cai, W., You, X.: Research on business process optimization based on quality improvement perspective. Ind. Eng. Manag. **06**, 161–168 (2017)
12. Yu, X., Lei, X., Liu, H.S.: Outsourcing risk analysis based on failure mode and consequence analysis extension model. J. Tongji Univ. (Nat. Sci. Edn.) **44**(02), 309–316 (2016)
13. Wang, Y., Huang, M.: The theoretical exploration of the international climate fund's financing and the allocation of funds—an analysis of global pareto optimal and fiscal balance [J/OL]. China Knowl. Netw. (2019-09-04) [2019-12-27]. http://kns.cnki.net/kcms/detail/50.1023.C.20190904.0858.002.html

How Does Censorship Shape Citizens' Participations of Mobile Government Social Media? A Value Perspective

Miao Zhang[1] and Shuiqing Yang[2(✉)]

[1] School of Education Science and Technology, Zhejiang University of Technology, Hangzhou 310014, China
[2] Department of Information Management and Engineering, Zhejiang University of Finance and Economics, Hangzhou 310018, China
hustxtysq@qq.com

Abstract. Governments aim to provide trustworthy and timely information to citizens interactively through mobile government microblogging services (GMS). Drawing on self-regulation theory and internet censorship literature, a research model reflected the impacts of citizens' censorship perceptions on their participations of mobile GMS was developed. A structural equation modeling (SEM) approach was employed to test the proposed research model by using data collected from 315 mobile GMS users in China. The structural modeling analysis revealed that internet censorship negative affect extrinsic value (e.g., social value and information value) and intrinsic value (e.g., hedonic value and emotional value) which further determine mobile GMS citizens' lurking behavior and contributing behavior. Self-censorship negatively influences emotional value which positively affects mobile GMS citizens' lurking behavior and contributing behavior.

Keywords: Mobile government social media · Participation · Internet censorship · Self-censorship

1 Introduction

Along with the explosive growth of social media and mobile technology, mobile government social media services (GSM) have penetrated across the public sector worldwide (Sharma et al. 2018; Yang et al. 2018). According to the 43nd China Internet Development Statistics Report, the number of government social media accounts on Sina microblog platform had achieved 139, 270 by the end of September 2019 (CNNIC 2019). Relying on mobile GSM, public agencies and bureaucracies can provide ubiquitous and convenient public services to citizens which significantly changed the ways of citizen-government communications (Guo et al. 2016) and citizen-citizen interactions (Li et al. 2018; Yang et al. 2018). By embracing mobile GSM, citizens not only can passively consume public information and services, but also can actively contribute knowledge and contents in the mobile GSM community (Ding et al. 2019). However, although the mobile GSM spreads very fast and received considerable acceptance by a

G. Salvendy and J. Wei (Eds.): HCII 2020, LNCS 12216, pp. 211–221, 2020.
https://doi.org/10.1007/978-3-030-50350-5_17

huge number of followers, the rate of citizens' sustaining participation is still very low (Li et al. 2018). For example, even though the Hangzhou government's GSM "Hangzhou Announcement" had gained more than 3.6 million followers (Hangzhou-Announcement 2019), its continuous participation rate reflected by sharing, liking, and commenting of administrative affair topics still remains very low. The success diffusion of mobile GSM depends on citizens' continuous participation rather than initial acceptance (Yang et al. 2018). Therefore, it is important to understand the factors that determine citizens' mobile GSM continuous participation behavior.

In academics, despite many studies have devoted to understanding mobile social media usage behaviors (Ahmad and Khalid 2017; Sharma et al. 2018; Yang et al. 2018), rare of research has investigated citizens' participation behaviors by including both contributing and lurking behaviors, especially in the mobile GSM context. Nowadays, citizens who use mobile GSM not only can visit and acquire information, but also can post and contribute content in the mobile GSM community (Yang and Zeng 2018). Considering both contributing and lurking behaviors thus would provide a holistic insight to understand citizens' mobile GSM participation behavior. In addition, extant studies usually focused on the benefits of mobile social media usage (Ahmad and Khalid 2017; Yang et al. 2018), rare of research has examined the role of censorship in forming the users' benefits evaluation and consequent usage behavior of mobile social media. Even though a number of studies have recently examined the impacts of censorship on mobile social media usage behavior (Li et al. 2018; Wang and Mark 2015), they usually focused on the extrinsic internet censorship. Little research has investigated the influences of both extrinsic internet censorship and intrinsic self-censorship on mobile GSM participation behavior. To better understand how censorship may affect citizens' mobile GSM participation behavior, both the extrinsic and intrinsic censorship should be taken into considerations. What's more, extant related studies tend to examined the factors that influence user participation behavior from the performance-based perspective by utilizing the leading technology acceptance model (TAM) or its extensions (Abu-Shanab 2017; Sharma et al. 2018). Despite TAM and its expanded models offer a useful theoretical basis in explaining technology usage behavior, these theories can't explain "why and how" individuals choose a special social media to meet their needs (Guo et al. 2010). Thus, the process underly citizens' contributing and lurking behaviors in the context of mobile GSM has seldom been examined. A careful review of the related literature suggests that Bagozzi's self-regulatory framework which reflected the self-regulatory processes might provide an explanation why citizens visit and contribute content in the mobile GSM community (Bagozzi 1992).

Based on the self-regulatory framework (Bagozzi 1992), the present study intends to explore citizens' mobile GSM participation behavior by focusing on the impacts of internet censorship and self-censorship on their self-regulatory processes. Specifically, the present study investigates: 1) *How do citizens' appraisals (e.g., internet censorship and self-censorship) affect their emotional reactions (e.g., social value, information value, hedonic value, and emotional value), and subsequently influence their coping response (e.g., lurking behavior and contributing behavior)? 2) What are the roles of internet censorship and self-censorship in shaping citizens' emotional reactions and subsequent participation behavior?*

2   Literature Review

Mobile government social media has received an increasing attention from scholars and practitioners in recent years (Ahmad and Khalid 2017; Li et al. 2019; Sharma et al. 2018; Yang et al. 2018). The provision of information is important for government adoption of GMS, even though this feature is often integrated into other government social media applications. A study of small U.S. local governments suggests that the provision of online information services is related to the adoption of Twitter, while the provision of online trading services is related to the adoption of Facebook (Gao and Lee 2017). On the other hand, information acquisition plays a determinant role in shaping citizens' GMS use intention. In regard to general usage of social media, Gan and Wang (2015) showed that the fulfillment of information expectation is the most important motivator for China's internet users to choose microblogging, in contrast with the choice of WeChat. By analogue, GMS users regard information seeking as their most important need, as revealed by a study in China.

More than acquiring information, sharing information with others stimulates GMS usage. On microblogging platforms, sharing information can be achieved by two kinds of behavior: posting and reposting (Boyd et al. 2010; Java et al. 2007). Reposting means that an original post is simply forwarded by micro-bloggers without any permission, thereby making information spread quickly and easily. As such, microblogging platforms especially facilitate the spreading and sharing of news (Kwak et al. 2010; Lee and Ma 2012; Rudat and Buder 2015). The enabler of fast information diffusion on social media has also evoked a considerable number of studies devoted to investigating government–citizen communication in emergency management (Hong et al. 2018; Thomas and Lisl 2012; Wukich and Mergel 2015). As pointed out by Medaglia and Zheng (2017), the government social media literature still lacks research which focuses on user behaviors, let alone in the context of internet censorship.

3   Theoretical Background and Research Hypotheses

Drawing on Bagozzi's self-regulatory framework (1992) and the censorship related literature, the present study develops a research model that reflects the impacts of internet censorship and self-censorship on citizens' self-regulatory processes in the mobile GSM context (Fig. 1). It depicts that citizens' appraisal including internet censorship and self-censorship will negatively affect their emotional reactions including extrinsic and intrinsic value, which will further positively affect their coping behavior including lurking and contributing behaviors. Theoretical justifications of the proposed hypotheses are discussed below.

Lazarus (1991) proposed a theoretical framework of appraisal-emotional reactions-coping response. The process of self-regulation refers to an individual's ability to change or adjust his assessments, feelings, desires, and behaviors for better results (Bagozzi 1992; Gotlieb et al. 1994). Based on the process of self-regulation, we proposed the following hypotheses.

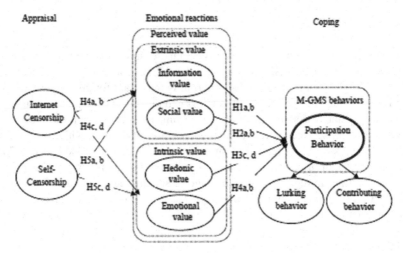

Fig. 1. Research model

3.1 Perceived Value and Participant Behaviors

Two types of participant behaviors in the online community were identified: lurkers and contributors (Phang et al. 2015). Lurkers are passive participants who access and obtain information, but do not provide content in the online community (Phang et al. 2015). Contributors are primarily content producers or publishers who actively share information, ideas, experience or knowledge with others in the online community (Lai and Chen 2014; Zhao et al. 2012). As for contributors, sharing information, especially via reposting, is a prominent feature of microblogging usage behavior. It suggests a higher level of interactivity than acquiring information and, on GMS platforms, it means a higher level of citizen engagement or participation (Mergel 2013). Therefore, we consider participant intentions of acquiring information and sharing information separately.

Information value that underlies the GMS' content will lend an impetus to citizens' behavioral intentions. Prior researches have suggested that social value or motivations for maintaining social relationships and building social capital increase users' willingness to share knowledge online (Chiu et al. 2006; Wasko and Faraj 2005). Therefore, the following hypothesis is proposed:

Hypothesis 1. Information value will positively affect a citizen's lurking behavior (a) and contributing behavior (b) by using mobile GSM.
Hypothesis 2. Social value will positively affect a citizen's intention to (a) acquire information and (b) share information by using mobile GMS.

The impact of hedonic value and emotional value on social media use intentions have also validated by previous studies (Yang et al. 2018). For example, the content for marketing a city's tourism will possibly increase the local residents' sense of identification (Nahapiet and Ghoshal 2000), thereby increasing their hedonic gratification. Considering previous literature that has documented the impact of hedonic value and emotional value on social media use behaviors, we can thus put forward the following hypothesis:

Hypothesis 2. Hedonic value will positively affect a citizen's lurking behavior *(a) and contributing behavior (b) by using mobile GSM.*
Hypothesis 3. Emotional value will positively affect a citizen's lurking behavior *(a) and contributing behavior (b) by using mobile GSM.*

3.2 Censorship and Participant Behaviors

China is adopting the strictest internet censorship policy, which has attracted the many research attention. Bamman et al. (2012) noticed that There are signs that China's Internet censorship practices include web filtering, search filtering, chat censorship, and blog censorship. For various reasons, social media censorship of collective action incidents is the rigorous in China. Based on the existing study (Wang and Mark 2015), we included both internet censorship and self-censorship into the research model. Internet censorship is defined as the opinions of Internet users on the existence of censorship (Wang and Mark 2015). Jamali and Shahbaztabar (2017) showed that internet filtering or censorship makes users feel being controlled and deprived of freedom, therefore triggering their negative emotions such as anger, disgust, sadness, and anxiety. Following the previous studies, have the following:

Hypothesis 4. Internet censorship will negatively affect (a) information value, (b) social value, (c) hedonic value, and (d) emotional value.
Hypothesis 5. Self-censorship will negatively affect (a) information value, (b) social value, (c) hedonic value, and (d) emotional value.

4 Research Methodology

4.1 Instrument

To ensure the content validity, the constructs in the present study were all adapted from the previous studies. The instrument was measured with seven-point Likert scales ranging from one (strongly disagree) to seven (strongly agree). The present study conducted a backward-translation procedure to ensure the translation validity. Then, the present study performed a pilot study on 20 mobile government social media users to further validate the measurements.

4.2 Sample

The empirical data for model testing were obtained through a web-based survey which conducted on WJX.CN. As a famous online survey website in China, WJX.CN has over 2.6 million active users with diversified backgrounds in its sample pool. The sample service of WJX.CN was adopted for data collection. As the aim of our study is to investigate the mobile government social media continuance behaviors, the target participants need to have the mobile government microblogging services. Eligible respondents were invited by WJX.CN to participate in our survey and whose who didn't have mobile GSM experiences are automatically filtered out by the pre-setting screening questions. Finally, 315 valid responses were obtained.

5 Data Analysis and Results

5.1 Reliability and Validity

Cronbach's alpha and composite reliability (CR) as two widely used indicators were adopted to test the internal reliability of the instrument. As showed in Table 1, the values of Cronbach's alpha range from 0.725 to 0.876, and the values of CR range from 0.820 to 0.913, indicating a good reliability of the instrument. In addition, the loadings of the items are all higher than the suggested criteria threshold of 0.7, and the values of AVE are all greater than the recommended benchmark level of 0.5, exhibiting a good convergent validity. To test the discriminant validity of the instrument, the cross-loading matrix was calculated. The internal-construct loadings of the respective construct were greater than the cross-loadings on other constructs, indicating a good discriminant validity.

To further examine the discriminant validity of the instrument, we compared the correlation coefficients of the inter-construct with the corresponding square root values of the AVE. The correlation coefficients for each construct are all lower than its corresponding square root values of the AVE, demonstrating a good discriminant validity.

The present study preformed two widely used statistical analyses to test the possible severity of common method bias (CMB) on the self-reported data. First, a Harman's one-factor test was performed on the eight key constructs in the proposed research model. The results reveal that no single factor can explain most of the covariance, suggesting that CMB was not a serious concern in this study. Second, following the procedure suggested by Podsakoff et al. (2003) and Liang et al. (2007), this study added a new factor in the measurement model as the common method factor, which loaded all indictors of the constructs in the original model. The results show that the loadings of original factors were all significant at $P < 0.001$ level, while the loadings of the common method factor were not significant. This indicated that CMB again was not a problem in our study.

5.2 Hypothesis Testing

Partial least squares (PLS) is a component-based SEM method, which has been widely adopted in the social behavior literature. Compared with the covariance-based SEM methods, PLS can handle both uni-dimensional and multi-dimensional variables model (Hair et al. 2011). In the present study, participation behavior is conceptualized as the multi-dimensional variable which includes both lurking and contributing behaviors. Thus, PLS is more suitable for the model testing in our study.

The results of model estimating were showed in Fig. 2, which indicates that seven over eight proposed hypotheses are supported by the statistical data. Specifically, the impacts of Internet censorship on social value, information value, hedonic value and emotional value were all negative significant, therefore validating hypotheses H1a, H1b,

Table 1. Scale properties

Variable	Item	Standard Loading	Cronbach's Alpha	CR	AVE
Lurking behaviors (LUB)	LUB1	0.838	0.863	0.907	0.709
	LUB2	0.852			
	LUB3	0.853			
	LUB4	0.824			
Contributing behaviors (COB)	COB1	0.862	0.872	0.913	0.723
	COB2	0.861			
	COB3	0.854			
	COB4	0.822			
Hedonic value (HEV)	HEV1	0.876	0.839	0.903	0.756
	HEV2	0.862			
	HEV3	0.869			
Emotional value (EMV)	EMV1	0.844	0.814	0.820	0.604
	EMV2	0.766			
	EMV3	0.714			
Information value (INV)	INV1	0.874	0.778	0.900	0.818
	INV2	0.863			
Social value (SOV)	SOV1	0.773	0.803	0.883	0.715
	SOV2	0.885			
	SOV3	0.874			
Internet censorship (PIC)	PIC1	0.864	0.790	0.874	0.698
	PIC2	0.808			
	PIC3	0.832			
Self-censorship (SEC)	SEC1	0.734	0.725	0.852	0.746
	SEC2	0.975			

Note: HEV = Hedonic value; SOV = Social value; INV = Information value; EMV = Emotional value; PIC = Internet censorship; SEC= Self-censorship; LUB= Lurking behaviors; COB= Contributing behaviors.

H1c and H1d. The impact of self-censorship on emotional value was negative significant, thus supporting hypotheses H2d. However, the hypothesized paths from self-censorship on social value, information value, and hedonic value were not significant, therefore, hypotheses H2a, H2b, and H2c were not supported. The hypothesized paths from social value, information value, and emotional value to participation behavior were all significant, thus supporting hypotheses H3a, H3b, and H3d. However, the influence of hedonic value on participation behavior was insignificant, thus H3c was not supported. The R^2 for participation behaviors is 0.503, which shows a reasonable explanation of the variance for the mobile GSM participation behavior. The impacts of perceived value on both lurking behavior and contributing behavior were also tested. As shown in Fig. 2, the impacts of social value, information value, and emotional value on lurking behavior and contributing behavior were all positively significant. The influence of hedonic value on lurking behavior and contributing behavior was not significant. The R2 for lurking behavior and contributing behavior were 0.396, and 0.359, respectively.

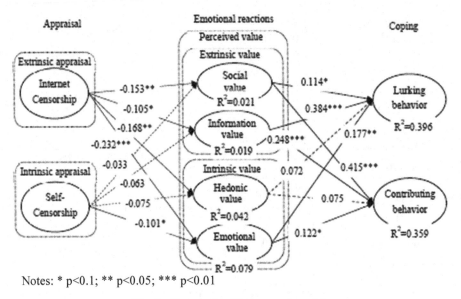

Notes: * p<0.1; ** p<0.05; *** p<0.01

Fig. 2. Test results of the research model.

6   Discussion

Based on self-regulation theory and internet censorship literature, the present study examined the influences of citizens' censorship perceptions on their participations of mobile GMS. The results reveal some interesting findings.

First, in terms of extrinsic appraisal, the present study found that Internet censorship negatively affects social value, information value, hedonic value and emotional value. This indicated that Internet censorship can decease citizens' both extrinsic value and intrinsic value including social value, information value, hedonic value and emotional value. The reason may be that Internet censorship is a very broad concept, including various web filtering which affect both extrinsic value and intrinsic value. In terms of intrinsic appraisal, the present study found that self-censorship negatively affects intrinsic value (e.g., emotional value) but not extrinsic value. This suggests that self-censorship as an intrinsic appraisal did not trigger extrinsic reactions.

Second, in terms of extrinsic reactions, the present study found that social value and information value both positively affect citizens' lurking behavior and contributing behavior. Specifically, in terms of the path coefficient and significant levels, social value exerts a stronger influence on contributing behavior when compared with lurking behavior. On the other hand, information value has a greater impact on lurking behavior when compared with contributing behaviors. This suggests that when citizens perceived a high level of social value, they will more likely to contribute on mobile GMS. When citizens perceived a high level of information value, they will more likely to get information by using mobile GMS.

Third, in terms of intrinsic reactions, the present study found that emotional value positively affects citizens' lurking behavior and contributing behavior. Specifically, compared with contributing behavior, social value exerts a stronger influence on lurking behavior in terms of the path coefficient and significant levels. This indicated that emotional value plays an important role in shaping citizens' lurking behavior and contributing behavior. However, the influence of hedonic value on lurking behavior and contributing behavior were non-significant. The possible reason is that the main intention of citizens to use mobile GMS is for getting information and interacting with others rather than pursuing hedonic value. The mangers of mobile GMS such can take action to improve citizens' extrinsic and intrinsic value to enhance their lurking behavior and contributing behavior. Our study such not only offer insights into the theoretical study of mobile GMS, but also help the managers to manage the platform of mobile GMS.

References

Abu-Shanab, E.A.: E-government familiarity influence on Jordanians' perceptions. Telematics Inform. **34**(1), 103–113 (2017)

Ahmad, S.Z., Khalid, K.: The adoption of M-government services from the user's perspectives: empirical evidence from the United Arab Emirates. Int. J. Inf. Manag. **37**(5), 367–379 (2017)

Bagozzi, R.P.: The self-regulation of attitudes, intentions, and behavior. soc. Psychol. Q. **55**(2), 178–204 (1992)

Bamman, D., O'Connor, B., Smith, N.: Censorship and deletion practices in Chinese social media. First Monday **17**(3) (2012). https://doi.org/10.5210/fm.v17i3.3943

Boyd, D., Golder, S., Lotan, G.: Tweet, tweet, retweet: conversational aspects of retweeting on Twitter. In: 2010 43rd Hawaii International Conference on System Sciences (2010)

Chiu, C.-M., Hsu, M.-H., Wang, E.T.G.: Understanding knowledge sharing in virtual communities: an integration of social capital and social cognitive theories. Decis. Support Syst. **42**(3), 1872–1888 (2006)

CNNIC: 44th statistical survey report on internet development in China. [R/OL]. (2019-08-30) [2019-9-12] (2019). http://www.cnnic.net.cn/

Ding, Y., Shuiqing, Y., Chen, Y., Long, Q., Wei, J.: Explaining and predicting mobile government microblogging services participation behaviors: a SEM-neural network method. IEEE Access **7**, 39600–39611 (2019)

Gan, C., Wang, W.: Uses and gratifications of social media: a comparison of microblog and WeChat. J. Syst. Inf. Technol. **17**(4), 351–363 (2015)

Gao, X., Lee, J.: E-government services and social media adoption: experience of small local governments in Nebraska state. Gov. Inf. Q. **34**(4), 627–634 (2017)

Gotlieb, J.B., Grewal, D., Brown, S.W.: Consumer satisfaction and perceived quality: complementary or divergent constructs? J. Appl. Psychol. **79**(6), 875–885 (1994)

Guo, J., Liu, Z., Liu, Y.: Key success factors for the launch of government social media platform: identifying the formation mechanism of continuance intention. Comput. Hum. Behav. **55**(Part B), 750–763 (2016)

Guo, Z., Tan, F.B., Cheung, K.: Students' uses and gratifications for using computer-mediated communication media in learning contexts. Commun. Assoc. Inf. Syst. **27**(1), 339–378 (2010)

Hair, J.F., Ringle, C.M., Sarstedt, M.: PLS-SEM: indeed a silver bullet. J. Mark. Theory Pract. **19**(2), 139–152 (2011)

Hangzhou-Announcement: The official Weibo of the News office of Hangzhou municipal government [R/OL]. (2019-02-16) [2019-03-21] (2019). https://m.weibo.cn/u/5211979483

Hong, L., Fu, C., Wu, J., Frias-Martinez, V.: Information needs and communication gaps between citizens and local governments online during natural disasters. Inf. Syst. Front. **20**, 1027–1039 (2018)

Jamali, H.R., Shahbaztabar, P.: The effects of internet filtering on users' information-seeking behaviour and emotions. Aslib J. Inf. Manag. **69**(4), 408–425 (2017)

Java, A., Song, X., Finin, T., Tseng, B.: Why we Twitter: understanding microblogging usage and communities. In: Proceedings of the 9th WebKDD and 1st SNA-KDD 2007 Workshop on Web Mining and Social Network Analysis. ACM (2007)

Kwak, H., Lee, C., Park, H., Moon, S.: What is Twitter, a social network or a news media? In: Proceedings of the 19th International Conference on World Wide Web. ACM (2010)

Lai, H.M., Chen, T.T.: Knowledge sharing in interest online communities: a comparison of posters and lurkers. Comput. Hum. Behav. **35**(6), 295–306 (2014)

Lazarus, R.S.: Emotion and Adaptation. Oxford University Press, New York (1991)

Lee, C.S., Ma, L.: News sharing in social media: the effect of gratifications and prior experience. Comput. Hum. Behav. **28**(2), 331–339 (2012)

Li, Y., Wang, H., Zeng, X., Shuiqing, Y., Wei, J.: Effects of interactivity on continuance intention of government microblogging services: an implication on mobile social media. Int. J. Mob. Commun. (2020, in press). https://doi.org/10.1504/IJMC.2020.10028671

Li, Y., Yang, S., Chen, Y., Yao, J.: Effects of perceived online–offline integration and internet censorship on mobile government microblogging service continuance: a gratification perspective. Gov. Inf. Q. **35**(4), 588–598 (2018)

Liang, H.G., Saraf, N., Hu, Q., Xue, Y.J.: Assimilation of enterprise systems: the effect of institutional pressures and the mediating role of top management. MIS Q. **31**(1), 59–87 (2007)

Medaglia, R., Zheng, L.: Mapping government social media research and moving it forward: a framework and a research agenda. Gov. Inf. Q. **34**(3), 496–510 (2017)

Mergel, I.: A framework for interpreting social media interactions in the public sector. Gov. Inf. Q. **30**(4), 327–334 (2013)

Nahapiet, J., Ghoshal, S.: Social capital, intellectual capital, and the organizational advantage* A2, Chap. 6. In: Lesser, E.L. (ed.) Knowledge and Social Capital, pp. 119–157. Butterworth-Heinemann, Boston (2000)

Phang, C.W., Kankanhalli, A., Tan, B.C.: What motivates contributors vs. Lurkers? An investigation of online feedback forums. Inf. Syst. Res. **26**(4), 773–792 (2015)

Podsakoff, P., MacKenzie, S., Lee, J., Podsakoff, N.: Common method biases in behavioral research: a critical review of the literature and recommended remedies. J. Appl. Psychol. **88**(5), 879–903 (2003)

Rudat, A., Buder, J.: Making retweeting social: the influence of content and context information on sharing news in Twitter. Comput. Hum. Behav. **46**, 75–84 (2015)

Sharma, S.K., Al-Badi, A., Rana, N.P., Al-Azizi, L.: Mobile applications in government services (mG-App) from user's perspectives: a predictive modelling approach. Gov. Inf. Q. **35**, 557–568 (2018)

Thomas, H., Lisl, Z.: Use of microblogging for collective sense-making during violent crises: a study of three campus shootings. J. Am. Soc. Inf. Sci. Technol. **63**(1), 34–47 (2012)

Wang, D., Mark, G.: Internet censorship in China: examining user awareness and attitudes. ACM Trans. Comput.-Hum. Inter. (TOCHI) **22**(6), 31 (2015)

Wasko, M.L., Faraj, S.: Why should I share? Examining social capital and knowledge contribution in electronic networks of practice. MIS Q. **29**(1), 35–57 (2005)

Wukich, C., Mergel, I.: Closing the citizen-government communication gap: content, audience, and network analysis of government tweets. J. Homeland Secur. Emerg. Manag. **12**(3), 707–735 (2015)

Yang, S., Hui, J., Yao, J., Chen, Y., Wei, J.: Perceived values on mobile GMS continuance: a perspective from perceived integration and interactivity. Comput. Hum. Behav. **89**(1), 16–26 (2018)

Yang, S., Zeng, X.: Sustainability of government social media: a multi-analytic approach to predict citizens' mobile government microblog continuance. Sustainability **10**(12), 4849 (2018)

Zhao, L., Lu, Y., Wang, B., Chau, P.Y., Zhang, L.: Cultivating the sense of belonging and motivating user participation in virtual communities: a social capital perspective. Int. J. Inf. Manag. **32**(6), 574–588 (2012)

Author Index

Printed in the United States
By Bookmasters